CYRIL OF AI

As ruler of the Church of Alexandria and president of the Third Ecumenical Council of 431, Cyril was one of the most powerful men of the fifth century and played a decisive role in the history of his times. He was an important thinker who defined the concept of christological orthodoxy for the next two centuries. Cyril is also often regarded as an unscrupulous and power-hungry cleric who was responsible for the murder of the female philosopher Hypatia and for the overthrow of the archbishop Nestorius.

Cyril of Alexandria presents key selections of Cyril's writings in order to make his thought accessible to students. The writings are all freshly translated and an extended introduction outlines Cyril's life and times, his scholastic method, his christology, his ecclesiology, his eucharistic doctrine, his spirituality and his influence on the Christian tradition. Brief introductions and notes to the individual selections provide valuable contextualization and elucidation of the ideas contained in them.

Norman Russell is a freelance lecturer and translator. He is the author, with Benedicta Ward, of *The Lives of the Desert Fathers: The Historia Monachorum in Aegypto* (1980).

THE EARLY CHURCH FATHERS
Edited by Carol Harrison
University of Durham

The Greek and Latin fathers of the Church are central to the creation of Christian doctrine, yet often unapproachable because of the sheer volume of their writings and the relative paucity of accessible translations. This series makes available translations of key selected texts by the major Fathers to all students of the early church.

Already published:

MAXIMUS THE CONFESSOR
Andrew Louth

IRENAEUS OF LYONS
Robert M. Grant

AMBROSE
Boniface Ramsey

ORIGEN
Joseph W. Trigg

GREGORY OF NYSSA
Anthony Meredith

JOHN CHRYSOSTOM
Wendy Mayer and Pauline Allen

CYRIL
OF
ALEXANDRIA

Norman Russell

London and New York

First published 2000
by Routledge
11 New Fetter Lane, London EC4P 4EE

Simultaneously published in the USA and Canada
by Routledge
29 West 35th Street, New York, NY 10001

Routledge is an imprint of the Taylor & Francis Group

Typeset in Garamond 3 by
Keystroke, Jacaranda Lodge, Wolverhampton
Printed and bound in Great Britain by
MPG Books Ltd, Bodmin

British Library Cataloguing in Publication Data
A catalogue record for this book is available from the British Library

Library of Congress Cataloging in Publication Data
Cyril, Saint, Patriarch of Alexandria, ca. 370–444.
[Selections. English. 2000]
Cyril of Alexandria / [translated by] Norman Russell.
p.   cm. – (The early church fathers)]
Includes bibliographical references and index.
1. Theology, Doctrinal. I. Russell, Norman. II. Title. III. Series.
BR65.C952 E5 2000
270.2′092–dc21   99–055830

ISBN 0–415–18250–6 (hbk)
ISBN 0–415–18251–4 (pbk)

CONTENTS

PREFACE

Cyril of Alexandria (c. 378–444) has been a controversial figure from the fifth century to the present day. In the English-speaking world our perception of him, moreover, has been coloured by Gibbon's damning portrait of him in the forty-seventh chapter of *The Decline and Fall of the Roman Empire*, where he is represented as the murderer of Hypatia and the bully of the Council of Ephesus. His writings, described by Gibbon as 'works of allegory and metaphysics, whose remains, in seven verbose folios, now peaceably slumber by the side of their rivals', are little read.

Cyril, however, deserves better. He was certainly a man of iron will and a consummate ecclesiastical politician. But he was also a theologian of the first rank and a biblical commentator whose insights can still be illuminating today. Within the last five years several important books on Cyril have appeared. The first of these was M.-O. Boulnois' magisterial *Le paradoxe trinitaire chez Cyrille d'Alexandrie*. The same year (1994) saw the publication of J.M. McGuckin's *St Cyril of Alexandria: The Christological Controversy*, and L.J. Welch's *Christology and Eucharist in the Early Thought of Cyril of Alexandria*. Just recently there have been two further fine studies of Cyril's christology: B. Meunier's *Le Christ de Cyrille d'Alexandrie*, and A.H.A. Fernández Lois' *La cristología en los commentarios a Isaías de Cirilo de Alejandría y Teodoreto de Ciro*. Cyril is less well served with translations. Although his complete letters have been translated by J.I. McEnerney in the Fathers of the Church series, and valuable selections of letters and shorter texts may be found in L.R. Wickham's *Cyril of Alexandria: Select Letters* and in McGuckin's book mentioned above, of the longer works only *On the Unity of Christ* is available in a modern English translation (by McGuckin). The aim of the present volume is to make some of Cyril's longer works more accessible. Selections are offered from two works not previously translated into English, the *Commentary on Isaiah* and *Against Julian*, and from two available only in Victorian versions, the *Commentary on John* and the *Five Tomes Against Nestorius*. The *Explanation of the Twelve Chapters* is added to these as a key text from the immediate aftermath of the Council of Ephesus.

The quotations from L.R. Wickham's *Cyril of Alexandria: Select Letters* (Oxford, 1983) are reproduced by permission of Oxford University Press.

I should like to thank Sebastian Brock, who gave me expert advice on some of the relevant Syriac literature, Lawrence Welch, who furnished me with a proof copy of his book when it was otherwise unobtainable, and Mina Goritsa, who sent me several important publications from Greece. I am also most grateful to Abel Fernández Lois for answering my enquiry concerning Jerome's influence on Cyril, and to Andrew Louth, who read the entire manuscript and made many valuable suggestions. I owe a special debt of gratitude to Carol Harrison, the General Editor of the series, for her helpful advice and encouragement. The errors and infelicities of language that remain are, of course, my own.

Norman Russell
27 June 1999
Feast of St Cyril of Alexandria

ABBREVIATIONS

ACO	*Acta Conciliorum Oecumenicorum*, ed. E. Schwartz, Berlin
ANF	*The Ante-Nicene Fathers*, eds A. Roberts and J. Donaldson, Edinburgh
BJRL	*Bulletin of the John Rylands Library*, Manchester
BLE	*Bulletin de Littérature Ecclésiastique*, Toulouse
CCL	*Corpus Christianorum*, Series Latina, Turnhout/Paris
CHR	*The Catholic Historial Review*, Washington
Chr. Un.	Cyril, *Quod Unus sit Christus*
C. Jul.	Cyril, *Contra Julianum*
C. Nest	Cyril, *Libri quinque contra Nestorium*
C. Thdt.	Cyril, *Contra Theodoretum*
Cod. Theod.	*Codex Theodosianus*
Cr. St.	*Cristianesimo nella storia*, Bologna
CSCO	*Corpus Scriptorum Christianorum Orientalium*, Louvain
DACL	*Dictionnaire d'Archéologie Chrétienne et de Liturgie*, eds F. Cabrol and H. Leclercq, Paris
DHGE	*Dictionnaire d'Histoire et de Géographie Ecclésiastiques*, eds A. Baudrillart, A. de Meyer and E. Van Cauwenbergh, Paris
Dial. Inc.	Cyril, *Dialogue on the Incarnation*
Dial. Trin.	Cyril, *Dialogues on the Trinity*
DOP	*Dumbarton Oaks Papers*, Washington
DR	*Downside Review*, Bath
DTC	*Dictionnaire de Théologie Catholique*, eds A. Vacant, E. Mangenot and E. Amann, Paris
Eccl. Hist.	*Ecclesiastical History*
Ep.	*Epistula*
Eph. Th. Lov.	*Ephemerides Theologicae Lovanienses*, Louvain

Expl. xii cap.	Cyril, *Explanatio duodecim capitum*
GCS	*Die griechischen christlichen Schriftsteller*, Leipzig/Berlin
In Is.	Cyril, *Commentary on Isaiah*
In Jo.	Cyril, *Commentary on John*
In Lc.	Cyril, *Commentary on Luke*
In Ps.	Cyril, *Explanation of the Psalms*
In Zach.	Cyril, *Commentary on Zechariah*
JEH	*Journal of Ecclesiastical History*, London
JRS	*Journal of Roman Studies*, London
JTS	*Journal of Theological Studies*, Oxford
LXX	Septuagint version
Med. Stud.	*Medieval Studies*, Toronto
MSR	*Mélanges de Science Religieuse*, Lille
NPNF	*A Select Library of Nicene and Post-Nicene Fathers of the Christian Church*, eds P. Schaff and H. Wace, Edinburgh
ODCC[3]	*The Oxford Dictionary of the Christian Church*, 3rd edn., ed. E.A. Livingstone, Oxford
PG	Migne, *Patrologia*, series Graeco-Latina
PGL	*Patristic Greek Lexicon*, ed. G.W.H. Lampe, Oxford
PL	Migne, *Patrologia*, series Latina
PO	*Patrologia Orientalis*, Paris
Rev. Thom.	*Revue Thomiste*, Paris
REA	*Revue des Etudes Augustiniennes*, Paris
RHE	*Revue d'Histoire Ecclésiastique*, Louvain
RSR	*Recherches de Science Religieuse*, Paris
RTL	*Revue théologique de Louvain*, Louvain
SC	*Sources Chrétiennes*, eds H. de Lubac and J. Daniélou, Paris
Stud. Pat.	*Studia Patristica*. Papers presented to the International Conference on Patristic Studies held in Oxford, successively Berlin, Oxford, Kalamazoo, Louvain
Thes.	Cyril, *Thesaurus de sancta et consubstantiali Trinitate*
Vet. Chr.	*Vetera Christianorum*, Bari
VLAGLB	*Vetus Latina. Aus der Geschichte der lateinischen Bibel*, Freiburg im Breisgau
ZKG	*Zeitschrift für Kirchengeschichte*, Gotha, then Stuttgart

Part I

INTRODUCTION

1

THE MAKING OF A BISHOP

EARLY LIFE

When Cyril died in 444, he and his uncle Theophilus, whom he had succeeded on the throne of Alexandria in 412, had ruled the Alexandrian Church for a total of fifty-nine years. For as long as anyone could remember they had dominated the ecclesiastical politics of the East Roman world. Between them they had deposed two archbishops of Constantinople, declared leading teachers of the Antiochene tradition heretical, and pursued ecclesiastical and theological courses of action, the one against Origenism, the other against Antiochene christology, which made them enemies throughout the East. It does not come as a surprise that someone should have written to a friend on the occasion of Cyril's death:

> At last with a final struggle the villain has passed away.
> ... His departure delights the survivors, but possibly disheartens the dead; there is some fear that under the provocation of his company they may send him back again to us. ... Care must therefore be taken to order the guild of undertakers to place a very big and heavy stone on his grave to stop him coming back here.[1]

Cyril and his uncle Theophilus belong to the new era inaugurated by Theodosius I's laws against polytheism, an era characterized by Christian violence not only towards pagans and Jews but also towards dissident fellow-believers.[2] Christians today are repelled by many aspects of the careers of Theophilus and Cyril. Their determined campaigns against their opponents attracted adverse comment even in their lifetime.[3] But what differentiates them from their episcopal contemporaries is not so much their aggressive power politics as the

3

scale of the resources, both material and intellectual, available to them.

Cyril was born in about 378 at Theodosiou in Lower Egypt, which was his father's hometown.[4] His mother came from Memphis, the ancient capital, at that time still a stronghold of polytheism. We know nothing of his father's family, but John of Nikiu informs us that Cyril's maternal grandparents were Christians.[5] They died comparatively young, leaving an adolescent son, Theophilus, and a daughter scarcely out of infancy. Shortly afterwards, perhaps during the resurgence of paganism under the emperor Julian in 362–3, Theophilus, who was then sixteen or seventeen, left Memphis for Alexandria, taking his little sister with him. There he enrolled himself in the catechumenate and thus came to the attention of the bishop, Athanasius. After baptizing the orphans, Athanasius took them under this wing. He placed the girl in the care of a community of virgins, where she remained until she was given in marriage to Cyril's father. The boy was marked out for higher things. Athanasius took him into his household and arranged for him to complete his studies under his supervision. As a highly intelligent Christian with no family ties, Theophilus could evidently be of service to the Church of Alexandria.[6]

Theophilus' early ecclesiastical career has been reconstructed by his biographer, Agostino Favale.[7] In about 370 he was admitted to the clerical state and for the last three years of Athanasius' life served as his secretary. When Athanasius died, Theophilus was too young to be considered for episcopal office. Five days before his death on 2 May 373 Athanasius designated Peter II as his successor. In 378 Peter was succeeded by his brother Timothy. In the meantime Theophilus was rising up the ecclesiastical ladder. In about 375 he was ordained deacon and began to teach publicly. It was in this period that Rufinus, who spent six years at Alexandria studying at the catechetical school under Didymus the Blind, attended lectures given by Theophilus and was impressed by him.[8] When Timothy died in 385, Theophilus was about forty years old and as archdeacon of Alexandria well positioned to take over the episcopate.

Theophilus succeeded to the throne of St Mark on 20 July 385. Cyril was then about seven years old, the age at which a child was first sent to school. As the only son of the family, it is possible that his uncle supervised his education.[9] His studies up to the age of sixteen or so would have been typical of those followed by any boy, whether pagan or Christian, from a reasonably well-off back-ground.[10] After receiving a thorough grounding in reading, writing and arithmetic at primary school, he would have gone to a grammarian, a *grammatikos*, for his secondary education. This would have consisted of a detailed study of classical literature, the principal pillars of which were Homer, Euripides, Menander and Demosthenes, together with a much more superficial treatment of mathematics, music and astronomy. After secondary school Cyril no doubt went to study with a rhetor, for the evidence of his writings shows that he pursued linguistic studies at a high level. He writes an elaborate Attic Greek, remarkable for its revival of obsolete words and its many neologisms, yet precise and well suited to his purposes.[11] He is also a master of the rhetorician's techniques of controversy.

Whether Cyril pursued formal philosophical studies is more difficult to determine. It is generally accepted that Cyril was not a philosopher. He works with images and metaphorical language rather than with the systematic development of ideas.[12] On the other hand it has been established that Cyril had a good knowledge of Aristotelian and Porphyrian logic.[13] Aristotle's *Organon*, *Topics* and *Categories* and Porphyry's *Isagoge* have all left their mark on his early writings. He handles technical Aristotelian terms in a confident manner, exploiting the relationship between substance and accidents and making extensive use of syllogistic reasoning. All this suggests a close acquaintance with the lecture rooms, especially as at this period the Alexandrian philosophical school was particularly noted for its work on Aristotle.[14] Marie-Odile Boulnois believes that besides acquiring an expertise in Aristotelian logic, Cyril also became acquainted with the exegetical methods of Platonism, but that he then distanced himself from a philosophical culture that had set itself the task of defending paganism.[15] Certainly in later life Cyril presented himself as an anti-Hellenist: 'Hellenic learning is vain and pointless,' he said, 'and requires much effort for no reward.'[16] When he was preparing his materials for *Against Julian* he read widely in such works as Porphyry's *History of Philosophy*, the Hermetic Corpus, and a treatise of Alexander of Aphrodisias on providence. He first went to Christian authors, however, as guides to help him find what he needed.[17] And at Ephesus in 431, when he found his orthodoxy under attack, it was the ecclesiastical side of his education that he chose to emphasize: 'We have never entertained the ideas of Apollinarius or Arius or Eunomius, but from an early age we have studied the holy scriptures and have been nurtured at the hands of holy and orthodox fathers.'[18] These holy and orthodox fathers would have been Didymus the Blind, Gregory of Nazianzus, Basil of Caesarea and, above all, Athanasius, echoes of whose works are found throughout his writings. The secular authors who would have nourished his early education are rarely mentioned.

The first secure date we have for Cyril is 403, when he accompanied his uncle to the Synod of the Oak, the council that deposed John Chrysostom.[19] By then he would have been at least a lector and perhaps also secretary to his uncle, as Theophilus had been to Athanasius. By the time Theophilus died on 15 October 412, Cyril had therefore had at least nine years' experience at the centre of power. Such experience was to stand him in good stead from the outset. The secular authorities had evidently had enough of the disturbances caused by the 'Egyptian Pharaoh', as one of his contemporaries called Theophilus,[20] and fearing a continuation of his policies under his nephew, supported the candidature of the archdeacon, Timothy. Cyril, however, had already built up a strong power base, which no doubt included the *parabalani*, the members of the guild of hospital porters, who were later to serve him as a private militia.[21] In spite of military support for Timothy, Cyril's faction, after three days of rioting, gained the upper hand. On 18 October Cyril was installed on the throne of St Mark.[22]

THE POWER STRUGGLE WITH
THE PREFECT

Cyril's episcopate shows a remarkable continuity of policy with that of Theophilus. The lynchpins of this policy were first, maintaining a relentless pressure on pagans, heretics and Jews; second, cultivating a close alliance with Rome (though his unwillingness to revise Theophilus' condemnation of John Chrysostom kept relations cool for the early part of his episcopate); third, resisting the expansion of the episcopal authority of Constantinople; and fourth, retaining the support of the monks. There are also continuities of style. Like his uncle, Cyril knew how to mobilize popular forces in the pursuit of his aims.[23] The excesses of the Christian mob were to be the subject of several reports to Constantinople. And as his conduct at Ephesus was to show, he had fully absorbed from Theophilus how to manipulate ecclesiastical politics to his advantage. We see him using unscrupulous tactics to present a *fait accompli* to the Antiochenes and then buying support in Constantinople to have his actions confirmed by the emperor – all from the highest motives. Furthermore, in loyalty to his uncle he opposed the rehabilitation of John Chrysostom for as long as he decently could and also maintained a public stance against

Origenism even though he had no time for anthropomorphite views.[24] Of course, there were discontinuities too, but these are more in the sphere of personal morality. Cyril did not emulate the theological opportunism of his uncle, who had attacked anthropomorphism but had then become an anti-Origenist when he saw that such a move would enhance his power base by ensuring the support of the simpler monks. Nor did he adopt his uncle's cynical approach to dealing with recalcitrant clergy by persecuting them on trumped up charges. It is the continuities in the public sphere, however, that leave the stronger impression.[25] In Cyril's own time he was regarded as 'his uncle's nephew'[26] and in the later Coptic tradition as 'the new Theophilus'.[27]

According to Socrates, the Church historian, Cyril's first action as bishop was to eject the Novatianists and seize their churches and other property.[28] His next move was against the Jews. In Socrates' account (his informant was an Alexandrian Jewish doctor who subsequently became a Christian) the Jewish community had gathered in the theatre to hear the publication of an edict by Orestes, the prefect of Alexandria, on theatrical shows, which the Jews liked to attend as part of their Sabbath recreation but which the prefect wanted to control as a source of public disorder. In the audience were some members of the bishop's party who had come to take note of the proceedings. Among these was a primary school master called Hierax, who used to lead the applause at Cyril's sermons and was regarded by the Jews as a trouble-maker. When his presence was observed, it was reported to Orestes, who had him arrested and interrogated under torture. As soon as Cyril was informed of this, he summoned the Jewish leaders and threatened them with reprisals if they took an aggressive line against the Christians. The immediate sequel to this was the outbreak of intercommunal violence in the neighbourhood of a church called Alexander's. The Jews raised an outcry in the streets one night that the church was on fire. When the Christians ran out to save the building, the Jews ambushed them and killed a number. Cyril, true to his word, took immediate countermeasures. At daybreak he made a tour of the Jewish quarter in person at the head of a large crowd and seized the synagogues in the name of the Church. Jews were driven out of their homes and their property plundered by the mob.[29]

John of Nikiu adds a significant detail. The Jews were wholly despoiled, he says, 'and Orestes the prefect was unable to render them any help'.[30] The Jews, it appears, were victims of a power struggle between the bishop and the prefect. In the disturbances that accompanied the imposition of Arian bishops in the fourth century the Jews had always sided with the authorities. Athanasius represents them as enthusiastic participants in the sacking of the cathedral and the harrying of the orthodox when Gregory the Cappadocian made his entry into the city in 339.[31] Fifty years later 'a mob of Greeks and Jews', according to Theodoret of Cyrrhus, drove out Athanasius' successor, Peter II, with the blessing of the prefect.[32] We may surmise that in the riots preceding Cyril's election the Jews had assisted the troops deployed by the authorities in support of his rival, Timothy.[33] Now Cyril, on the pretext of the Alexander's church incident, had turned the tables on them. His actions must have infuriated Orestes. They were clearly against the law, which required the authorities to 'repress with due severity the excess of those who presume to commit illegal deeds under the name of the Christian religion and attempt to destroy or despoil synagogues'.[34] Moreover, the Jews were vital to the city's economy. They played an important part in the shipping business, and it was one of the prime responsibilities of the prefect to see that the annual grain fleet was despatched to Constantinople.[35] Cyril's attempt at reconciliation – holding out the book of the Gospels for Orestes to kiss – was rejected. A public display of submission to Christ, and by implication to his minister, was not calculated to enhance the prefect's authority. Orestes submitted a report of the whole affair to Constantinople. Cyril sent in a counter-report claiming that the Christians had been provoked.[36]

During the next few months the rift between bishop and prefect deepened. Orestes, although a Christian, began to lean more heavily on pagan advisers to counterbalance the overbearing authority of the Christian bishop. After the fall of the Serapeum in 391 many pagan intellectuals had left Alexandria. One who remained was the philosopher Hypatia, the daughter of the mathematician Theon.[37] She was highly respected by Christians as well as pagans. It was she and not the bishop who was granted the right of *parrhēsia*.[38]

Hypatia was not a militant pagan but her privileged access to Orestes was a snub which Cyril could not endure. The campaign of intimidation he began to bring to bear on Orestes is illustrated by two incidents. In the first the monks were called in from Nitria. Five hundred of them, 'resolved to fight on behalf of Cyril',[39] descended on the city. They waylaid the prefect in his carriage and shouted out abuse, accusing him of being a pagan. Orestes remonstrated with them but stones began to fly, one of them striking him on the head and covering his face with blood.[40] The perpetrator, a monk called

Ammonius, was arrested and interrogated so severely that he died. Rival reports from the prefect and the bishop were again sent to the emperor. Cyril attempted to score a propaganda victory by exposing Ammonius' body in a church and declaring him a martyr. But the more sober-minded element of the Christian population saw this as a cheap attempt to put further pressure on the prefect.[41]

In the second incident a Christian mob led by a cleric, a lector called Peter, attacked Hypatia as she was being driven through the city. She was seized from her carriage and dragged into the Caesareum, the former temple of the imperial cult, which was now the cathedral. There she was stripped and stoned to death with broken roof tiles.[42] Her body was then hacked to pieces and burned. John of Nikiu claims that afterwards 'all the people surrounded the patriarch Cyril and named him "the new Theophilus", for he had destroyed the last remains of idolatry in the city'.[43] Hypatia's body had indeed been treated like the cult images of the pagan temples, which had been broken up and burned as dwelling-places of the demons.[44]

The murder of Hypatia took place in March 415.[45] In the following year the imperial government responded with an edict reprimanding the bishop indirectly for exceeding his authority ('It pleases our Clemency that clerics should have nothing in common with public affairs or matters pertaining to a municipal senate') and regulating the affairs of the *parabalani*. Their number was reduced to 500, the names to be approved by the prefect of Alexandria, who was also to vet new members when vacancies occurred.[46] Although the number was increased to 600 and control was restored to the bishop seventeen months later,[47] honour seems to have been satisfied. We hear of no further difficulties with the prefect of Alexandria for the rest of Cyril's episcopate.

THE YEARS OF CONSOLIDATION

For the next twenty-eight years Cyril directed one of the greatest institutions of the Roman world.[48] The term 'patriarch' does not appear until after his death,[49] but the reality of patriarchal power had been exercised by the bishops of Alexandria since the beginning of the fourth century. Canon 6 of the Council of Nicaea (325) had confirmed the jurisdiction of Alexandria over the bishops of Egypt, Libya and the Pentapolis (i.e. Cyrenaica), some seventy-five in all. Each of them looked to the incumbent of the Alexandrian throne as his direct superior. Only the bishop of Alexandria had the right to perform episcopal ordinations, even in Cyrenaica, where the bishops were metropolitans. At Church Councils the Egyptian bishops always took their lead from their hierarch and voted as a bloc.[50]

The Alexandrian Church to which Cyril acceded was extremely wealthy. It had two regular sources of income: the contributions sent in from each diocese and the revenues it drew from its property.[51] From the middle of the fourth century the Alexandrian Church had begun to acquire land in the nomes, the administrative districts of the Delta and the Nile valley. As it did not enjoy tax exemption, there was no incentive for the government to block the growth of its holdings. These were small and scattered to begin with, not becoming great estates until the sixth century. But we have documentary evidence of an estate in the Arsinoite nome belonging to the Church of Alexandria in Theophilus' time which was large enough to need the services of two stewards.[52] There is also evidence that the Church of Alexandria had interests in Nile shipping.[53] The treasury that Cyril inherited from his uncle is therefore likely to have been a healthy one. Theophilus had spent large sums on building churches but he was a careful steward of the Church's wealth and in any case had been able to replenish the treasury from his despoliation of temples.[54]

The episcopal residence since about 360 had been the Caesareum, a huge complex of colonnaded buildings on an eminence overlooking the harbour, which had originally been built as a temple to the deified Caesar. It had been re-dedicated to St Michael, but was known to the end of the Roman period by its original name.[55] There is no evidence for any catechetical or ecclesiastical school in Alexandria after the death of Didymus the Blind in 398.[56] But the Caesareum would have housed at least a library and a secretariat besides other administrative offices under the supervision of the archdeacon. From this centre Cyril conducted the affairs of the Alexandrian Church until his death.

Apart from his annual festal letters to the bishops of Egypt, we have no precise dates for Cyril's writings until the outbreak of the Nestorian controversy. But to this early phase of his episcopate we can assign in their probable order of publication his two works on the Pentateuch, the *Adoration and Worship of God in Spirit and in Truth*, and the *Glaphyra* (or 'Elegant Comments'), his two works on the christological significance of the prophets, the *Commentary on the Minor Prophets* and the *Commentary on Isaiah*, and finally a series of works of a more dogmatic nature, the *Thesaurus*, the *Dialogues on the Trinity*, and the *Commentary on the Gospel of St John*.

A vignette of Cyril's pastoral work, preserved for us by Sophronius of Jerusalem, probably also belongs to this period.[57] It relates to the translation of the relics of Cyrus and John to Menouthis, a coastal town a few miles east of Alexandria. Menouthis was famous for its temple of Isis, a healing centre which attracted even Christians.[58] In order to draw Christians away from Isis, Cyril set up a rival shrine to which he transferred from St. Mark's church in Alexandria the relics of the Diocletianic martyrs Cyrus and John, the former of whom, according to tradition, had been a doctor who had treated the poor without charge. The survival of Cyrus' name in the modern place-name, Aboukir (Abu-Kyr), suggests that Cyril's strategy was successful.[59]

2

THE EARLY WRITINGS

Peter Brown in a recent study has drawn attention to 'the seeming dissonance between late Roman upper-class culture and late Roman political reality'.[1] There is a comparable 'seeming dissonance' between the ecclesiastical literary culture of the period and the harsh realities of church politics. At first sight the works that Cyril produced in the tranquillity of his study early in his episcopate seem remote from the practical business of running his immense diocese. When the Egyptian bishops assembled at a synod, they did not come to debate theological points with their Alexandrian colleague. They came to receive instructions from their patriarch. Powerful as Cyril was, however, the art of persuasion was still vital to him. The theoretical relationship between Christianity and Judaism could not be established by burning a few synagogues, nor could erroneous views on the nature of the Trinity or the person of Christ be countered by episcopal fiat. Moreover, the episode of the attempted canonization of Ammonius had warned Cyril early in his episcopate that educated public opinion could not be taken for granted. It needed to be wooed.

Cyril had a combative cast of mind, sharpened on Aristotelian dialectics and steeped in the study of the Bible. He became a bishop at a time of greatly increased tension between Christians, pagans and Jews as a result of the Theodosian laws of 391. The popular violence against the temples unleashed in that year by the imperial prohibition of pagan worship spilled over into attacks on synagogues. At first the government tried to control this. A rescript of 393 made the destruction of synagogues illegal.[2] But by 416 Judaism, which had hitherto been a *religio*, was being referred to as a *superstitio*.[3] And in 423 a further rescript, while reiterating the prohibition on the burning of synagogues, decreed that no new ones were to be built or existing ones repaired.[4] It is against this background of Judaism's deteriorating legal status that Cyril developed his theological position on the Mosaic laws and the prophetic writings of the Old Testament.

THE CHALLENGE OF JUDAISM

Cyril's first work, the *Adoration in Spirit and in Truth*, is presented in the form of a dialogue between Cyril and a questioner called Palladius.[5] Palladius is troubled by two of the sayings of Christ: Matthew 5:17–18 (I have come not to abolish the law and the prophets but to fulfil them) and John 4:23 (true worshippers will worship the Father in spirit and in truth). How are these two texts to be reconciled? It seems to Palladius that the second implies the abolition rather than the completion of Jewish worship. In reply Cyril gives an exegesis of a selection of passages from the Pentateuch with the aim of developing the idea of worship in spirit and in truth by showing how the 'types and shadows' of the Old Testament find their fulfilment in the realities of the New. Indeed, the ultimate purpose of the *Adoration* is to demonstrate the concordance of the two Testaments and to prove that the Christians, not the Jews, are the true heirs to the promises of God.[6]

In the course of carrying out this programme, Cyril sets out in the early books of the *Adoration* an outline history of salvation. First he delineates the problem. Human beings are orientated towards vice and are in servitude to the enemy. How are they to reject evil, throw off the yoke of slavery, and return to the beatitude of their primitive state? The first man was created by God and stamped with his image and likeness by the Holy Spirit, who is the 'breath of life' (Gen. 2:7). Nevertheless, at the instigation of Satan, 'that wicked and God-hating beast', he freely chose to disobey God. As a result of his disobedience he was expelled from paradise and came under the power of corruption and death. The law of Moses was given as a partial remedy to this situation, but human beings were unable to find a way out on their own. The intervention of God himself was needed, which finally took place with the coming of Christ. Christ put an end to the old situation because in his own person he recapitulated the life of Adam, though without submitting to sin. Now believers by uniting themselves with Christ can benefit from his victory over sin and death.[7]

The festal letters that were sent out to the Egyptian bishops early each year in order to announce the date of Easter confirm and amplify this outline of salvation history. The approaching feast provided a suitable occasion for reviewing the whole sweep of the divine economy, which Cyril sees in terms of four phases.[8] The first is the human condition after the Fall, dominated as it is by the devil, sin and corruption. The second is the incarnation of the Word, who reveals God and liberates us from sin. The third is the redressing of the situation. The opposition of the Jews and of Satan leads Christ to his passion. But his death reveals his divine identity. He descends into hell and liberates the dead. The final phase is the resurrection of Christ and his ascension to the Father as the first-fruits of a new humanity. This is followed by the gift of the Spirit, which incorporates believers into the new humanity and assimilates them to Christ.

The festal letters and the *Adoration in Spirit and in Truth* illustrate some of Cyril's chief characteristics as a theologian and exegete. First of all, soteriological concerns are uppermost. It is these that determine his christology, just as his christology shapes his trinitarian theology. Secondly, he is fundamentally a Paulinist, deploying and developing many of the leading themes of Paul's epistles.[9] Thirdly, symmetries are important to him. The time of Adam is followed by the time of Christ, the descending movement of God by the ascending movement of man, kenosis by exaltation. Cyril's polemics are directed against those who are perceived by him to block this descending and ascending pattern of salvation. These are principally the Jews, who historically had attempted to block the descending movement of God by rejecting Christ and bringing him to his passion and death, and in Cyril's own time were attempting to block the ascending movement of the faithful, so to speak, simply by being who they were. In the Jewish view, the Old Testament was *their* Bible, which the Christians were misusing. From the Christian side, the continued existence of the Jews was a standing reproach to their own scheme of things. It was essential to Cyril's theological viewpoint that the prophets should look forward to Christ and that the Jews should be rejected and replaced by the Gentiles.

The Jews were not merely a theoretical problem to Cyril. In the letters of Isidore of Pelusium we have evidence of contacts between Christians and Jews on an intellectual level at the beginning of the fifth century in which Jews more than hold their own against Christian opponents. Isidore was a holy and ascetic priest of Pelusium, a great port in the north-east corner of the Delta, who maintained a vast correspondence with a large circle of people, including his archbishop, Cyril.[10] Among his correspondents was a man called Adamantius, who had been unsettled by a discussion with a Jew on the virgin birth. Adamantius was told to tell the Jew that there was nothing in Christianity that was foreign to the law and the prophets. But the Scriptures needed to be read correctly, which meant christologically.[11] Another correspondent was Ophelius, a schoolmaster who was engaged in a disputation with a Jew on Deuteronomy 18:15: 'The Lord your God will raise up for you a prophet like me from among you.' Christians took this to refer to Jesus, but the Jews to Joshua (the same name as Jesus in Greek) the son of Nun. Isidore gave Ophelius seven arguments of a logical and linguistic nature that he could use against the Jew.[12] There was also a bishop called Isidore who had been challenged by Jews to explain Haggai 2:9 on the rebuilding of the temple: 'For the glory of this house shall be great, the latter more than the former, says the Lord Almighty.' This, he was told, refers to the Church, which has replaced the temple, 'for Jewish things have come to an end'.[13] Against a Jewish inquirer who objected to the Eucharist as an innovation he defended Christian worship as the true fulfilment of the Law.[14]

The evidence presented by Isidore provides us with a more immediate context for Cyril's anti-Jewish polemics than the 'profound change of mood'[15] we have already noted with regard to the legal status of Judaism.[16] It was essential to the Christian view of salvation history that with the coming of Christ 'Jewish things' should have come to an end. The 'types and shadows' of the Old Testament had been succeeded by the reality of the New, the temple by the Church, the Passover by the Eucharist. The blows suffered by Judaism in the first and second centuries were regarded with quiet satisfaction by Christians for they confirmed the Christian view that they and not the Jews were the heirs to the divine promises. Yet the Jews would not go away. It had been an immense shock to Christianity when the Emperor Julian, who knew precisely where to aim his blows against the Church (his exclusion of Christians from public teaching posts had caused more consternation among Christian intellectuals than all the previous persecutions), undertook to assist the Jews in the rebuilding of the temple in Jerusalem. This was not according to the divine plan, as far as Christians were concerned, and profound relief greeted the abandonment of the project.[17] The Jews, however, and not only Jews but also Christians attracted to Judaism, continued to hope for a full restoration of the practices of the Old Testament. In his *Commentary on Zechariah*, dating from the first decade of the fifth century, Jerome vividly evokes the hopes of Jews for a restored Jerusalem:

15

The Jews and Judaizing Christians promise themselves at the end of time the building-up of Jerusalem, and the pouring forth of waters from its midst, flowing down to both seas. Then circumcision is again to be practised, victims are to be sacrificed and all the precepts of the laws are to be kept, so that it will not be a matter of Jews becoming Christians but of Christians becoming Jews. On that day, they say, when the Christus will take his seat to rule in a golden and jewelled Jerusalem, there will be no more idols nor varieties of worship of the divinity, but there will be one God, and the whole world will revert to solitude, that is, to its ancient state.[18]

With their apocalyptic hopes for final vindication, their complaints that Christians had misappropriated their Scriptures and their learned exegesis of the Hebrew text (to which Christian commentators continued to be indebted[19]) the Jews could not simply be ignored.

If it had not been for the Nestorian controversy, it is probably as a biblical commentator that Cyril would have been remembered. Like all patristic exegetes he distinguishes between the *historia*, the historical or literal meaning, and the *theoria* the spiritual significance.[20] Amongst Christian Platonists such as Origen or Gregory of Nyssa, the *theoria* was often interpreted as an allegory of the ascent of the soul to God. For Cyril, however, with his strongly christocentric emphasis, the spiritual sense always leads to some aspect of the mystery of Christ. In the preface to the *Glaphyra* he discusses his method:

> First we shall set out the historical events in a helpful fashion and explain these matters in a suitable way. Then lifting this same narrative out of type and shadow we shall refashion it and give it an interpretation which takes account of the mystery of Christ, having him as the goal – if indeed it is true that the end of the law and the prophets is Christ (cf. Rom. 10:14).[21]

By the time Cyril comes to write his commentaries on Isaiah and the minor prophets he has learned much from Jerome's exegetical methods,[22] but his fundamental orientation remains the same. Whatever is best in the spiritual interpretation 'looks to the economy relating to Christ'.[23]

The position of Moses in Cyril's scheme reflects this approach. In *Against Julian* Moses is exalted as the greatest of all teachers of wisdom, the inspirer of Plato and the entire Greek philosophical tradition. With regard to paganism Cyril has no doubt that Moses, as the paradigm of wisdom, belongs to the Church. With regard to Judaism, however, Moses becomes a more complex figure. On the one hand he is a type of Christ, representing symbolically ('in shadow') the salvific work of God that is to be achieved in its fullness in Christ. Thus when Moses seizes the tail of the serpent and turns it back into a rod (Ex. 4:4), he foreshadows Christ restoring humanity to its pristine state. When he puts his leprous hand into the fold of his cloak and draws it out restored to health (Ex. 4:6), he foreshadows Christ taking humanity into the bosom of God and restoring in it the divine image. When he pours onto the ground the water that turns to blood (Ex. 4:9), he is prefiguring the waters of baptism.[24] On the other hand Moses is also contrasted with Christ.[25] The fact that Moses was commanded to remove his shoes — these being 'a sign of death and corruption, for every shoe is made from the remains of dead and decaying animals' — in the presence of the theophany of the burning bush symbolizes the inaccessibility of Christ to those unwilling to shed the Mosaic law and its 'paedagogic' worship:

> For no one is justified in the law. It was necessary for him who wishes to know the mystery of Christ to put away beforehand the worship in types and shadows, which is superior neither to corruption nor to sin. Then he will know and enter into the holy land — that is, the Church. For those who have not rejected worship according to the law are subject to corruption, as the Saviour himself clearly said: 'Truly, truly I say to you, unless you eat the flesh of the Son of Man and drink his blood, you have no life in you' (Jn 6:53).[26]

The provisional character of the Mosaic dispensation is confirmed by other images. Moses is the servant of the household who must make way for the householder's son.[27] The law which he introduced is the plough that breaks up the soil of the people of God so that they are prepared to receive the seed of the Gospel.[28] The 'Jewish way' must be replaced by the 'evangelical way'.

If Moses is a type of Christ, it is because Christ has superseded him. Cyril's chief means of expressing this is through the Pauline image of Christ as the second Adam. The fundamental symmetry is already there in Paul: as one man, Adam, introduced death, so one man, Christ, introduced the fullness of life (Rom. 5:12–19; 1 Cor. 15:20–3).

Cyril applies to this image Irenaeus' idea of recapitulation. The whole of humanity is recapitulated in Christ, just as it was present originally in Adam. This is the meaning of the Pauline phrase, 'in Christ'. The chief content of the idea of recapitulation is the newness of life achieved in Christ. Christ is the second first-fruits, the second root, the representative example of the new humanity. He transforms the old, opening up a new path for us. The following passage from the *Commentary on John* spells out the implications that the image of the second Adam holds for Cyril:

> Next, wishing to clarify in turn the different modes of recapitulation, Paul once said: 'For God has done what the law, weakened by the flesh, could not do: sending his own Son in the likeness of sinful flesh and for sin, he condemned sin in the flesh, in order that the just requirement of the law might be fulfilled in us, who walk not according to the flesh but according to the Spirit' (Rom. 8:3–4); and on another occasion: 'Since therefore the children share in flesh and blood, he himself likewise partook of the same nature, that through death he might destroy him who has the power of death, that is, the devil, and deliver all those who through fear of death were subject to lifelong bondage' (Heb. 2:14–15).
>
> That these are the two modes of recapitulation necessarily entailed by the account of the incarnation of the only-begotten Son, Paul has explained to us. But that there is another mode that includes these others the wise John has taught us. For he writes about Christ in the following way: 'He came to his own home, and his own people received him not. But to all who received him, who believed in his name, he gave the power to become children of God; who were born, not of blood nor of the will of the flesh nor of the will of man, but of God' (Jn 1:11–13).
>
> It is therefore manifest, in my view, and plain to all that it is especially for these reasons that, being God and by nature from God, the Only-begotten became man in order to

condemn sin in the flesh, kill death by his own death and make us sons of God, regenerating those on earth in the Spirit and bringing them to a dignity that transcends their nature. For surely it was well planned that by this method the race that had fallen away should be recapitulated and brought back to its original state, that is to say, the human race.[29]

Of the three modes of recapitulation to which Cyril draws attention, the moral (condemnation of sin), the physical (killing of death) and the spiritual (becoming sons of God through the Spirit), it is the third that brings the Church into direct competition with Judaism. Who are the sons of God? Are they the physical descendants of Israel? No, says Cyril. The Jews repudiated Christ and remain attached to the types and shadows of the Scriptures. In consequence Israel has been replaced by the Gentiles:

What more, then, should one say, or what is remarkable about those who believe in Christ compared with Israel, since the latter too is said to have been begotten by God, according to the text, 'Sons have I begotten and brought up, but they have rejected me' (Is. 1:2)? To this I think one should reply as follows: First, that since 'the law has but a shadow of the good things to come instead of the true form of these realities' (Heb. 10:1), even this was not given to the descendants of Israel for them to have in a literal sense but was depicted in them typologically and figuratively 'until the time of the reformation' (Heb. 9:10), as Scripture says, when it would become apparent who those were who more appropriately and more accurately called God their father because of the Spirit of the Only-begotten dwelling within them. For the descendants of Israel had 'a spirit of slavery inducing fear', while Christians have 'a spirit of sonship' eliciting freedom, 'which enables us to cry "Abba! Father!"' (Rom. 8:15)[30]

Just as Moses has been superseded by Christ, so the physically constituted people of God has been superseded by a people constituted by the Spirit. This spiritual Israel, which is the Church, is characterized by a double participation in the divine life, a corporeal one maintained through the Eucharist and a spiritual one brought about by the reception of the Holy Spirit at Baptism. The eucharistic body is the real body of the Word endowed with his power. It is described as a co-worker, not consubstantial with the Word but deriving its efficacy through being united to that which is life by nature. 'When we taste of it, we have that life in ourselves since we too are united (*synenoumenoi*) with the flesh of the Saviour in the same way that the flesh is united with the Word that dwells within it.'[31] It restores us to the Adamic state, to incorruption, when it is mingled (*anakirnamenon*) with our bodies.[32] The Eucharist lies at the heart of Cyril's piety.[33] In the *Commentary on John* he defends it on the one hand against those who through excessive reverence abstain from receiving it, thus cutting themselves off from the source of life, and on the other against the Jews, who 'should not suppose that we have invented some kind of new mystery' and 'become angry at being called from types to reality'.[34] Foreshadowed in the manna of the desert and the paschal lamb, the Eucharist enables the believer to participate corporeally in Christ as intimately as the earthly body of Christ participated in the Word.

Such participation in Christ is made possible by the Holy Spirit. It is the Spirit that restores us to the divine image and likeness:

> You should be aware that we call the human spirit an offspring of the Spirit, not because it comes from him by nature, for that is impossible, but because in the first place, with regard to its origin it was called through him from non-being into existence, and secondly, with regard to the dispensation of the Incarnation, it was remodelled by him to make it conform more closely to God, impressing upon us his own stamp and transforming our understanding, as it were, to his own quality. This, I believe, is also the correct way of interpreting the sayings that Paul addressed to some people: 'My little children, with whom I am again in travail until Christ be formed in you!' (Gal. 4:19) and also: 'For in Christ Jesus I have begotten you through the Gospel' (1 Cor. 4:15).[35]

The baptized henceforth live with the divine life. They become by participation that which the Son is by nature:

> We therefore ascend to a dignity that transcends our nature on account of Christ. But we shall not also be sons of God ourselves in exactly the same way as he is, only in relation to him through grace by imitation. For he is a true Son who has

his existence from the Father, while we are sons who have been adopted out of his love for us, and are recipients by grace of the text: 'I have said, you are gods and all of you sons of the Most High' (Ps. 82:6).[36]

The deification of the believer is correlative to the incarnation of the Word, the working out in the individual of the descending and ascending pattern of salvation which we have already noted with regard to the true Israel. Like Athanasius, Cyril sees in Christ a paradigmatic transformation of the flesh, the promotion of our nature in principle through union with the Word from corruption to incorruption, from human inadequacy to the dignity of deity. But there is also a new emphasis. The recovery of the divine image and likeness takes place pre-eminently in our inner life and involves the will. We are called to a spiritual transformation through a dynamic participation in Christ by means of Baptism and the Eucharist, and not only in Christ but in the life of the Trinity as a whole. For the Son and the Spirit together bring about our filiation and sanctification. Through them we have access to the Father and so arrive at deification. *Theopoiēsis*, Cyril's preferred term for deification until the controversy with Nestorius, is the goal of human life. We do not merely become images of the image. Through Christ we participate in the source of divine being itself, sharing a community of life with the Father, Son and Holy Spirit as gods and sons of the Most High.[37]

THE REFUTATION OF ARIANISM

Athanasius frequently compared the Jews to the Arians. In his view they were two sides of the same coin: 'For the Jews said: "How, being a man, can he be God?" And the Arians: "If he were very God from God, how could he become man?"'[38] The Arians 'have shut themselves up in the unbelief of the present Jews',[39] for although they approach the problem of the person of Christ from a different starting-point, they reach a similar conclusion. Athanasius put his finger on the central difficulty of the Arians, albeit in a tendentious fashion: how to affirm a God who is utterly transcendent and yet also knowable and accessible to human beings. If there are no distinctions in the *ousia* of the Godhead, how does the second person of the Trinity attain any real solidarity with ourselves?

In Cyril's day the current form of Arianism was that of the Anomoeans, Aetius and Eunomius. These radical neo-Arians, who became bishops of Antioch and Cyzicus, respectively, in 362 and 360, derived their sobriquet from holding that there was an essential dissimilarity between the ungenerated Father and the generated Son. Aetius is blamed by Socrates for having arrived at this opinion through having come under the spell of Aristotle's *Categories* (which he had probably absorbed, like Cyril, as a student in Alexandria).[40] Certainly together with Eunomius, who began his career as his pupil and secretary, he acquired a reputation for 'a relentless dialectic' that has persisted to the present day.[41]

Aetius died in 367 and Eunomius in 394. We hear of Arian communities that revered their memory in Antioch and Constantinople but not in Alexandria itself.[42] Who, then, were Cyril's opponents? The First Ecumenical Council had condemned two bishops of the Pentapolis, Theonas of Marmarice and Secundus of Ptolemais, for holding Arian views in 325.[43] In the early fifth century Arianism seems still to have been flourishing in the area. Synesius of Ptolemais issued an encyclical letter to his clergy between 411 and 415 warning them of the teaching of a certain Quintianus, who was propagating 'the most godless heresy of Eunomius'.[44] Perhaps the presence of Arian teachers in this corner of his patriarchate was sufficient to stimulate Cyril to write against them. But as G.M. de Durand remarks, Cyril probably had no need of a stimulus of this kind to rouse him to action.[45] Not only did he have Athanasius and the Cappadocians as his model, but Arianism was still a living force in the Church at large, 'devouring the souls of simpler folk with an open gaping mouth'.[46]

The central issue on which Cyril opposes Eunomius is the question of the knowledge of God. According to Socrates, Eunomius held that our knowledge of the divine *ousia* is not inferior to God's knowledge of himself.[47] This is a hostile account that puts Eunomius' linguistic theory in the worst possible light. What Eunomius is more likely to have claimed, as Maurice Wiles argues, is 'to know enough about the *ousia* of God, about what it is to be God, to be able to exclude what he regarded as Cappadocian mystification and to ensure that our Christian language refers, that our speech about God has a purchase on reality'.[48] In opposing Eunomius, Cyril set himself the task of showing how a radically transcendent God could be reconciled with a Saviour who is fully divine (because only God can save) and yet one with us (because only thus can salvation be received by us).

According to Eunomius, language can give us access to the divine nature because the divine names are directly revealed by God and correspond to the reality of the things they signify. The divine intellect does not operate in a discursive manner. It comprehends the whole of reality in one act and expresses all in one word. A single term can therefore express the nature of God. For Eunomius that fundamental term is *agennētos*, 'ingenerate' or 'unengendered', which is not simply an *epinoia*, or mental construct, but defines the *ousia* of God.[49]

Against Eunomian realism Cyril defends the incomprehensibility of God and the deficiency of language. There is an infinite distance between the divine glory and the human word. How, then, can we talk about God? Cyril makes a distinction between existence and essence. We can know that God exists, but we do not know what he is by nature. Ontologically he is *hyperousios* – beyond essence or substance.[50] 'The divine nature,' says Cyril, 'is ineffable and cannot be comprehended by us in its fullest possible form, but only in what it accomplishes and effects.'[51]

The best way we can approach this transcendent reality is by analogy and from a multiplicity of points of view:

> Starting from a great number of contemplations, we gather knowledge, not without sweat and effort, as if in a mirror. And by assembling in our minds a conspectus of conceptual images as if in riddles and by means of very fine and, so to speak, polished mental representations, we acquire stability in faith. But since among creatures and beings subject to generation and decay nothing has been structured to resemble the supreme nature and glory in a precise and unique manner, it is with effort that we comprehend that which is connected with it and snatch from each existent thing in a useful way that which contributes to making it manifest.[52]

When we finally come into the presence of God, our partial knowledge will disappear, just as the stars shining resplendently in the night sky give way to the light of the sun.[53] But in the meantime we must work with figures and feeble images of reality. Cyril himself demonstrates this approach in his discussions of the Trinity. Usually he begins with metaphors and images before moving on to conceptual language. Guided by him, we shall follow his method.

Cyril's images, as Boulnois has pointed out, are not just rhetorical figures permitting a comparison between two terms.[54] They actually stand in the place of concepts, or rather, they convey difficult concepts in symbolic form. The context of the struggle against Arianism means that with regard to the first two persons of the Trinity the emphasis is on unity rather than diversity, but the use of metaphor means that the aspect of diversity is always present. The images used by Cyril are the following: source and stream, root and fruit, light and radiance, fire and heat, honey and sweetness, intellect and word, breath and spirit, flower and fragrance.[55] None of these is entirely his own invention. Their cumulative effect, however, lends a richness to his exegetical writing and demonstrates the value of the multiple analogical approach to the representation of complex theological ideas. Although our language is inadequate, we can say something in this way that gives us an insight into reality.

Source and stream, root and fruit, light and radiance, intellect and word are all well-established images in earlier patristic literature.[56] As pairs of terms, each of which entails the other, they are of great value in expressing on the one hand the co-eternity of the Father and the Son, and on the other their unity in diversity, their community of substance together with their separate identity. An image which Cyril does develop in an original way, however, is that of flower and fragrance.[57] In the *Commentary on Isaiah* he brings together a number of biblical texts on this theme: a flower shall grow out of the root of Jesse (Is. 11:1 LXX); the rod of Aaron put forth almond blossoms (Num. 17:8); Christ is a flower of the plain, a lily of the valleys (Song 2:1 LXX); he is the fragrance of the knowledge of God (2 Cor. 2:14).[58] These texts indicate, Cyril suggests, three different things: that Christ is like the fragrance of the Father, that in him human nature blossomed once again, and that the Holy Spirit produces a spiritual fragrance in the believer.

In the *Dialogues on the Trinity* and the *Commentary on John* Cyril develops these suggestions more fully. 'Everything,' he says, 'has, so to speak the fragrance of its own nature.'[59] Smells are not identical with the things from which they emanate, yet they take one directly to the particular nature of each species. The Son is the fragrance of the Father – distinct from his source yet inseparable from it and expressive of its unique nature. The procession of the Holy Spirit may also be compared to the dissemination of a fragrance. Commenting on John 16:15 ('All that the Father has is mine; therefore I said that he will take what is mine and share it with you'), Cyril says that this refers to the Spirit. It proves that the Spirit does not possess his wisdom by participation in the Son, which would make him ontologically inferior to him.

No, it is as if one of the most scented flowers gave out a fragrance that spreads and is sensed by the people in the vicinity: 'he will take what is mine'. What is signified is a natural relationship, not a participation in something separate. One takes it that this applies equally to the Son and the Spirit.[60]

When he returns to the same text in the *Commentary on John*, Cyril takes the image even further: 'If 'he will take what is mine', it is because (the Spirit) is consubstantial with the Son and proceeds through him as befits God, who possesses in its perfection all the virtue and all the power of the Son.'[61] The Holy Spirit is like 'a living and active fragrance from the substance of God, a fragrance which transmits to the creature that which comes from God and ensures participation in the substance which is above all substances.'[62] Not only does the Spirit transmit knowledge of the divine nature, as in the earlier texts, but participation in the divine nature as well. Another aspect of the operation of the sense of smell thus suggests itself to Cyril:

If in effect the fragrance of aromatic plants impregnates clothing with its own virtue and in some way transforms into itself that in which it finds itself, how does the Spirit not have the power, since it issues from God by nature, to give by itself to those in which it finds itself the communication of the divine nature?[63]

Human nature is endowed by grace with that which the Spirit has by nature. In this way the image of the transmission of a fragrance is able to contribute to the idea of the deification of the believer.

In the end, however, images are not sufficient in themselves to answer rational arguments without the help of philosophical concepts. As a student of Aristotelian logic, Cyril was well equipped to fight Eunomianism with its own weapons. He recognizes the limitations of analogy: that which transcends us does not conform to the conditions of our own world.[64] At the same time he does not overestimate the ability of the human mind to arrive at divine truth by intellectual processes.[65] Yet the Eunomians have made a rational case and if it is to be refuted, it must be on rational grounds.

Before discussing Cyril's philosophical models of the Trinity, let us briefly review his technical terms, as he himself does at the beginning of the *Dialogues*.[66] The Nicene Creed, which is set down as a benchmark, raises the first problem, that of the word *homoousion*.

Cyril's interlocutor, Hermias, protests that this is an innovative term not found in the Scriptures.[67] Cyril replies that this does not prevent the word being used if it corresponds to the truth. Other unscriptural expressions such as 'incorporeal' and 'without form' are used of God without anyone raising any objection. But there is in fact biblical justification for the term. God himself declared to Moses 'I am the one who is (*ho ōn*)' (Ex. 3:14). The present participle of the verb 'to be', *ōn*, revealed as his name by God himself, allows us to apply the derived noun, *ousia*, to God. If the Son is of the same nature as the Father he may therefore legitimately be called *homoousios*, of the same *ousia* or substance.[68] The term *homoiousion*, of similar substance, is to be rejected because if the Son is only similar to God, he is not in fact God and therefore cannot be our Saviour and Redeemer.[69] There is no middle way. Christ is either a created being or God. Then how can he be a mediator? The answer is by the self-emptying dispensation of the Incarnation.

The *homoousion* establishes the oneness of God. But what does the threeness consist in? A distinction is to be made between *ousia* and *hypostasis*; the former referring to the reality common to all three, the latter to the existence proper to the Father, the Son and the Holy Spirit.[70] *Physis*, or 'nature', is equivalent to *ousia*, while *prosōpon*, or 'person', is equivalent to *hypostasis*. These distinctions are derived from the Cappadocians, who had already done the work to establish the equivalence of *hypostasis* and *prosōpon*.[71] But in Cyril's terminology there is a certain fluidity which can sometimes lead to uncertainty of meaning. Although in his trinitarian theology *ousia/physis* is distinguished from *hypostasis*, in his christology *physis* is identified with *hypostasis*. Moreover, the equivalence of *hypostasis* and *prosōpon* is not absolute. *Prosōpon* has not yet established itself as a technical term and Cyril often uses it with its fundamental meaning, 'face', to the fore. When he uses *hypostasis* Cyril is therefore emphasizing the individual subsistence of the divine Persons; when he uses *prosōpon* he tends to be describing a subject responsible for its actions.[72] These equivocal meanings of *physis* and *prosōpon* will cause difficulties later in his polemics with the Antiochenes.

Another key term with an equivocal meaning is *idios*, 'proper' or 'own'.[73] Like Athanasius, Cyril uses *idios* in both a trinitarian and a christological context. The Son is the Father's own because he does not belong to the created order. The body is the Word's own because it has been taken into union with the Word in an intimate and inseparable manner. Within the trinitarian context Cyril usually employs *idios* to designate that which belongs to the common divine nature. But sometimes, like the Cappadocians, he uses *idios* to define that which distinguishes the Persons.[74] With regard to Eunomianism 'it is in the distinction between natural properties and hypostatic properties that the key to the Cyrillian refutation resides'.[75] To ascertain whether the Eunomian term *agennētos*, 'unengendered', is a property of the divine nature or of the hypostasis of the Father, one must ask, 'Compared to what is he unengendered?'[76] Clearly to the second person of the Trinity. 'Unengendered' cannot refer to the divine nature as such but only to the distinction between the Father and the Son. The Eunomians, however, claim not only that 'unengendered' is proper to the divine substance but that it is the divine substance. In Cyril's view this is to confuse *idion* with *ousia/physis*, to take a property for the divine nature itself. *Agennētos* may be used as a theological term but only as a property of the Father.

The threefold nature of God and the numerical order of the Persons are biblical data. The disciples were commanded by the risen Christ to baptize 'in the name of the Father and of the Son and of the Holy Spirit' (Mt. 28:19). Moreover, hints of the plurality of the Godhead are already present in the Old Testament. More than once Cyril draws attention to the significance of the first person plural in the text, 'Let us make man in our image' (Gen. 1:26) and to the appearance of the Lord to Abraham in the form of three men (Gen. 18:1–3).[77] How, then, are these three hypostases to be defined?

Cyril's approach is through the names that the New Testament gives to them.[78] The Arians saw the names 'Father' and 'Son' as metaphorical because if God had really engendered a son, that would imply change in him, which is impossible. Cyril defends the divine generation as something mysterious and beyond comprehension which really does express the ontological relationship between the first two Persons of the Trinity. In order to counter Arian accusations of anthropomorphism, however, he needs to prove the reality of divine paternity without submitting the Father to the limitations of the human condition. This he does by applying to Arian views a logical critique. For example, on the subject of generation and will, Eunomius had argued that if the Father engendered the Son by an act of will, that would imply that the will of the Father pre-existed the Son and therefore that the Son is not co-eternal with the Father. Cyril counters this by a *reductio ad absurdum*. Is the Father good voluntarily or involuntarily? Either reply raises a problem because the question is wrongly conceived. The question on the generation of the Son is of a similar kind. The Father engendered the Son not by will but by nature, for no act of will pre-existed his generation.[79] Drawing on chapter 7 of Aristotle's *Categories*, Cyril argues that Father and Son are correlative terms which define the reciprocity of the first two persons of the Trinity.[80] Although 'Father' and 'Son' are human analogies, they do in fact express a truth, namely, that the Father is the source and principle of divinity and that the Son is also divine, not in an extrinsic way by participation in something prior to himself, but intrinsically, or 'by nature'.

The same arguments may be applied to the Spirit. Against both the Eunomians, for whom the Spirit was a creature like the Son, and the Macedonians, who accepted the divine dyad of Father and Son but found it difficult to fit a third hypostasis into the relationship, Cyril maintains that the Spirit is divine by nature, not by a relationship with the Son that is merely extrinsic. He encounters a difficulty, however, with the New Testament names, 'Holy' and 'Spirit', because these can apply to the divinity as a whole and do not seem adequate to the task of marking off the Spirit as a distinct divine hypostasis. Cyril makes the most of the available analogies. The original meaning of *pneuma* as 'breath', for example, is pressed into service. As intimately connected with the person who is breathing yet not part of him, *pneuma* is an image signifying the proper existence of the Spirit and his consubstantiality with the other two hypostases.[81] Most of the Spirit's appellations, however, are rather abstract. He is 'the quality of the deity',[82] 'the quality of the holiness',[83] 'the sanctifying power of the divinity',[84] the 'completion (*sympleroma*) of the Trinity'.[85] These suggest that the Spirit must inevitably remain largely anonymous. Cyril cannot draw from his name a definition of his proper mode of being as he can in the case of the Father and the Son. There is a hidden quality of the Spirit which defies elucidation.

Something may nevertheless be said about the mode of subsistence proper to the Spirit on the basis of two Scriptural texts, the Pauline 'Spirit which is from God' (*to ek tou theou*) (1 Cor. 2:12) and the Johannine 'Spirit of truth who proceeds from the Father' (*ho para tou patros ekporeuetai*) (Jn 15:26). If the name 'Spirit' does not yield satisfactory results, the prepositions *ek* ('from out of') and *para* ('from the side of'), and the verb *ekporeuein* ('to proceed') offer an alternative line of enquiry.[86]

The Spirit is 'from out of' the Father. Cyril almost never uses the preposition *ek* of the Spirit in relation to the Son.[87] It is the Father who is the fount and source of Godhead for both the Son and the Spirit:

Since the Son is from (ek) the Father, that is, from his essence, we conceive of him coming forth from him in an ineffable way and abiding in him. We also conceive of the Holy Spirit in the same way. For he is from him who is truly God by nature, but in no way separated from his essence. Rather, he issues from him and abides in him eternally, and is supplied to the saints through Christ. For all things are through Christ in the Holy Spirit.[88]

The Son is able to supply the Spirit to the saints on the economic level because on the theological level the Spirit is the proper (idion), not the extrinsic (ouk exōthen), possession of both the Father and the Son.[89] It is this that differentiates the third from the second Person of the Trinity and prevents him from being a second Son. As the idion of both the Father and the Son he can be poured forth 'from both' (ex amphoin) – that is to say, Cyril quickly adds, from the Father through the Son.[90] The preposition para can be used like ek to indicate the Spirit's principle of origin in the Father. It occurs less frequently, however, and usually in the context of discussions of the economic Trinity: the Spirit is received by the Son and distributed to the saints 'from the side of' the Father.[91]

The remaining term sanctioned by Scripture is 'procession'. Cyril uses it rarely, considering the bulk of his writings, and always with reference to the Father as the source of the Spirit's being – never to assert that the Spirit proceeds from the Son, or even from both the Father and the Son.[92] He defines the noun, ekporeusis, as a coming forth from the essence of God.[93] The Spirit 'proceeds' (ekporeuei) from the Father, yet at the same time is also the idion of both the Father and the Son, for the Son is not to be excluded tout court from the procession of the Spirit. The implications of the Spirit as the idion of the Son were later to cause considerable unease to Theodoret of Cyrrhus, who could accept the expression in view of the consubstantiality of the Persons but not if it implied that the Spirit took his very existence from the Son.[94] Cyril assured him that he accepted that the Holy Spirit proceeded from God the Father in accordance with the Lord's saying, but insisted that the Spirit was not alien (ouk allotrion) to the Son.[95] It is characteristic of Cyril's christology that he should have wished in this way to safeguard the Son's integration into the life of the Trinity as fully as possible.[96]

The most fruitful way of approaching the Spirit's proper mode of being is perhaps through his role in the economy of salvation. As the 'quality of the deity', the idion of the Father and the Son, the Spirit is entrusted with the communication to human beings first of the knowledge of God and secondly of participation in him. He does not do this in isolation, of course, from the other two Persons, but his role with regard to believers is a particularly intimate one. As the last in the order of processions from the Godhead, he is the first to initiate their return to God. In Baptism he remodels them not in his own image but in the image of the Son. In the Eucharist and the practice of the Christian life he deifies them by enabling them to participate in the divine life of Christ. The proper mode of his subsistence may elude us, but it is in him that we attain our salvation.

3

THE NESTORIAN
CONTROVERSY

The difference in tone between Cyril's writings against the Arians and those against Nestorius is striking. The latter are altogether more vehement and expressed in much more personal terms. With the appearance of Nestorius, Cyril felt himself challenged at the vital core of his faith, and not by a heretic on the margins of the catholic Church but by the bishop of the imperial city itself whose views inevitably commanded a wide audience. The fight against the enemy within was to call for all the resources that Cyril could muster.

Nestorius had been summoned to Constantinople by Theodosius II in the spring of 428 to succeed Sissinius, who had died on 24 December 427.[1] The intense rivalry between different clerical factions that followed the death of Sissinius prompted the emperor to look further afield for a successor. On the recommendation of John of Antioch, his choice fell on Nestorius, a native of Caesarea Germanicia in Commagene, who was at the time superior of the monastery of Euprepius, just outside Antioch.[2]

At his inaugural sermon in the presence of the emperor on 10 April 428, Nestorius exclaimed: 'Give me, O Emperor, the earth purged of heretics, and I will give you heaven in return. Assist me in destroying heretics, and I will assist you in vanquishing the Persians.'[3] Like that other fiery orator, John Chrysostom, who had come from Antioch to Constantinople a generation earlier, Nestorius was to antagonize powerful interests with his zealous approach to his new responsibilities. Within five days of his enthronement he began a ruthless persecution of Arians, Macedonians and Quartodecimans. The ugly disturbances that accompanied this programme did nothing to enhance his reputation. Nor did his harrying of the saintly Bishop Paul of the Novatianists, who was much admired in aristocratic circles. In these matters, however, Nestorius' actions were not very different from those of Cyril. What marks him off from his Alexandrian colleague is his much weaker political acumen, as evidenced further by his alienation of two very influential elements of Constantinopolitan society, namely, the monastic party and the Augusta Pulcheria.

The presence of urban monasteries in Constantinople was something new to Nestorius, for they seem not to have been a feature of Syrian monasticism. The monks of the capital exercised an influential spiritual ministry amongst the laity and many were highly revered. One such was the archimandrite Dalmatius, a recluse who had been one of Theodosius' earlier choices as a successor to Sissinius but had declined on account of his commitment to the enclosed life. He was to create a sensation in the summer of 431 when he appeared dramatically in public to demand the ratification of Cyril's decisions at Ephesus.[4] Another was Hypatius, archimandrite of a monastery in Chalcedon across the Bosporus, who was Pulcheria's spiritual adviser. Nestorius' orders that monks were to confine themselves to the liturgical routine of their monasteries and not engage in urban ministries earned him gratuitous opponents.

By an egregious error of judgement, however, Nestorius was to create an enemy for himself more powerful than any monk: the Augusta Pulcheria herself. Theodosius' elder sister was no ordinary Byzantine princess.[5] Although not technically a nun, she lived the life of a consecrated virgin in the imperial palace, devoting herself to prayer and good works. She had brought up her brother on the early death of their parents and in consequence maintained a powerful ascendancy over him throughout his life. Her combined status as Augusta and professed virgin gave her a unique role in ecclesiastical affairs. When Nestorius took possession of the cathedral of Constantinople, he found her portrait over the altar, which he had removed.[6] He also gave instructions that the robe she had donated as an altar cover was no longer to be used. Moreover, when Pulcheria attempted to enter the sanctuary to receive communion the following Easter, Nestorius closed the royal doors to her. She had apparently been accustomed to receiving communion in the manner of the clergy and the emperors, but Nestorius said that no woman could enter. 'Why?' she demanded. 'Have I not given birth to God?' – if a woman had given birth to God, surely a woman could enter the sanctuary, especially one whose consecrated virginity assimilated her to the Mother of God. Nestorius, shocked, replied that she had given birth to Satan.[7] The enmity thus generated was to be a major factor in Nestorius' downfall, for 'there is little doubt that Pulcheria understood attacks on the Theotokos as a personal affront'.[8] When Nestorius began to preach against the title *Theotokos*, the response was led by people close to Pulcheria.

THE DEVELOPMENT OF THE CRISIS

Towards the end of the summer of 428 a delegation came to Nestorius to ask his ruling on a disputed theological point. Should the blessed Mary be called *Theotokos*, 'she who gave birth to God', or *Anthrōpotokos*, 'she who gave birth to man'?[9] The first term seemed Apollinarian to the proponents of the second, the second adoptionist to the proponents of the first. Nestorius ruled that neither was wrong, but the expression *Christotokos* was a much better one because it was closer to the language of the New Testament. Looking back on this episode many years later, Nestorius claimed, somewhat disingenuously, that it was a local matter which he would have resolved in a perfectly reasonable manner had it not been for a combination of two factors: 'the ambition of those who were seeking the episcopate' and the interference of the 'clergy of Alexandria'.[10] By these two factors he meant Proclus, consecrated bishop of Cyzicus but prevented by the populace from entering his see, who had been the strongest of the local candidates passed over for the Constantinopolitan throne, and Cyril, the ever-watchful guardian of the theological traditions of Alexandria. That the dispute was not simply of local importance was to be proved by subsequent events.

Some weeks later, perhaps in November, a priest called Anastasius, who was a member of the entourage Nestorius had brought with him from Antioch, preached a sermon in the Great Church in which he denounced the term *Theotokos*: 'Let no one call Mary *Theotokos*, for Mary was only a human being, and it is impossible that God should be born of a human being.'[11] 'These words,' Socrates says, 'created a great sensation, and troubled many both of the clergy and the laity.'[12] A riposte was not long in coming. On 26 December, the day that had been recently instituted as a 'festival of virginity', Proclus preached an ecstatic sermon on the Mother of God in the presence of Nestorius and no doubt of the imperial ladies.[13] Mary, he declared, is the glory of the female sex. In her all women are honoured, for as mother and virgin she recovered for us what was lost in the Fall:

> She is the spiritual garden of the second Adam, the workshop of the unity of the natures, the celebration of the saving

exchange, the bridal chamber in which the Word espoused the flesh, the living natural bush which the fire of divine childbirth did not consume (cf. Ex. 3:2), the real swift cloud which supported corporeally him who rides on the cherubim (cf. Is. 19:1), the most pure fleece filled with heavenly dew (cf. Jud. 6:37, 38), from which the shepherd clothed the sheep.[14]

Mary is the unique bridge between God and humanity, the loom on which the seamless robe of the union was woven by the Holy Spirit. Through her, Christ who is both God and man entered the world without even destroying her virginity *in partu*:

> Emmanuel as man opened the gates of nature, but as God did not rupture the barrier of virginity. He came forth from the womb in a manner comparable to the way in which he entered by the faculty of hearing (cf. Lk. 1:38). He entered impassibly; he came forth ineffably, according to the prophet Ezekiel, who said: 'The Lord brought me back by way of the outer gate of the sanctuary that looks eastwards, and it was shut. And the Lord said to me, Son of man, this gate shall remain shut, it shall not be opened, and no one shall pass through it; for the Lord God of Israel shall enter by it and it shall be shut' (Ez. 44:2). Here is clear proof of holy Mary the *Theotokos*. Let all further disputation cease and let us be illuminated by the teaching of the Scriptures, that we may obtain the kingdom of heaven in Christ Jesus our Lord, to whom be glory for ever and ever. Amen.[15]

The sermon was greeted with rapturous applause, much to Nestorius' displeasure.[16] Early in the following year, 429, he began a series of lectures as a corrective to the use of the term *Theotokos* and the christology implied by it, which seemed to him dangerously close to Apollinarianism.[17] Nestorius was a powerful orator, able to respond to his audience's reactions and develop his points even in the face of hostility. He does not mince his words: 'That God passed through from the Virgin *Christotokos* I am taught by the divine Scriptures, but that God was born from her I have not been taught anywhere.' Those who call Mary *Theotokos* are heretics.[18]

If Anastasius' sermon had caused a sensation, Nestorius' lectures came as a bombshell. Opposition to him in the capital began to grow. A lawyer called Eusebius (later to be bishop of Dorylaeum) had a poster displayed in a public place accusing Nestorius and his party of teaching the adoptionism of Paul of Samosata.[19] Quotations from Paul and Nestorius – those from Nestorius including: 'Mary did not give birth to the divinity', 'How can Mary have given birth to one older than herself?' and 'He who was born of the Virgin was a man' – were arranged in parallel columns to suggest that there was very little difference between the two. As a nice touch, the presentation of quotations concluded with one from an Antiochene bishop, Eustathius, anathematizing those who held that there were two sons, the eternally begotten Son of the Father and the son born of Mary. With these mutual accusations of heresy, the crisis moved into a new phase.

The news of the disturbance created in Constantinople by Nestorius' lectures quickly spread abroad. Cyril seems to have been aware of it when he composed his paschal letter for 429. He makes no direct mention of Nestorius but he dwells on the unity of the person of Christ and refers to Mary as 'Mother of God' (*Mētēr Theou*).[20] Shortly afterwards, however, Cyril addressed an encyclical letter to the monks of Egypt in which he does deal specifically with the issues raised by Nestorius.[21] Most of the themes which he develops later in his letters and anti-Nestorian treatises are found in this letter. First he discusses the title '*Theotokos*', which he insists is implied by the divinity of Christ. It may not be Scriptural but it expresses the belief of the Apostles that Jesus Christ is God and is supported by patristic testimony. The title safeguards the true union of God and man in Christ because it excludes the idea that Christ is either merely a God-bearing man or else a God who simply uses the body as an instrument. Rational arguments from analogy are also employed. In the case of human beings God gives the soul but the flesh is formed in the womb, yet a human mother gives birth to the whole living being. The purpose of these arguments is to draw out the soteriological implications of the Incarnation. Anything that diminishes Christ reduces him to our level and makes it impossible for him to be a saviour. We are gods by grace; therefore he must be God by nature. Eucharistic questions are also raised. How do we participate in the flesh of Christ if he is a man like us?

Copies of the letter were soon forwarded to Constantinople. And before long visiting clergy brought Cyril news of Nestorius' reaction to it.[22] On hearing that Nestorius had expressed extreme annoyance, Cyril wrote him his first letter, *Andres aidesimoi*.[23] If Nestorius was upset, he said, he only had himself to blame, for he had started the disturbance. Nestorius, he was told, had asked why Cyril had not first written to him privately. Cyril's response was first that pastoral necessity demanded a public rebuke – it was essential to correct the view that Christ is not God but an instrument and tool of the deity and a God-bearing man – and secondly that by the time he wrote his *Letter to the Monks* the disturbance was no longer a domestic matter but had already assumed international proportions. Celestine of Rome and the Italian bishops, he added ominously, were following the affair with the greatest concern. Nestorius would be well advised to amend his theological line if he wanted to put a stop to an ecumenical scandal. The threat of Roman involvement would not have been wasted on Nestorius, and his final remark that he was ready to fight to the death for the faith of Christ showed that he was in deadly earnest.

Nestorius replied with a curt note, *Ouden epieikeias*.[24] He declares that Cyril's letter contains a lot about his own piety but nothing about brotherly love, not to put it more strongly than that. He responds with his own veiled threat: events will show who is right.

Nestorius now moved to assert the authority of the imperial see. There were always visiting ecclesiastics at Constantinople who had come to appeal to higher authority to have the wrongs redressed that they believed they had suffered in their local churches. Among these were several Western bishops exiled for their Pelagian views and a group of litigants from Alexandria. Nestorius wrote to Pope Celestine requesting information on the Pelagians, evidently with the intention of proceeding to a formal review of their case.[25] Moreover, he began investigating the complaints of the Alexandrians.[26] Apart from his initiatives on the canonical level, he also hardened his theological line. Towards the end of 429 he invited Dorotheus of Marcianopolis to preach in the cathedral – possibly on the anniversary of Proclus' sermon. The event was reported by Cyril to Celestine the following year.[27] Dorotheus had proclaimed: 'If anyone dares to call Mary *Theotokos*, let him be anathema.' Whereupon, according to Cyril, there were loud protests and a general exodus from the church.

On hearing of this episode Cyril sent Nestorius his second letter, *Kataphlyarousi*, which the Acts of Chalcedon date to February 430.[28] First he brushes aside the Alexandrian complaints that Nestorius is purporting to review – these are petty wrongdoers against whom Cyril has ample evidence. Then he sets out a succinct statement of his single-subject christology. The Word was not changed into flesh or transformed into a human being but was united hypostatically (*kath' hypostasin* – a novel expression in a christological context, which means 'fundamentally', 'not superficially') with flesh endowed with soul and reason. The single subject of the suffering and death of Christ is the impassible Word, who conquers death because he is by nature immortal and incorruptible.

> Scripture, after all, has not asserted that the Word united a man's role (*prosōpon*) to himself but that he has become flesh. But the Word's 'becoming flesh' is just the fact that he shared flesh and blood like us, made our body his own and issued as man from woman without abandoning his being God and his being begotten of God the Father but remaining what he was when he assumed flesh as well. This is the universal representation of carefully framed theology. This is the key to the holy fathers' thinking. This is why they dare to call the holy Virgin '*Theotokos*' – not because the Word's nature, his Godhead, originated from the holy Virgin but because his holy body, endowed with life and reason, was born from her and the Word was 'born' in flesh because united to this body substantially (*kath' hypostasin*).[29]

The campaign against Nestorius now began in earnest. All through the spring and summer of 430 Cyril worked energetically to marshal international support. The key to success lay in ensuring that the court was on his side. To this end he reworked one of his earlier treatises, the *Dialogue on the Incarnation*, bringing it to bear on the dispute with Nestorius, and sent it to Theodosius.[30] Two small treatises were also sent to the empresses, Pulcheria and Eudocia, and to the princesses, Arcadia and Marina.[31] Although Cyril was correct in attaching importance to the support of the imperial ladies, it was a mistake to try to enlist their help independently of Theodosius. The emperor was irritated by Cyril's blatant acknowledgement of where the power really lay.[32]

Ecclesiastical allies, of course, were also vital. Cyril wrote to Acacius of Beroea, the doyen of the Eastern bishops, who had participated with Theophilus in the Synod of the Oak which had condemned John Chrysostom. But Acacius was too old and experienced to be drawn in. The doctrinal issue, however, combined with the canonical implications of Nestorius' interest in the Pelagians' case, ensured that Rome would wish to be involved even without encouragement from Cyril. In the summer of 430 Cyril sent Celestine a dossier on Nestorius with a covering letter.[33] 'The longstanding custom of the churches persuades us to communicate with your Holiness,' he writes. The occasion prompting his communication is the sermon preached by Dorotheus, as a result of which people were staying away from Nestorius' liturgy. Presenting himself in a judicious and moderate light, Cyril reviews the progress of the crisis, touching on Nestorius' homilies, how they were brought into Egypt and caused a disturbance, his own *Letter to the Monks* and the good impression it made in Constantinople ('people wrote to thank me'), his forbearance in not breaking off communion with Nestorius but on the contrary his earnest efforts to recall him to orthodoxy. Enclosed with the letter was a collection of patristic testimonies, together with a selection from Nestorius' writings.

Rome gave the matter careful attention. Cyril's dossier was sent for assessment to John Cassian in Marseille as the foremost Western expert on Eastern affairs. After receiving a negative report from Cassian, Celestine convoked a synod of Italian bishops, which met early in August 430 and, unsurprisingly, pronounced against Nestorius. Celestine wrote to Cyril entrusting him with the execution of the synod's decisions in the East.[34] He also wrote to Nestorius, complaining of the poison on his lips and recalling him to his pastoral responsibilities.[35]

In the meantime pressure was building up in Constantinople for the convoking of an ecumenical council. The archimandrite Basil, one of the leaders of the monastic party, addressed a petition to the emperor complaining that monks and laymen who protested that Nestorius was teaching two sons were being subjected to beatings and imprisonment, and appealing for a general council.[36] Nestorius, still confident of the emperor's support, did in fact decide to call a council of his own, consisting of a representative selection of theologians – experts who could appreciate the subtlety of his arguments – from the dioceses under his control or friendly towards him. Once the idea of a council had been mooted, however, the momentum of events soon ensured that Nestorius' conception of it would be superseded. A general council was not in itself detrimental to Nestorius' interests provided, of course, it was held in Constantinople or its environs. What must have come as a shock to him was the decision – taken no doubt under the influence of Pulcheria – to hold the council in Ephesus, a metropolitan see hostile to Constantinople and, moreover, already a centre of devotion to the Virgin. The imperial sacras were sent out on 19 November, convoking the council at Ephesus on 7 June the following year, the feast of Pentecost.

Unaware of this development, Cyril had called a synod of

Egyptian bishops to confirm the decisions of the Italians. Buoyed up by their condemnation of Nestorius and by the papal mandate he had received, Cyril wrote his third letter to Nestorius, *Tou sōtēros hēmōn*.[37] Celestine had sought the healing of 'the sick doctor'.[38] Cyril wanted to force Nestorius into a corner in which his choices were either a humiliating capitulation or resignation and exile. He therefore appended to his letter the notorious Twelve Chapters, a set of propositions cast in the most uncompromising terms which anathematized those who did not subscribe to them. This letter, together with that of Celestine communicating the decisions of the Roman synod, was delivered to Nestorius at his residence by an Egyptian delegation after the liturgy on Sunday, 30 November.[39] If Cyril had known the effect his letter would have, it is doubtful whether he would have couched it in the form that he did.

Nestorius was taken aback by Cyril's starkly aggressive stance. He at once sent the Twelve Chapters to John of Antioch, with the result that the Antiochenes rallied to the defence of their Constantinopolitan colleague. Although urging Nestorius to show moderation and come to some compromise,[40] they did not recognize in Cyril's propositions a statement of orthodox belief. Two of their ablest theologians, Andrew of Samosata and Theodoret of Cyrrhus, wrote hostile critiques of the Twelve Chapters from an anti-Apollinarist viewpoint, to which Cyril felt bound to reply. In the months leading up to the council Cyril was fully occupied repairing the damage done to his cause.[41]

THE THEOLOGICAL ISSUES

What was really at issue in this dispute? Both sides agreed on the fundamentals of the Nicene faith, namely, that Christ was truly God and truly man. Each rejected the caricature drawn of it by the other, Nestorius denying that he was teaching two sons in the manner of Paul of Samosata, Cyril denying that he was propounding an Apollinarian Christ who was not fully human. Why, then, could they not come to an agreement? The reason was that, despite the disclaimers, each believed that heretical conclusions were necessarily implied by the logic of the other's language about Christ. Cyril, rooted in Athanasian soteriology, could not believe that a Christ who was the result of a merely extrinsic union between the Word and humanity, such as Nestorius seemed to teach, was capable of effecting our salvation. Nestorius, for his part, could only see Cyril's arguments through anti-Apollinarian spectacles.[42] If the Word did not unite himself with a human life that was complete in every respect, he could not be our Saviour, for as Gregory of Nazianzus had said, 'that which has not been assumed has not been healed'.[43] The issue was therefore ultimately about the nature of salvation. The clash arose from the fact that Cyril and Nestorius approached it from different starting-points, Cyril, working with a 'katagogic' model, asking how does the Word become human without ceasing to be divine, Nestorius, working with an 'anagogic' model, asking how is this man Jesus Christ divine without compromising his humanity.[44]

There was also a problem of terminology. The key words *ousia*, *physis*, *hypostasis* and *prosōpon* were still in the process of becoming technical terms and are used by both protagonists in a fluid, not to say confusing, manner. *Ousia* is 'substance' or 'essence', the irreducible being of something. In Aristotelian usage it could also mean the universal, the genus or the substratum. *Physis* has a range of meanings very similar to *ousia*. It signifies 'nature' or 'essence' or 'substratum'. But it also means nature as manifested in the physical world, and hence can be equivalent to *hypostasis*.[45] *Hypostasis* has the fundamental meaning of 'support' or 'substructure'. In philosophical usage it means 'subsistence', actual reality as opposed to appearance. In trinitarian theology it signifies substantive existence or a subsistent entity or concrete reality.[46] *Prosōpon* has an even broader range of meanings. Its fundamental meaning is 'face' or 'countenance', from which come the significations 'representation', 'guise', 'role', 'individual self', and finally 'concrete representation of an abstract *ousia*'.[47] From this it may be seen that these words form a spectrum in which meanings shade into each other. *Physis*, or 'nature' can sometimes mean *ousia* and sometimes *hypostasis*. *Hypostasis* can be equivalent to *prosōpon* or distinct from it. The Cappadocians had spoken of one *ousia* in three *hypostaseis*, which after Chalcedon was to become the accepted terminology, *physis* being understood as synonymous with *ousia* and *prosōpon* with *hypostasis*. In Cyril's usage, however, *physis* is equivalent to *hypostasis* and means a concrete individual reality, so that Cyril can speak indifferently of a single incarnate *physis* or a single incarnate *hypostasis* of God the Word, which Nestorius, understanding *physis* and *hypostasis* in terms of *ousia*, interpreted in an Apollinarian sense. Conversely, Nestorius' talk of two *prosōpa*, meaning two different roles, forming a prosopic union by conjunction, seemed to Cyril to entail two sons, one human and one divine, for he understood *prosōpon* in terms of *hypostasis*.

Was it all then a matter of linguistics? No, although the terminology hampered mutual understanding there were real differences in the christological models espoused so ardently by the two protagonists. Cyril's chief concern was to maintain the single-subject christology he had inherited from Athanasius. The Word of God was the subject of all the acts of Jesus Christ, for salvation is brought about by the eternal Son who has accommodated himself in the economy of salvation to human life. Two key texts from the New Testament support this: John's statement that the Word was made flesh (Jn. 1:14) and Paul's that the Son emptied himself in order to become one with us (Phil. 2:6–11). Enfleshment and kenosis are the fundamental concepts underlying Cyril's christology. As Cyril became aware of the strength of the Apollinarian charges that were being pressed against him, he stressed that Christ had a human mind and soul. This aspect of his christology had been present from the beginning but its implications for a human psychology of Christ had not been developed, for his main focus had been on the salvific activity of the Word. When Christ was troubled or distressed, or appeared to be ignorant, it was because the Word was accommodating himself to the conditions of human life. If Christ suffered on the human level, he suffered impassibly (*apathōs epathen*), a paradoxical expression that attempts to encapsulate the idea of genuine human experience but without inner conflict.

In Christ God was acting humanly. One of the phrases that Cyril uses to express this is the Apollinarian slogan, 'one incarnate nature of God the Word' (*mia physis tou Theou Logou sesarkōmenē*), which he mistakenly thought to be of Athanasian origin.[48] It must have been brought to his notice at the beginning of the controversy with Nestorius, for it appears for the first time in the *Five Tomes Against Nestorius*.[49] 'For the incarnate nature of the Word is immediately conceived of as one after the union', he says, and goes on to give as an analogy the oneness of the human person although made up of two dissimilar elements, soul and body. This should have excluded an Apollinarian interpretation, for a simultaneous oneness and twoness is maintained. But the analogy of body and soul (even though used by Theodore of Mopsuestia)[50] is not a particularly felicitous one from the Antiochene point of view, for if Word and flesh are compared to soul and body, it is a short step to the position that the Word occupies the place of the soul in Christ. Cyril repeats the formula with the same analogy without further elaboration in his letter to Eulogius.[51] It is only in his replies to Succensus' inquiries after the Council of Ephesus that he addresses the Antiochene objections. The problem was put to him succinctly in the following words: 'If there is only one incarnate nature of the Word, there must have been a sort of merger and mixture, with the human nature in him being diminished by its removal.' To this Cyril replies:

> Again they twist the facts, failing to recognize that the reality is one incarnate nature of the Word. If the Word who was begotten mysteriously of God the Father and who afterwards issued as man from woman by assumption of flesh (not lifeless flesh but flesh endowed with life and reason) is truly and actually one Son, he cannot be divided into two persons or sons but remains one, though not discarnate or incorporeal but possessing his very own body in inseparable union. To say this could not possibly mean or entail mingling, merger or anything of that kind, how could it? If we call the only-begotten Son of God become incarnate and made man 'one', that does not mean he has been 'mingled', as they suppose; the Word's nature has not transferred to the nature of the flesh or that of the flesh to that of the Word – no, while each element was seen to persist in its particular natural character for the reason just given, mysteriously and inexpressibly unified he displayed to us one nature (but as I said, *incarnate* nature) of the Son. 'One' is a term applied properly not only to basic single elements but to such composite entities as man compounded of soul and body. Soul and body are different kinds of thing and are not mutually consubstantial; yet united they constitute man's single nature despite that fact that the difference in nature of the elements brought into unity is present in the composite condition.[52]

Wickham remarks that this is the closest Cyril comes to the 'two natures' formula of Chalcedon.[53] Although there is only one incarnate nature of the Word, for the Word is a single subject, that oneness does not destroy the twoness – even the word 'one' can be an equivocal term for Cyril.

The term that Cyril seems to have devised himself to express the 'how' of the oneness is 'hypostatic' (*kath' hypostasin*). Both aspects of *hypostasis* are brought into play here, the sense of actual reality as opposed to appearance, and the sense of substantive existence. The hypostatic union was one that was real (i.e. ontological rather than moral) and personal (i.e. resulting in a concrete individual who was the single subject of the actions and experiences of Jesus Christ). One of the ways of expressing this was by the system of cross-reference known as the *communicatio idiomatum*.[54] Anything predicated of the divine Word could also be predicated of the assumed humanity and vice versa by virtue of the single hypostasis. The subject of the life of Jesus is the Word, who has emptied himself to accommodate himself to human life. The ignorance and fear shown by Jesus on occasion are evidence of such accommodation. These attributes cannot be assigned simply to the humanity, while others, such as the power manifested in the miracles, are assigned to the divinity. They must all refer to the single divine hypostasis who is the author of our salvation.

In his Third Letter to Nestorius, Cyril insists that all the sayings in the Gospels must be referred to a single *prosōpon*, the incarnate hypostasis of the Word.[55] To Nestorius this seemed as if Cyril was saying that Christ was the product of an Apollinarian *krasis*, or fusion, of the human and the divine. Nestorius preferred to speak of two *prosōpa* (meaning 'roles', as opposed to Cyril's single *prosōpon*, which meant 'hypostasis'). For him the humanity and the divinity each had to be given its due weight. Each was a separate reality which together made a single reality. Looking back on the controversy many years later from his desert exile, he set out his understanding of prosopic union as opposed to Cyril's hypostatic union:

You should not have accused me and calumniated me as if I did not confess a single *prosōpon* in two natures, or as if I set the natures apart in separation and division, as if they were separated in a spatial sense and distant from one another. For I have indeed called the 'dweller' him who necessarily dwells in the nature. The dweller is he who dwells in him who serves him as a dwelling, and he has his *prosōpon*, while he who serves as a dwelling has the *prosōpon* of him who dwells. So by the use of their *prosōpa*, as though they were making use of their own properties in an authoritative way, the former is the latter and the latter is the former, the former and the latter abiding just as they are in their natures. If he is truly God, we confess that he is truly God also in his nature and that he is complete, lacking nothing of the nature of the Father; and we confess that the man is truly man, complete in his nature, lacking nothing of the nature of men, neither in body nor in soul nor in knowledge; he has all this in our image, apart from sin. He is not without activity in his own nature. For although God makes use of these things in his own *prosōpon*, he makes use of them as of things appertaining to man, in the same way as the humanity makes use of the divinity in the things appertaining to divinity. For they have a union with regard to the *prosōpon* and not with regard to the *ousia*.[56]

By insisting that the union is on the level of *prosōpon* rather than *ousia*, Nestorius attempts to preserve a voluntarist element in his model of Christ: the union was not simply a mechanical one but involved Christ's human will. This is the aspect which lies behind the use of the term *synapheia*, conjunction, which drew such scorn from Cyril. Nestorius had said in one of his addresses: 'There is no division in the conjunction, or in the dignity, or in the sonship. There is no division in his being Christ, but there is division between the divinity and the humanity.'[57] Cyril protests at Nestorius' 'indivisible conjunction' (in spite of being himself a practitioner of the paradoxical statement). Anything suggestive of mere juxtaposition or proximity is utterly unacceptable as a synonym for 'hypostatic union', nor will Nestorius' arguments in favour of a nominal identity serve in its stead.[58]

When Cyril returns to christological themes in the years after the controversy he picks on 'conjunction' as indicative of Nestorius' fundamental error: 'But is this mere conjunction with the Word enough to allow him to group the proper glory of God and rise above the bounds of the created order? Does this make him an object of worship even though he is not God?'[59] For Cyril this is the crux of the matter. Christ is not simply a theological problem to be dissected and scrutinized; he is a Saviour to be worshipped and adored. The salvation he offers is a dynamic process that begins with the Word's accommodating himself to the human situation by a free act:

> If [the Word] had not been born like us according to the flesh, if he had not partaken of the same elements as we do, he would not have delivered human nature from the fault we incurred in Adam, nor would he have warded off the decay from our bodies, nor would he have brought to an end the power of the curse which we say came upon the first woman.[60]

That is why the term *Theotokos* is so important. In a single word it encapsulates the entire plan of salvation. 'You destroy the mystery of the economy of the flesh by saying that the holy Virgin should not be called *Theotokos*.[61] The Incarnation in principle transformed human nature as a whole, the Word refashioning it in his own flesh. This was the aspect of the Incarnation that Nestorius, with his emphasis on the moral rather than the ontological character of the union of the natures, found least acceptable. 'Why do you mock the beauty of truth and call the deification of the sacred flesh an apotheosis,' cries Cyril, 'all but scolding those who have chosen to hold an orthodox view for professing this?'[62] The Word descended into the human world in order to raise it up to the life of God. Participation in the divine life is the purpose of the sacraments. And without the deifying power of the Word they are emptied of their efficacy: 'If you detach the life-giving Word of God from the mystical and true union with the body and separate them entirely, how can you prove that it is still life-giving?'[63] Unless the incarnate body of Christ was filled with divine life we cannot ourselves be transformed:

> The body of the Word himself is life-giving, since he has made it his own by a real union transcending our under-standing and powers of expression. In a similar way, if we too come to participate in his holy flesh and blood, we are endowed with life completely and absolutely, because the Word dwells within us, both in a divine way through the Holy Spirit and in a human way through the holy flesh and the precious blood.[64]

This transformation is not to be understood in a mechanical sense. Participation in the Spirit is also needed along with participation in the eucharistic flesh of the Son:

> Therefore the Son does not change the least thing belonging to the created order into the nature of his own deity (for that would be impossible) but there is imprinted in some way in those who have become partakers of the divine nature through participating in the Holy Spirit a spiritual likeness to him and the beauty of the ineffable deity illuminates the souls of the saints.[65]

Through partaking of the Spirit and the body of Christ, devout Christians are lifted up to a new level of being. If the Word has not already deified by nature the flesh that he assumed at the Incar-nation, Christians cannot become gods by adoption and participate in the divine life. Cyril's single-subject christology is the necessary presupposition for his transformational spirituality.

THE COUNCIL OF EPHESUS

The bishops began to gather at Ephesus at the beginning of June 431. The first to arrive was Nestorius with sixteen bishops and a military escort under the command of a personal friend, Count Irenaeus. He met with a hostile reception from Memnon, the bishop of Ephesus, who with his forty Asian bishops was solidly pro-Cyril, and in view of the decisions of the Roman synod regarded Nestorius as a defendant whose case was to be heard at the coming council. Until the matter was resolved all the churches in Ephesus were barred to him. Cyril arrived next by sea with fifty of his suffragans (the instructions concerning metropolitans did not apply to Egypt) and a number of monks, including the formidable Shenoute.[66] The appointed day, 7 June, came and went. Then, on the following Friday, 12 June, Juvenal of Jerusalem arrived with sixteen bishops from Palestine.[67] There was as yet no sign of the papal delegation, nor of the Eastern bishops, who were travelling overland by the imperial postal service.

The Council of Ephesus is the first ecumenical council the proceedings of which we can follow in detail.[68] Cyril knew that the legal forms had to be observed punctiliously because the record of the proceedings would be scrutinized carefully in Constantinople before the emperor's assent would be given. Accordingly, an Alexandrian priest called Peter was appointed *Primicerius*, or head, of the notaries who were to see that the proceedings of the council were conducted according to legal precedent and were properly recorded. The practical arrangements for the council, however, remained in the hands of the emperor, who entrusted them to a senior court official, the Count Candidian.[69]

During the period of waiting for the Easterners discussions were held at Nestorius' lodgings that were to have repercussions on the fortunes of the protagonists. Theodotus of Ancyra and Acacius of Melitene in Armenia Secunda came to the council as supporters of Nestorius. They were alienated, however, by Nestorius' didactic manner and scandalized, as they were to relate to the council, by hearing him say that neither birth from the Virgin nor being fed at the breast could be attributed to God, and that a two or three-month old baby could not be spoken of as God.[70]

The boost to the morale of the Cyrillian party given by the defection to them of two such senior figures as Theodotus and Acacius was the first of two factors that persuaded Cyril that he could go ahead and convene the council in the absence of the Easterners. The second was the arrival on 21 June of an advance party, consisting of Alexander of Apamea and Alexander of Hierapolis, who brought a letter together with a verbal message from John. The letter spoke of the hardships suffered on the journey and said that the main party was 'five or six stages' from Ephesus.[71] The accompanying message was: 'The Lord John the bishop told us to say to your Reverence, "If I am late, do what you must do."'[72] John no doubt meant that Cyril could go ahead if he was delayed beyond the week needed to complete the remaining stages of the route. Cyril, however, used the message as a pretext for immediate action.[73] John *was* late, so he summoned the council to meet the following morning, Monday 22 June.

Later Nestorius was to complain that Cyril took over the council and dominated it completely.[74] It is true that a letter signed by sixty-eight bishops was delivered to Cyril urging him to wait for the Easterners.[75] But Cyril proceeded at all times according to the ecclesiastical canons and imperial regulations that governed such councils. His right to preside was undisputed. Nestorius was debarred because he was under canonical censure from Rome. Cyril was the most senior hierarch present and in any case until the arrival of the papal legates was Celestine's proxy.[76] Even if the Easterners had been there he would have been the natural president. Presiding at the council was one thing, however, and attaining a satisfactory result was another. Cyril himself, as will be seen, did not intervene very much in the proceedings. Nor could he force the bishops to keep to his agenda. The business side was handled by Peter, the chief notary. Although Cyril will have prepared the agenda with him and supplied him with the dossier of documents and the books which he was later to lay before the fathers, all depended on the mood of the assembly. No doubt the party lists were anxiously scanned for an assessment of voting intentions. But a result could only be attained if there was unanimity. The bishops did not come to a council to negotiate a compromise. They came to recognize, and under the Holy Spirit to affirm, the true faith. Unanimity was the guarantee that the Holy Spirit was speaking. Without it a council would fail. Cyril judged that conditions so favourable to a positive result were unlikely to occur again, so he moved quickly. The only impediment was the lack of co-operation of Count Candidian, without whose reading of the imperial sacra the council could not legally be opened. On the morning of 22 June Candidian wanted to disperse the assembly, but Cyril outmanoeuvred him. When challenged to substantiate his authority, Candidian read out the contents of the sacra, which act was then taken as imperial authorization for proceedings to begin.[77]

The bishops assembled in the cathedral of Ephesus, the Great Church of St Mary the *Theotokos*.[78] Formal discussion was delayed because first a delegation was sent to Nestorius to invite him to attend. The delegates waited for several hours in the courtyard of his lodgings, but he refused to receive them.[79] Proceedings thus began without him in the afternoon with Peter, who acted as the secretary of the council, reading a summary of the events which had led to its being convoked.[80] Cyril's most senior allies were Juvenal of Jerusalem and Flavian of Philippi (who was also proxy for Rufus of Thessalonica). At this early stage of the session it was Juvenal who took the lead. At the end of Peter's report he intervened to ask for the imperial sacra that had been sent to each of the metropolitans to be read out. It was thus established that sixteen days had already elapsed since the day appointed by the emperor for the opening of the council. When this point had been underlined by Memnon, Cyril spoke, giving his reasons for opening the council – the sickness of many of the bishops and the death of some – and proposing that a number of further imperial documents should be read.[81] Theodotus of Ancyra, however, intervened to say that those documents could be read in due course; what should come next was the matter of Nestorius' absence. His attendance was necessary if the bishops were to accomplish their business with a common mind and purpose. Hermogenes of Rhinocolura (one of Cyril's suffragans from a town on the Pelusium–Gaza road) testified that Nestorius had been informed of the opening of the council the previous day and had said (somewhat ambiguously), 'I will examine the matter, and if it is necessary for me to come, I shall come.'[82] Other bishops confirmed that this was so. Flavian of Philippi then intervened to say that a further delegation of seven bishops had been sent to Nestorius that morning. The note that they were to have delivered was read out and the leader of the delegation, Theopemptus of Cabasa (another of Cyril's suffragans from a town in the Delta), was called upon to give his evidence. Flavian then said that in accordance with canonical requirements (*Apostolic Canons* no. 74), yet a third summons had been issued to Nestorius later in the morning without result. Again the leader of the delegation, John of Hephaestus (another Egyptian from the Delta), was called upon to give his report. Nestorius' wilful absence in defiance of the canons having thus been established, the council could move on to its main business.

Juvenal of Jerusalem now proposed that the Symbol of Nicaea should be read. This was done by Peter, who then announced that he had a letter to hand written by Cyril to Nestorius, which, if called upon by the council, he would read. On being asked to do so by Acacius of Melitene, he read Cyril's Second Letter, *Kataphlyarousi*. Cyril then intervened, submitting that what he had written to Nestorius did not differ from the teaching of the Symbol of Nicaea, and called on their holinesses to express their judgement.[83] Juvenal led the response followed by the statements of a further 124 bishops testifying that they recognized in Cyril's letter the orthodox faith of Nicaea. Then Nestorius' reply was read and again Cyril requested a response from the council. This time there were thirty-four testimonies, led as before by Juvenal of Jerusalem, at the end of which the bishops cried out: 'If anyone does not anathematize Nestorius, let him be anathema.'[84]

The way was now clear for the council to proceed to the formal deposition of Nestorius. Juvenal called for Celestine's letter to be read out. Then Peter announced that he had to hand supporting letters of Cyril to Nestorius, which he would read if requested. On being invited to do so by Flavian, he read Cyril's Third Letter to Nestorius, *Tou sōtēros hēmōn*. This time the letter seems to have been heard in silence. No acclamations are recorded; the record simply states that after reading the letter and putting it in the minutes, Peter went on to say that he had further letters from Celestine.[85] The Twelve Chapters that conclude Cyril's letter had already been attacked by Theodoret of Cyrrhus, who had arrived early in Ephesus independently of John of Antioch, and from the start had served as Nestorius' chief theological spokesman. Theodoret was one of the dissidents who were boycotting the council, but clearly his arguments had struck a chord in the minds of the bishops. Their unease was not lost on Cyril. After the council, when events seemed to turn against him, he set himself to write an exposition of the chapters which was designed to soften their impact and consolidate the support of the moderates.[86]

Having minuted *Tou sōtēros hēmōn*, Peter announced that the bishops were present who had handed the letter to Nestorius the previous year. Flavian then called on them to give their testimony. Their leader, Theopemptus of Cabasa, said that they went on a Sunday after the liturgy to the episcopal residence and gave him the letter in the presence of the clergy and almost all the *illustri*.[87]

Another member of the delegation, Daniel of Darnis in Cyrenaica, added that they were told to return the next day for a response, but the doors were shut to them.[88] This phase of the proceedings concluded with Fidus of Joppa saying that Acacius and Theodotus could testify that Nestorius still held those opinions, whereupon Cyril called upon them to do so.

Peter then announced that he had books to hand of the Fathers with select passages marked in them which he would read if requested. This was the first time that a patristic florilegium was put forward for the establishment of doctrine. The practice seems to have been an innovation of Cyril's.[89] Flavian moved that the patristic testimonies should be read. Peter then said that he had passages from books by Nestorius to hand, and Flavian moved that they should be read too. Finally a letter to the council from Capreolus of Carthage was read with a Greek translation.[90] Then Cyril put the proposal: Is it your wish to affirm the primitive doctrines of the faith and depose the innovator? He had judged the moment well. The decision was unanimous. All 197 bishops present at the first session, led by Cyril, Juvenal and Flavian, filed up to the altar and put their signatures to the deed of deposition.[91]

Cyril was jubilant. He wrote home describing how the crowds waited outside all day and when the doors opened in the evening how they escorted the bishops to their lodgings with torches and incense. The whole city was illuminated in celebration.[92] In the elation of the moment he told the people of Alexandria that he would be home as soon as the legal papers were prepared.

The following morning notice of deposition was served on Nestorius, 'the new Judas'.[93] Letters were also sent to Constantinople to make sure that the decision of the council would become as widely known as possible in order to make it difficult for the emperor not to ratify it.[94] For nothing, of course, was law without the imperial assent. Separate reports were sent to the emperor by the Synod, Nestorius, and Candidian.[95]

The arrival of John of Antioch's party on 26 June led to a dramatic turn of events. John was understandably furious that Cyril had not waited and immediately proceeded to hold his own council, attended by the dissident bishops.[96] The council found Cyril's Twelve Chapters tainted with the teachings of Apollinarius, Arius, and Eunomius and deposed both Cyril and Memnon, reporting the result to the emperor.[97] The Ephesians reacted by closing the churches to John and the forty-two other bishops who had signed the deed of deposition.[98]

Theodosius' response on receiving so many conflicting reports was to send to Ephesus an official on the staff of the Master of Offices called Palladius with letters annulling all that had been done at the partial gatherings over which Cyril and John had presided and ordering that the council should reassemble and confirm the true faith.[99] The two sides, however, refused to be brought together.[100] Moreover, by participating in the Johannine council, Candidian had compromised himself with the Cyrillians, with the result that he was no longer able to represent the emperor. Consequently, an official of the highest rank was sent out to replace him, the *magister* John, Count of the Sacred Largesses, with a different set of instructions, this time confirming the depositions of Nestorius, Cyril and Memnon.[101]

In the meantime the arrival of the Roman legates on 10 July had encouraged the Cyrillians. The council was re-convened at once at Memnon's residence for a second session in order to hear Celestine's letter. Five further sessions followed at intervals until the end of July.[102]

Count John arrived at the beginning of August and immediately put Cyril, Memnon and Nestorius under arrest. In order to resolve the impasse the emperor decided to hold a colloquy of theological experts within easy reach of the capital. Seven bishops were chosen from John's party and seven from Cyril's, the chief spokesmen on each side being Theodoret of Cyrrhus and Acacius of Melitene, respectively.[103] The delegates met on 11 September[104] at the Rufinianai Palace near Chalcedon, where they conducted their discussions in the presence of the emperor himself. The progress they made was reported back by John's delegates to his group at Ephesus in a series of letters. Their report that Acacius' mention of a passible Godhead upset the emperor encouraged the Easterners,[105] but in the end the results were inconclusive. The only positive outcome was that the Easterners put forward a statement accepting the Virgin as *Theotokos* that was to be the basis of the Formulary of Reunion of 433.[106] The momentum was gradually lost. Nestorius, who had lost his stomach for a fight, petitioned to be allowed to return to his monastery near Antioch.[107] A new bishop, Maximian, a man inoffensive to all parties, was chosen to succeed him as bishop of Constantinople and the consecration was arranged for 25 October.[108] The sacra of dismissal was sent to Ephesus, releasing the bishops.[109] Cyril, however, anticipating the course of events, had already left.[110] He returned to Alexandria on 24 October to a triumphant welcome.[111]

THE SEARCH FOR UNITY

The fact of the matter was, however, that the council had failed. Cyril's gamble in presenting John of Antioch with a *fait accompli* on his arrival at Ephesus had not paid off. Instead of accepting the majority decision, the Easterners repudiated what was done on 22 June, thereby denying the council the unanimity that would have brought peace to the Church.

For the next two years Cyril made strenuous efforts to retrieve the situation.[112] Friendly relations were soon established with the new bishop of Constantinople.[113] But only the government could do what was needed to heal the rift with the Eastern bishops, and the government was not particularly well disposed towards Cyril, as Cyril himself was perfectly aware. The long apologia he addressed to Theodosius on his return to Alexandria bears ample testimony to his sense of insecurity concerning his standing with the emperor.[114] The government acted in the following year, when an imperial commissioner, Aristolaus, was despatched to the East with instructions to bring about a solution, by force if necessary. If Cyril and John could not reach an agreement, they were summoned, each accompanied only by a few theological experts, to attend a conference before the emperor at Nicomedia – precisely the solution that Nestorius had proposed the year before Ephesus.[115] This was a period of great danger for Cyril, who saw clearly that there was a real possibility that Ephesus could be set aside and even that Nestorius could return to Constantinople. We know this from a fascinating letter from Cyril's archdeacon, Epiphanius, to Maximian of Constantinople, which mentions the strong pressure that was being applied to Cyril to withdraw the Twelve Chapters – 'Aristolaus has been pressing him to implement the imperial decrees' – and reveals that Cyril had sunk into a state of deep depression.[116] The letter was intended to be highly confidential, for it goes on to specify whom Maximian should approach behind the scenes and precisely what he should bestow in the way of gifts (including carpets, inlaid furniture and gold) in order to facilitate the formulation of a new imperial policy more favourable to Alexandria.[117] Ultimately there were only two possible solutions. Either the deposition of Nestorius had to be confirmed by the Easterners, and that precluded the withdrawal of the Twelve Chapters, for these were the real basis on which Nestorius had been condemned, or there had to be a return to the *status quo ante*, which would have entailed Cyril's own deposition and banishment.

These were the issues at stake when the tribune and notary Aristolaus, accompanied by the *magistrianos* Maximus, arrived in Antioch in the early summer of 432.[118] He carried with him, besides the imperial rescripts addressed to John and Cyril, letters from Theodosius to Acacius of Beroea and Symeon Stylites. Acacius and Symeon both had international reputations as holy men. In approaching them the emperor was following a well-established path for the resolution of an impasse.[119] Acacius, who was now over a hundred years old, was particularly well placed to act as a mediator. Not having attended the council, he stood outside the conflict and was revered by Cyril and the Antiochenes alike. At his prompting John held a synod at Antioch. The resulting letter from John was then entrusted by Acacius to Aristolaus, who brought it to Cyril. John insisted that the Antiochenes took their stand on the faith of Nicaea, as interpreted by Athanasius, without any additions: 'we reject the doctrines recently added either by letters or by chapters.'[120] When Cyril read this letter, he was dismayed: 'They wanted everything written by me,' he wrote to Acacius of Melitene, 'to be null and void.'[121] Nevertheless he set himself to compose a conciliatory letter to the elder Acacius in which he expressed his motives and his desires in a carefully considered way. This masterly letter was to create the conditions for reconciliation between Alexandria and Antioch.[122]

On the question of the withdrawal of his letters Cyril was adamant. He could not suppress his writings if those of Nestorius were still circulating. But he was aware of the problems caused by the Twelve Chapters and was anxious to limit their scope: 'My Chapters were written with such force only to withstand the teachings of Nestorius.'[123] If once peace had been established there was anyone still unhappy about them, he was invited to write privately to Cyril, who would elucidate them further. He wanted it to be understood clearly that he emphatically denied holding the opinions of Apollinarius, or Arius, or Eunomius, and stood firmly, like John, on the faith of the 318 fathers of Nicaea without adding anything. On the level of human respect, Cyril declared that at the request of the emperor he forgave those who had harmed him. The Egyptian bishops, outraged at the way that Cyril had been treated, were more difficult to bring round, but Aristolaus 'so calmed matters that he opened up for me an easy path towards peace.'[124] Peace was what Cyril wanted to see re-established. But it had to be accomplished in such a way that none of the bishops would dissent from it. 'For then it will be ecumenical and will avoid creating many other schisms in the process of healing this one.'[125]

The letter went down very well with the Easterners. Acacius passed it on to John, who studied it with his theological advisers. Theodoret pronounced it a complete *volte-face* – 'diametrically opposed to what he was writing before'.[126] In his view Cyril, if sincere, had removed the main impediment to union: 'we find his letter in agreement with what we say and completely opposite to the Twelve Chapters.'[127]

Aristolaus now returned to Alexandria accompanied by Paul of Emesa, who was briefed to conduct negotiations on behalf of John. Paul brought a letter from John, in which he welcomes Cyril's recent letter to Acacius of Beroea and expresses the hope for a complete healing.[128] He mentions the letter of Athanasius to Epictetus as an authoritative exposition of the faith of Nicaea and expresses full confidence in Paul of Emesa. But he gives nothing away. Nor did Cyril like its tone.[129]

The negotiations in Alexandria took some time.[130] Paul himself was perfectly willing personally to anathematize Nestorius and signed a document to that effect,[131] but this did not count for much if John was not prepared to sign on behalf of the Church of Antioch. Progress, however, was made in the weeks that followed. Aristolaus, as we have seen, was applying pressure behind the scenes. The Creed drawn up by the Antiochenes at Ephesus was accepted by Cyril with some small additions. This symbol of faith was inserted into the letter *Euphrainesthōsan hoi ouranoi*, usually referred to in its Latin form, *Laetentur coeli* ('Let the heavens rejoice'), which was entrusted to Aristolaus on the strict understanding that it was not to be delivered to John unless John first signed the anathematization of Nestorius.[132]

The public was prepared for the coming declaration of unity by a sermon delivered by Paul in the cathedral of Alexandria on Christmas Day 432.[133] When Paul proclaimed: 'Mary the *Theotokos* therefore gives birth to Emmanuel', the congregation burst into applause, crying out, 'That is the true faith! That is what we wanted to hear!'[134]

> Mary the *Theotokos*, [Paul went on,] therefore gave birth to Emmanuel, and Emmanuel is God incarnate. For God the Word who before the ages was ineffably and inexpressibly begotten of the Father in the last days was born of a woman. Having assumed our nature perfectly, and having taken humanity to himself from the first moment of conception, and having made our body a temple for himself, he came

forth from the *Theotokos*, the same perfect God and perfect man. By a union (*syndromē*) of the two perfect natures, I mean the Godhead and the manhood, he became for us one Son, one Christ, one Lord.[135]

Such a full statement of Cyril's single-subject christology was received with the greatest enthusiasm. There were shouts of 'Worthy!' and 'Welcome, orthodox bishop!' What Paul had proclaimed was a paraphrase in the Alexandrian idiom of the statement that Cyril had sent to John:

> Accordingly we acknowledge our Lord Jesus Christ, the only-begotten Son of God, to be perfect God and perfect man made up of soul endowed with reason and of body, begotten of the Father before the ages in respect of his Godhead and the same born in the last days for us and for our salvation of Mary the Virgin in respect of his manhood, consubstantial with the Father in Godhead and consubstantial with us in manhood. A union of two natures has been effected and therefore we confess one Christ, one Son, one Lord. By virtue of this understanding of the union which involves no merging, we acknowledge the holy Virgin to be *Theotokos* because God the Word was 'made flesh' and 'became man' and united to himself the temple he took from her as a result of her conception. As for the terms used about the Lord in the Gospels and apostolic writings, we recognize that theologians treat some as shared because they refer to one person, some they refer separately to two natures, traditionally teaching the application of the divine terms to Christ's Godhead, the lowly to his manhood.[136]

There were those who thought that by accepting the last clause of this formula Cyril was giving in to a two-subject christology. But as we have seen in relation to his trinitarian theology, he was well aware of the limitations of language and happy to accept a variety of approaches provided the essential truths were safeguarded. After repeating the Antiochene formula, he goes on to reassure John on two points: first that his christology is not crypto-Apollinarian, and secondly that it does not imply the passibility of the Word.[137] With regard to the first point, when he says that Christ is from heaven he does not mean that the flesh is of heavenly rather than human origin. There is no mixture or confusion of the human and the divine in

Christ. With regard to the second point, he confirms the impassibility of the Word: it is only by economy that the Word attributes to himself the suffering in the flesh.

Under pressure from Aristolaus, John finally gave way. He wrote to Cyril rehearsing the events of the previous year and concluding with the anathematization of Nestorius and the recognition of Maximian as his successor.[138] Officially the schism was over.

CYRIL'S LAST YEARS

For the remaining eleven years of his life Cyril worked hard to consolidate his victory, but no longer from the centre of world affairs. True to his word, he responded to private inquiries with careful expositions of his teaching, encouraging his more sober allies and calming the hotheads. From this period we have the letter to Acacius of Melitene explaining what had been achieved and reassuring through Acacius those of his supporters who thought he had conceded too much.[139] John of Antioch had been giving out, no doubt to reassure his own extremists, that Cyril had accepted the two natures.[140] Cyril insists that the phraseology of the Formulary of Reunion, which seems to separate the natures but which Cyril takes to be the one Lord speaking both divinely and humanly, was necessary in order to allay Antiochene fears of Apollinarianism.[141] Two letters to Successus, a Cilician bishop who strongly supported Cyril, are important for their exposition of christological doctrine.[142] In them Cyril attributes the origin of the idea of two distinct Sons to Diodore of Tarsus.[143] He also responds to a keen Syrian inquirer, the deacon Maximus, with a letter analysing the Nicene Creed,[144] and to a Palestinian deacon called Tiberius with a letter dealing with christological difficulties set out as a series of propositions.[145] The same Palestinian correspondent, now apparently a priest, elicited a further important statement from Cyril on Christian anthropology, the *Doctrinal Questions and Answers*.[146]

Other compositions of a longer nature supplement the letters. In 438 Cyril was asked by Theodosius to accompany the empress Eudocia on a pilgrimage to Jerusalem. There it was brought to his attention that a different christology to that of Ephesus was being promoted in the East on the basis of the writings of Nestorius' teacher, Theodore of Mopsuestia.[147] On his return to Alexandria, Cyril produced a series of works attacking Theodore of Mopsuestia and Diodore of Tarsus as pseudo-theologians. These works were

Against Diodore and Theodore, whom he now identified as the originators of the errors taught by Nestorius,[148] *Against the Synousiasts*, a riposte to a work of the same title by Diodore attacking Apollinarius, in which Cyril corrects Apollinarius from his own perspective,[149] and the dialogue *On the Unity of Christ*, his most mature expression of his christology, which again attacks the school of Diodore and Theodore.[150] The fruits of this campaign were to be reaped at the Fifth Ecumenical Council of 553, when the writings of Theodore and those of Theodoret that criticized Cyril's Twelve Chapters were condemned.

Cyril had his works copied and kept to hand in order to place with suitable recipients as the occasion arose.[151] John of Antioch, of course, would not have been an appropriate recipient for a polemical christological work. To him Cyril sent his copious refutation of the Emperor Julian's *Against the Galilaeans*, the multi-volume *Against Julian*.[152] Cyril had no doubt begun *Against Julian* many years previously, probably before the beginning of the Nestorian crisis. He returned to it, however, in the last decade of his life, perhaps giving it its final redaction at this stage.[153]

On a more domestic level, Cyril did not neglect his pastoral responsibilities to his Egyptian clergy. He wrote to the bishops of Libya and the Pentapolis, instructing them to be more careful about whom they promoted to the priesthood, as scandal had been given by the ordination of unsuitable candidates: newly married men and monks ejected from their monasteries.[154] He also wrote to Calosirius, a bishop of the Arsinoite nome (the Fayyum), directing him to put a stop to anthropomorphite ideas that were circulating in the monasteries in his area. Calosirius was, moreover, to correct erroneous notions concerning the Eucharist, namely, that the consecrated elements lost their efficacy if they were reserved for another day, and to keep a watchful eye on Messalian tendencies among the monks. Furthermore, he was to take steps to isolate the Meletians from contact with the orthodox.[155]

Cyril always kept his finger on the spiritual pulse of the desert. A late source sheds a characteristic light on his relationship with the monks. The story is told in the *Apophthegmata Patrum* of an unnamed monk living in Lower Egypt who believed that Melchizedek was the Son of God.[156] Such ideas are known to have circulated in Egypt – Epiphanius gives an account of a sect calling itself Melchizedekians.[157] When the monk's views were reported to Cyril, he sent an emissary to put a question to him in the form of an *aporia*, a theological doubt. Could the monk help Cyril decide the truth of the matter? Was Melchizedek a man or the son of God? The monk asked for some time to think and pray about it and came to the conclusion, through seeing a vision of the patriarchs, that Melchizedek was a human being after all. By his tactful approach Cyril delicately guided the monk away from a dangerous opinion. And through the vision the monk was able to accede to his bishop's teaching without loss of face.

Cyril died on 27 June 444. John of Antioch had predeceased him in 441 and had been succeeded by his nephew Domnus. Of the other protagonists, Juvenal and Theodoret were to live to take part in the next Ecumenical Council, held at Chalcedon in 451, that was to complete the work begun at Ephesus. Nestorius, who on account of his continued literary activity was banished from his monastery of Euprepius first to Petra and then to the Great Oasis in Upper Egypt, also outlived Cyril, dying perhaps in 450.[158] In the dispute with Cyril he had the last word. Bearing the hardships of his exile with fortitude and dignity, he wrote in the Great Oasis the apologia that has ensured him admirers to the present day.[159]

4

THE CYRILLIAN LEGACY

The complex figure of Cyril stands behind every phase of the christological controversies of the next century or so.[1] Cyril often expressed himself in strong terms, but he was by no means inflexible. His central intuition, that the Word was the dynamic single subject of both the divine and the human acts of Christ was in conflict with the more symmetrical Antiochene understanding of two mutually interpenetrating natures. Yet in the *Laetentur* letter he was able to accommodate the Antiochene tradition and point the way towards a fuller rapprochement. Even Theodoret came eventually to acknowledge the strength of Cyril's position. The more intransigent side of Cyril, however, as expressed in the *mia physis* slogan and the Twelve Chapters, proved to have greater popular appeal, with consequences for ecclesiastical unity that are still with us today.

The *mia physis* slogan, in particular, became a source of conflict within a few years of Cyril's death.[2] Cyril had interpreted 'one incarnate nature of God the Word' in an orthodox way, but it could easily be taken to imply that there were two natures before the union but only one after it. This was the teaching of Eutyches, an archimandrite of Constantinople and extreme Cyrillian, who emphasized the unity of Christ at the expense of his humanity. Eutyches was condemned in November 448 at a Home Synod (*synodos endēmousa*), at which his writings were judged against the standard of orthodoxy set by Cyril's Second Letter to Nestorius and the Formulary of Reunion, but he refused to accept the verdict. Protected by Chrysaphius, a powerful palace official, he wrote letters to a number of hierarchs protesting the orthodoxy of his teaching. His cause was taken up with enthusiasm by Dioscorus, Cyril's successor at Alexandria, who put pressure on Theodosius to summon a general council in order to exonerate Eutyches. This council met at Ephesus in August 449. Proceedings were controlled by Dioscorus, who was evidently hoping to repeat Cyril's success at Ephesus eighteen years previously. Unlike Cyril, however, Dioscorus neglected to secure the support of Rome. The Roman legates had brought with them Leo's *Tome to Flavian*, which was to play such an important role at Chalcedon, but they were prevented from reading it out. Instead Eutyches was allowed to hold the floor and win a supportive vote from the 113 fathers assembled at the council with the help of intimidation brought to bear by soldiers, monks and *parabalani*, who burst in at a prearranged signal. The way in which the vote was secured prompted Pope Leo to dub the synod 'the Robber Council'.[3]

The sudden death of Theodosius from a riding accident in July 450 led to a change of imperial policy which within fourteen months was to result in the annulment of the synod of 449 and the deposition of Dioscorus. Theodosius' sister, the Augusta Pulcheria, lost no time in getting rid of Chrysaphius, thus depriving Eutyches of his political support. She then took as her consort the Latin-speaking soldier, Marcian, who like her was sympathetic to the views of Pope Leo. A new ecumenical council was summoned in order to deal with the twin threats of Nestorianism and Eutychian monophysitism.

The council which met at Chalcedon in October 451 was the most representative held to date. It was attended by more than 450 fathers from all the eastern provinces of the empire, including Illyria (at that time dependent ecclesiastically on Rome), which in itself ensured that no one theological tradition would triumph to the exclusion of the others. The Cyrillian tradition was represented by the second letter to Nestorius and the *Laetentur* letter to John of Antioch, which incorporated the Antiochene Formulary of Reunion. The Latin-speaking tradition was represented by Leo's *Tome to Flavian*. The more extreme Cyrillian position, as expressed by the Twelve Chapters, was irreconcilable with the two natures teaching of Leo's Tome and was therefore excluded. The Council of Ephesus of 431 had produced no new symbol of faith, declaring as a matter of principle that nothing was to be added to the symbol of the 318 fathers of Nicaea. Under imperial pressure, however, the fathers of the Fourth Ecumenical Council drew up a new symbol of faith which sought to combine the oneness of Christ as a single subject with the duality implicit in his being 'perfect God and perfect man'.[4] Phrases from Cyril's amended text of the Formulary of Reunion were combined with Leo's understanding of the two natures. The resulting Definition of Christ as one person or hypostasis 'made known in two natures' without confusion or change was a skilful synthesis of the traditions of both East and West, but it lacked popular appeal and was widely seen as a betrayal of Cyril.[5]

Before the council had even finished its work, a Palestinian monk called Theodosius returned to Jerusalem to sound the alarm that the bishops were proclaiming a Nestorian Christ. Juvenal, who had won the independence of Jerusalem from Antioch at the council, nevertheless returned home to a hostile reception. In Egypt Dioscorus, who had been deposed by the council and exiled to Gangra in Paphlagonia, was succeeded by Proterius, who proved so unpopular that on the death of the Emperor Marcian in 457 he was murdered by a rioting mob. In the meantime the people of Alexandria had already elected Timothy Aelurus, who was to become the leader of the opposition to Chalcedon.[6]

Timothy Aelurus was an orthodox, if narrow, Cyrillian.[7] He opposed the Eutychians as well as the Chalcedonians, but his uncanonical election led to his being sent into exile at Gangra by the new emperor, Leo. Leo was succeeded by Zeno in 474 but in the following year Zeno was driven out of Constantinople by the usurper Basiliscus. Basiliscus summoned Timothy to the capital, and for the next twenty months Timothy controlled imperial ecclesiastical policy. The result was the Encyclical of Basiliscus (475), which condemned the 'innovations' of the Council of Chalcedon.[8] Timothy returned to Alexandria, where he pursued a moderate policy with regard both to theology (he accepted the double consubstantiality of Christ with God and with man) and to ecclesiastical discipline (repentant Proterians were not re-anointed like apostates). The overthrow of Basiliscus by the Emperor Zeno in 476, however, led to the setting aside of the Encyclical. Timothy's advanced age saved him from renewed exile, for within a few months he was dead.

The new ecclesiastical policy inaugurated by Zeno was inspired by the Patriarch Acacius, who had played a leading role in restoring the emperor to his throne. The immediate problem was the situation in Alexandria, where the Cyrillian majority was at loggerheads with the Proterian adherents of Chalcedon. Acacius, although sympathetic towards the views of Timothy Aelurus could not go so far as to condemn Chalcedon because of the twenty-eighth canon of that council, which for the first time gave Constantinople a proper patriarchate second in rank to that of Old Rome. The edict which was published in 482 came to be known as the *Henotikon* of Zeno.[9] Like the Encyclical of Basiliscus it takes as its standard the faith proclaimed by the 318 fathers of Nicaea that was confirmed by the 150 fathers of Constantinople and followed by the fathers who had been convened at Ephesus. It goes further than the Encyclical, however, in placating majority opinion in the East by also accepting as authoritative the Twelve Chapters of Cyril, 'whose memory is pleasing to God'. Nevertheless it attempts to steer a middle course by making no reference either to the *mia physis* formula or to the Tome of Leo. Instead it condemns in general terms any innovations made by anyone 'either in Chalcedon or in any synod whatever'. The Alexandrians would have liked to have seen an unequivocal condemnation of Chalcedon. Peter Mongus, Timothy's successor, subscribed to the edict all the same, but the extremist monastic party seceded, becoming known as the *Akephaloi*, 'the headless ones', on account of their lack of episcopal leadership. In spite of an initially favourable reception, at least in the East, the *Henotikon* did not achieve its purpose. Not only did it provoke a schism with Rome – the prelude, as Grillmeier has called it, of the *status schismatis* between East and West[10] – but it failed to reconcile the monophysite extremists in both Egypt and Palestine.

The *Henotikon* policy was continued by Zeno's successor, Anastasius, but with the accession of another Latin-speaking soldier, Justin, in 518 there came a new change of direction, once again in favour of Chalcedon. Chalcedon, however, had no hope of acceptance in the East on the popular level unless it could be shown to be in harmony with the teaching of Cyril. A determined effort was made in the reign of Justin's nephew, Justinian, to interpret Chalcedon in a 'katagogic', Cyrillian manner. The phrase used to express this, in order to make it absolutely clear that the 'one person' of the Definition was one of the Trinity, was the 'theopaschite' formula, 'one of the Trinity suffered in the flesh'.[11] This 'neo-Chalcedonianism', or 'Cyrilline Chalcedonianism', as it is often called, remained the official policy of the empire and received conciliar endorsement at the Fifth Ecumenical Council of 553.[12] By then, however, the conservative Cyrillian East had already been lost. Severus of Antioch, the last great patriarch of a united Antiochene Church, was driven into hiding as a result of the change of policy of 518, and continued to oppose Chalcedon and the Tome of Leo from a Cyrillian standpoint until his death in 538. Justinian made an attempt to reconcile him to the Imperial Church, but he was condemned in 536 by a *synodos endēmousa* as both a Nestorian and a Eutychian (by some extraordinary logic) and banished to Egypt.[13] In 543 Jacob Baradaeus was consecrated bishop of Edessa and succeeded in establishing a secessionist church with its own hierarchy, the 'Jacobites' or 'Monophysites', as their opponents called them. At the same time the Coptic Church, centred on the desert monasteries, was emerging in Egypt.

This very brief sketch of the christological debate in the century following Cyril's death perhaps suffices to give some idea of his pervasive influence. Most Eastern Christian communities defined themselves in relation to Cyril's teaching. The more strict Antiochenes, who recoiled from the Apollinarianism they detected in Cyril's writings and could not accept the Formulary of Reunion, flourished on the eastern borders of the empire and in Persian territory, calling themselves the Church of the East.[14] Those who were able to interpret Chalcedon in a Cyrillian manner remained in communion with the Imperial Church and were known as Melchites. The narrower Cyrillians, however, who regarded Chalcedon as incompatible with the Twelve Chapters, the only side of Cyril to which they gave real weight, were lost permanently to the Imperial Church in the sixth century and survive today as the Oriental Orthodox Churches. In the West Cyril was also venerated as a standard of orthodoxy but he was not well understood, for the Latins tended to contrast him too sharply with Eutyches, Dioscorus and Apollinarius.

Cyril's prestige has always remained high, at least in official ecclesiastical circles. In the seventh century Anastasius of Sinai called him 'the seal of the Fathers', and in the nineteenth Pope Leo XIII proclaimed him a Doctor of the Church.[15] Yet he is not read much today except by students of the history of doctrine. This is partly due to the surge of sympathy for Nestorius following the publication of his apologia at the beginning of the twentieth century, which added to the hostility long felt towards Cyril on account of the murder of Hypatia.[16] Cyril, however, deserves our attention. On the historical level a better understanding of his teaching could do much to dispel the standard notion that the failure of Chalcedon in the East was the result of 'ignorance, stupidity, stubbornness, or even separatist nationalist aspirations'.[17] On the dogmatic level he is the greatest patristic exponent of a christology 'from above'. On the spiritual level he is a theologian and biblical exegete well worth studying for the many insights he offers into the fundamental meaning of the Christian faith.

Part II

TEXTS

GENERAL INTRODUCTON TO
THE TEXTS

The following texts have been chosen to complement McEnerney's translation of the letters and the selections already published by Wickham and McGuckin. The emphasis has therefore fallen on the early works with nothing, except perhaps the passages from *Against Julian*, later than 431. Cyril, however, never changed his fundamental theological viewpoint. After 431 he searched for ways of expressing his convictions in words which did not antagonize his opponents, but at no time did he entertain any doubts about the position he was defending. The earlier exegetical works on Isaiah and St John's Gospel are therefore valuable for showing how he handled soteriological themes before Nestorius became an issue. In the *Five Tomes Against Nestorius* we see him working out at length the arguments that would be summarized in the dogmatic letters. The *Explanation of the Twelve Chapters* marks the beginning of a new phase when he is forced onto the defensive and realizes that he must reassure those who do not share his tradition that his views do not deviate from orthodoxy. The treatise *Against Julian* is the product of his hours of leisure, when he could turn his mind to the less pressing challenge still presented by intellectual polytheism.

The task of translating Cyril's writings began in his own lifetime. Indeed, Cyril himself saw to it that Latin translations were supplied of the documents that he was sending to Rome.[1] In Constantinople, the papal agent, Marius Mercator, was also supplying Rome with translated material throughout the Nestorian crisis. In the Middle Ages, however, Cyril was little known in the West. It was only in the Renaissance that he came into prominence, partly through his importance at the Council of Florence of 1438–9 as the principal Greek patristic witness to the *Filioque*, and partly through the value of *Against Julian* as a mine of ancient philosophical texts.[2]

These two aspects of Cyril, his trinitarian theology and his witness to ancient philosophy, ensured him a wide readership when his works began to be printed in Latin translation at the beginning of the sixteenth century. His first translator was George Trapezuntius, a member of the brilliant circle of Greek emigrés surrounding Cardinal Bessarion, best known as a translator of Aristotle. The first work George translated, at the request of Pope Nicholas V, was the *Commentary on John*, which he called an 'opus certe divinum'.[3] It was printed for the first time in Paris in 1508 by Wolfgang Hopyl and was reprinted in 1520 and 1524. George also translated the *Thesaurus*, which was likewise printed by Hopyl and went into several editions. *Against Julian* was translated by the German reformer, Johannes Oecolampadius, who also translated the *Dialogues on the Trinity* and *On Adoration in Spirit and in Truth*. These were first published in Basle by André Cratander in 1528 in a three-volume Latin edition of Cyril which included the two translations by George Trapezuntius.

Interest in Cyril's anti-Nestorian works was stimulated by the exigencies of Reformation polemics. The publication of the text of the *Five Tomes Against Nestorius* – one of the first of Cyril's works to be printed in Greek – edited with a Latin translation by Bishop Antonius Agellius and issued by the Typographia Vaticana in 1607, was a by-product of Pope Paul V's project to publish the acts of the ecumenical councils from the original documents preserved in the Vatican Library. The condemnation of Nestorius was seen as an important witness to the ubiquity of papal authority in the patristic period.

The resurgence of interest in Cyril in the nineteenth century was again prompted by considerations of ecclesiastical controversy. Edward Bouverie Pusey was eager to include Cyril in his Tractarian series, the Library of the Fathers of the Church, particularly on account of Cyril's apparent support for the *Filioque*.[4] The emphasis today tends to fall on Cyril's place in the history of doctrine. His biblical exegesis is comparatively neglected. Yet it is rich without being fanciful and often capable of providing material for spiritual reflection. Moreover, we are perhaps more ready now than in the recent past to appreciate the value of symbol in theological discourse. Long passages from the commentaries on Isaiah and on John have accordingly been included in the present selection. The reader may perhaps still find in them an echo of the divinity discerned by George Trapezuntius.

Each piece is accompanied by an introduction and explanatory notes. The marginal references in majuscule refer to the columns of Migne; those in minuscule refer to the page numbers of Aubert, which are also reproduced in Migne, Pusey and Schwartz. Square brackets around marginal references indicate that the adjoining text does not begin at the top of the page or column. The biblical quotations are given in the Revised Standard Version, except where the RSV has been adapted to reflect the Septuagint version of the Old Testament. The Psalms are numbered according to the Hebrew version.

COMMENTARY ON ISAIAH

INTRODUCTION

The *Commentary on Isaiah* belongs to the early years of Cyril's episcopate. It is perhaps his first verse-by-verse commentary on a major book of the Bible, dating, together with his *Commentary on the Twelve Minor Prophets*, from the period 412–25, after his two works on the Pentateuch and before his anti-Arian compositions, the *Thesaurus*, the *Dialogues on the Trinity* and the *Commentary on John*.[1]

Cyril mentions in his preface that there were already several satisfactory commentaries in circulation.[2] He is probably referring principally to the commentaries of Eusebius, Jerome and Pseudo-Basil.[3] Of these the most influential was that of Eusebius of Caesarea.[4] Jerome borrowed heavily from it for the first Latin commentary, as did the Greek commentary attributed to Basil of Caesarea.[5] At first sight Cyril, too, seems heavily dependent on Eusebius. He writes in a similarly restrained style, giving emphasis to the historical context and only occasionally resorting to allegory. Like Eusebius, he gives apostolic status to Isaiah as the prophet *par excellence* of the coming of Christ. He also shares with Eusebius a conviction that the Jews have been replaced by the Christians as the people of God and that the spiritual Jerusalem is the Church. The influence of Jerome, however, seems to have been more direct. The evidence of the text suggests that Cyril consulted him on a number of points of detail, especially in matters of linguistics and Jewish interpretation.[6] Indeed much of what seems to be Eusebian may in fact have been mediated through Jerome.[7]

How, then, did Cyril gain access to Jerome? It is not unlikely, in view of the close links that had existed between Jerome and Theophilus during their joint campaign against Origenism, that on his succession to the episcopate Cyril would have found several of

Jerome's works, including the *Commentary on Isaiah* (written in 410), in his uncle's library.[8] Cyril does not seem to have had any knowledge of Latin, but we know that there were translators on whose services he could have called. When he sent his dossier on Nestorius to Pope Celestine in 430, he said in his covering letter that he had had the excerpted passages translated, 'this being possible for us in Alexandria'.[9] Celestine in turn bears witness that he had had no difficulty in understanding all that his Alexandrian colleague had written to him, thanks to Cyril's emissary, the deacon Posidonius.[10] By contrast, Celestine wrote to Nestorius that he had not been able to reply to him because his letters had had to await translation into Latin.[11] It therefore seems reasonable to suppose that there was a group of translators in Alexandria who made Jerome accessible to Cyril by translating into Greek if not the whole commentary at least a selection of the more significant passages. In any event, there were no obstacles to Cyril's becoming acquainted with Jerome.[12]

In the absence of a critical text, the translation has been made from Migne, PG 70, 9–1450.

TEXT

Prooem. (PG 70, 9A–13B)

9A The word of the holy prophets is always obscure. It is filled with hidden meanings and is in travail with the predictions of divine mysteries.[13] For the end of the law and the prophets is Christ, as Scripture says (cf. Rom. 10:4). It is necessary, I maintain, that those who wish to elucidate such subtle matters should be keen, if they are to proceed in a logical manner, to make a thorough examination of all the symbolic details of the text with real spiritual insight, establishing first the precise literal meaning[14] and then interpreting the spiritual sense,[15] that readers might derive profit from every aspect of the text and that the explanation of its meaning might clearly be seen not to be deficient in any respect. I know, of course, that a number of previous writers have already dealt with these matters and have produced long treatises on them. These are perfectly adequate, in my opinion. It is therefore not ignoble to appeal to diffidence as a motive for not adding to them and to allow oneself to be

71

persuaded to remain silent, on the grounds that one has nothing new to add to what has already been said by others, but instead would only be repeating the same points and running through the same spiritual themes. Yet even if this turns out to be the case, there is certainly no harm done, for those who attend readings are confirmed in the truth through hearing the majority speaking in unison. Accordingly, I have persuaded myself to overcome my diffidence in the conviction that the sweat and labour expended in a good project is better than a life of leisure. Nor have I entirely abandoned the hope that occasionally I shall be able to find something new and different to say, seeing that God has made the path to be followed in matters of spiritual speculation a broad one. For it is written: 'Thy commandment is exceedingly broad' (Ps. 119:96).

12A

Blessed Isaiah, then, prophesied during the reigns of Uzziah, Jotham, Ahaz and Hezekiah. We shall now say something about the times of these kings and explain in a cursory fashion how each spent his life. For we shall see from this that the word of the prophecy was appropriate and most apposite in relation to the events of those days.

B

Now Uzziah, who is also called Azariah, was a good man. He advanced in glory and power until he gained control over the nations bordering Judah, imposed taxes on many of them and compelled them to accept his rule. He founded cities and acquired others, extending the borders of the land of the Jews. Then he experienced something characteristically human. Overcome by a combination of luxurious living and excessive glory, he began to acquire inflated ideas and gripped by the disease of arrogance he rebelled against the divine law itself. For he thought that he ought to crown himself with the prerogatives of the divine priesthood. He attempted to enter into the divine temple and himself offer incense to God and fulfil what was laid down by the law in a way that contravened the law. On account of this he

C

became a leper there and then and lost every scrap of his honour. For a person suffering from leprosy is pronounced an abomination by the law.

His reign was succeeded by that of his son Jotham, a devout man except that he did not remove the high places, as Scripture says (cf. 2 Kgs 15:35), but the Israelites still sacrificed to the works of their own hands, going up into the mountains and hills and sacrificing under the oak and poplar, under the well-canopied tree, as Hosea says, because the shade was good (cf. Hos. 4:13).

When Jotham died the sceptre passed to Ahaz, a most loathsome man, a hater of God, a man filled with the utmost depravity. He closed the divine temple itself, and he did not allow the sacrifices laid down by the law to be offered to the God of all, and he forbade the customary festivals of the Jews, and setting up altars in every part of Jerusalem he commanded that things made by human hands should be worshipped and that the host of heaven should be adored. And indeed he even 'passed his own children through fire' (2 Chron. 28:3 LXX), that is, he burnt them as a sacrifice to the impure demons, and in short there was no impiety towards which he did not aspire.

Hezekiah reigned after him, a pious and devout man, and a promoter of righteousness. He was a zealot for everything that was good, and a performer of the divine will. He gave orders that everything should be done and should prevail in a manner contrary to the unlawful acts of Ahaz. For he opened the doors of the temple and then gave instructions that sacrifices and libations should be offered to God and that he should be honoured by priestly ministrations according to the law. And indeed he saw to the restoration after many years of the law concerning the Passover. He destroyed sanctuaries and altars and idols made by human hands and commanded soothsayers and false prophets and the bands of singers of spells to fall silent, and he was a good man in the eyes of God.

Thus in the period of the reigns we have just mentioned the God of all was sometimes provoked to anger, when Israel fell into idolatry, and sometimes relented and showed clemency, when Israel changed and became pious through the virtue of the ruler. Consequently, the word of the prophecy is mixed. There are times when it utters the most dire threats, when Israel became impious, but it also introduces a note of promise to the virtuous. And everywhere mention is made of the redemption of Christ, and it is said that in the course of time Israel will be banished from intimacy with God, and will be succeeded by the multitude of Gentiles justified by faith in Christ. It therefore seems to me that the blessed prophet Isaiah was very rightly crowned not only with the grace of prophecy but also the distinction of apostolicity. For he is at the same time both a prophet and an apostle, and in his writings there are discourses which do not fall short of the splendour of the Gospel proclamations.[16]

ISAIAH'S VISION

In Is. 1.4 (PG 70, 169A–176B)

6:1–3   In the year that King Uzziah died I saw the Lord of hosts sitting upon a throne high and lifted up; and the house was full of his glory. Around him stood the seraphim; each had six wings: with two they covered their faces, and with two they covered their feet, and with two they flew. And one called to another and said: 'Holy, holy, holy is the Lord of hosts; the whole earth is full of his glory.'

[169B]   Visions were not revealed to the blessed prophets by God one after another or in a continuous fashion. Instead they were revealed at intervals as it seemed good to the Lord, and at the times which he who reveals profound secrets and knows what [172D] is hidden chose to appoint. [. . .][17] That the prophet saw 173A the Son in the glory of God the Father nobody can doubt, since John manifestly wrote about him: 'Isaiah said this because he saw his glory and spoke of him' (Jn 12:41). Observe the exalted dignity appropriate to God and the authority exercised over all creation. For God is on a throne high and lifted up, crowned impressively with the distinctive splendours of his rule. The highest powers, who are said not to be transcended by anything created, stand around him, occupying the position of household servants, and honour him with their praises. They say that the whole earth is full of his glory. I take it that we should not think of the divine throne as lifted up in a physical sense. For that would be
B foolish and absurd. The divine throne is set up on high in the sense that the glory of God's rule is regarded as transcending every intelligible nature. The sitting on it seems to indicate the steadfastness, as it were, and the enduring nature and immutability of God's blessings.[18] For the divine David also sings in this way: 'God sits on his holy throne' (Ps. 47:8).

And indeed the prophet Jeremiah says to him: 'For thou art enthroned for ever, and we are perishing for ever' (Bar. 3:3). For created nature is always and at all times subject to decay, and it is this that endows originated being with its due limit. On the throne, as I have said, is seated the wisdom who is the craftsman and creator of all things. That is to say, her immutability is unshakeable.[19] Isaiah says that the house is full of his glory. For since Israel had not yet behaved impiously towards our Lord Jesus Christ, the glory of God filled the house in Jerusalem. But when they rejected his rule, they fell into impious ways. It was on that account that they heard the saying: 'Behold, your house is forsaken and desolate' (Mt. 23:38).

In each of the seraphim, Isaiah says, are implanted six wings, so that with two they cover their face, with two their feet and with the remaining two they fly. The word 'seraphim' means 'fiery' or 'burning'.[20] For there is nothing cold in the higher powers since they are especially close to God. That is why we ourselves, when we cleave to him by faith and a good way of life that follows the law punctiliously, also become fervent in spirit and ardent in our love for God. The fact that the seraphim veil their faces and their feet with their wings and fly with one pair of them is a symbol of their not being able to see either the beginning or the end of the concepts or thoughts concerning God. For the head and the face indicate the beginning, and the feet the end. For the divine is without beginning and knows no end. With regard to what lies in between – I refer to time, in which things which were once non-existent were brought into being – we can scarcely grapple with it. They fly because they have nothing that is mean. On the contrary, their minds are always raised up towards God. For the highest powers do not think about the things below, as we do, but keep their minds fixed on ineffable and sublime thoughts. And their mouth is full of praises. For they sing a doxology and they do it by turn, not because they become tired, in my view, but rather because they cede the honour to each other, receiving and giving back the doxology as a gift. For everything in heaven is done in due order. They say the 'Holy' three times and then conclude the doxology with the 'Lord of hosts', setting the Holy Trinity within a single divine nature.[21] For by common consent we say that the Father subsists, and similarly with the Son and the

75

Holy Spirit. And there is no principle that divides each of those named and separates them into different natures. On the contrary, we conceive of a single Godhead in three hypostases. Our evidence for this is provided by the holy seraphim, who also say that the whole earth is full of his glory, predicting what is to be and announcing in advance

B the mystery of the dispensation that has been brought about by Christ. For before the World became flesh the whole world was ruled by the demon, the wicked one, the serpent, the apostate. And the creature was worshipped rather than the Creator and Maker. But when the only-begotten Word of God became man, the whole earth was filled with his glory. For every knee shall bow to him, and every tribe and tongue shall confess him and serve him, as Scripture says (cf. Phil. 2:10, 11). The blessed David also predicted this in the spirit, for he said: 'All the nations thou hast made shall come and bow down before thee, O Lord' (Ps. 86:9). This was fulfilled when a multitude of nations was called, all of them bowing down to him who for our sake became like us yet for his own sake remained supreme over all things.

In Is. 1.4 (PG 70, 180D–184A)

6:6, 7 And there was sent to me one of the seraphim, and he had in his hand a burning coal which he had taken with tongs from the altar. And he touched my mouth and said: 'Behold this has touched your lips; your guilt will be taken away, and you will be cleansed of your sins.'

The divine Paul writes of the holy angels that they are all
181A 'ministering spirits sent forth to serve, for the sake of those who are to obtain salvation' (Heb. 1:14). The point he is making is not obscure. For amongst the higher powers all things are done in due order, and with them there are limitations of honour or ministry, and boundaries are set for the glory of each by God who apportions all things as he sees fit. Yet there is a single yoke laid upon all, and they serve at the bidding of the Lord, not regarding their servitude as unworthy, but counting the reality of it as a source of honour and glory. Accordingly, the mystery of Christ is prefigured in the eyes of the prophet, in a manner very well ministered to by the higher powers. One of the seraphim is sent with a burning

B
coal which he has taken with tongs from the altar. This was a symbol of Christ, who for our sake and on our behalf offered himself to God the Father as a spiritual sacrifice, pure and undefiled, and a fragrant offering (cf. Eph. 5:12).[22] Thus it was very appropriate that he should be taken from the altar. But why he should be compared to a burning coal needs to be explained.

It is customary in the inspired Scriptures to compare the divine nature to fire. That is how God was seen by blessed Israel on Mount Horeb, or Sinai, on the day of assembly (cf. Deut. 4:10, 11). This is also how he was also seen by blessed Moses himself as he was tending sheep in the desert, when he appeared in the form of the burning bush and conversed with him (cf. Ex. 3:1–6). Now the coal is by nature wood, only it C is entirely filled with fire and acquires its power and energy. Our Lord Jesus Christ himself, in my view, may very appropriately be conceived of in the same way. 'For the Word became flesh and dwelt among us' (Jn 1:14). But although he was seen by us as a man, in accordance with the dispensation of the Incarnation, the fullness of the Godhead nevertheless dwelt in him, by means, I would emphasize, of the union. Thus it may be seen that he has the energies most appropriate to God operating through his own flesh. Accordingly, he touched the bier and raised the widow's dead son (cf. Lk. 7:11–16). And indeed by spitting and anointing their eyes with mud, he enabled the blind to see (cf. Jn 9:6, 7). Emmanuel is therefore very appropriately compared to a burning coal, for when he touches our lips he wipes away our sins completely and cleanses us of our transgression.

D
Then how will he touch our lips? When we acknowledge belief in him. Thus the divine Paul writes: 'The word is near you, on your lips and in your heart (that is, the word of faith which we preach); because, if you confess with your lips that Jesus is Lord and believe in your heart that God raised him from the dead, you will be saved. For man believes with his heart and so is justified, and he confesses with his lips and so is saved' (Rom. 10:8–10). Therefore let our lips be touched by 184A the divine coal, who burns up the sweepings of our sin, and consumes the rubbish of our transgression, and makes us fervent by the Spirit. What is meant by taking with tongs is neatly explained by faith in Christ and knowledge of him, which we receive by the tongs, as it were, of the teachings or

predictions to be found in the law and the prophets. Hence the word of the holy apostles also confirms the truth in every way. For by quoting testimonies from the law and the prophets, they convince their hearers, and all but touch their lips with the burning coal themselves as they prepare them to confess their faith in Christ.

THE PROPHECY OF THE MESSIAH

In Is. 1.4 (PG 70, 204A–205D)

7:14–16   Behold a virgin shall conceive in the womb and shall bear a son and you shall call his name Emmanuel. He shall eat butter and honey. Before he knows how to reject evil he will choose the good. For before the child knows good and evil, he will reject evil and choose the good. And the land you are afraid of because of the two kings will be abandoned.

204B   Some of those who have translated the divine Scriptures have rendered this: 'Behold a young woman shall conceive in the womb.' It seems to the Jews that the mother of the Lord should be indicated by the expression 'young woman' and should not rather be called a virgin.[23] For they think it possible to invalidate the power of the mystery if she is called a young woman rather than a virgin. One may note their ignorance on a number of levels. First, even if the virgin is called a young woman, that does not exclude her from being a virgin. Secondly, they say that the prophet uttered the words 'Behold, a young woman shall conceive in the womb and shall bear a son' about the wife of Ahaz, so that we should take this to refer to the birth of Hezekiah. But without examining the words of the prophecy, they rashly seize on what seems right to them and then think that they have
C   proved their point through this alone. But, my friends, one might say to them, who has called Hezekiah Emmanuel? Or how can it be proved that before he had knowledge of good and evil he rejected wickedness and chose the good? We therefore say farewell to their quibbling and welcome what is right and true, believing that in this prophecy God is indicating the

holy Virgin to us. For in this way there will truly be a miracle and a great sign in both its depth and its height that has come about in accordance with the divine promise. For he who is from above, and is by nature the only-begotten Son of God the Father, emptied himself and was brought forth from a virginal womb according to the flesh, receiving his generation not from the human emission of seed but from the power and energy of the Holy Spirit. For that is why it was said to the holy Virgin by the mouth of the blessed Gabriel: 'The Holy Spirit will come upon you, and the power of the Most High will overshadow you' (Lk. 1:35). She will in consequence, it says, bear a son. And you, O house of David, the prophet says, who has now ceased to trust in God and seek a sign from him in confirmation of what he has promised on account of worshipping idols instead of him, you will call his name Emmanuel, that is, you will acknowledge that God has appeared in human form. For it was when the only-begotten Word of God appeared like us that he became 'God with us'. He who transcends the whole of nature became as we are.[24]

Observe how in order to show that he was truly God as well as man, the prophet assigned to him attributes that were both divine and human. For when he says that he was given food suitable for infants, namely butter and honey, he is trying to assure us that he came to be in the flesh in reality. Then he goes on to teach that although he did indeed become flesh he was nonetheless as God superior to sin, for he adds at once: 'For before the child knows good and evil, he will reject evil and choose the good.' For human beings who have not yet arrived at puberty and have not attained that age which is crowned with prudence, are not in any position to be able to discern what is vicious and what is good. But once they have reached the appropriate age, they are able to make a free choice as to what should be done. The divine and supreme nature, unlike our own, but in keeping with the sublime character that is peculiar and appropriate to it, is ever inaccessible to wickedness. And it repudiates the ways of viciousness, for it is not put to the test from that quarter, nor does it experience any annoyance, for it rejects wickedness by virtue of its nature, or rather, of its essence. This is no different, in my opinion, to saying about light that it is incompatible with darkness. For light and the absence of light cannot be present simultaneously. The phrase 'he will

79

C reject evil and choose the good' therefore signifies that it belongs to the divine nature to be irrevocably fixed on the good. This is also true with regard to Christ. For even though he came into being according to the flesh through the Holy Virgin, since he was God by nature and the Word begotten by God, he was holy as God both from the womb and before it, or rather before all ages, seeing that he did not lose his own prerogatives on account of the human nature. Neither did he ignore what pertains to human nature on account of the dispensation of the Incarnation, in order that he might be believed to have become like us in reality, and might sanctify this created nature of ours.

He says furthermore that the land about which he is suspicious and alarmed on account of the two kings will be abandoned. This is similar to saying openly: 'When the Virgin who is pregnant gives birth, you, O house of David, will call his name Emmanuel. Then all who trouble the holy land will abandon her. For she is not yet accessible to those who

D wish to penetrate her.' This is a spiritual saying. For when Emmanuel was born, the real holy land and city, which is the Church, became the good thing that was hoped for.[25] She was trampled on by every enemy, who finding her disinclined to fight departed, leaving her to be saved by God. 'For I shall be to her, says the Lord, a wall of fire surrounding her and I will be the glory within her' (Zech. 2:5).

THE NATURE OF THE MESSIAH

In Is. 2.4 (PG 70, 309B–316B)

11:1–3 There shall come forth a rod from the root of Jesse and a flower shall grow out of the root, and the Spirit of God shall rest upon him, the spirit of wisdom and understanding, the spirit of counsel and might, the spirit of knowledge and piety, and the spirit of the fear of God shall fill him.

309C Having been granted foreknowledge by illumination from above, the prophet makes a clear prediction of what is to be. For it had been said in recent times to the blessed David by God who is Lord of all: 'One of the fruit of your loins will I set on your throne' (Ps. 132:11). Since he knows all things, he implanted in the holy prophets foreknowledge of what was to be, and this was proclaimed by them, that the mystery might be attested from all quarters and might be believed as a fact. And so he says that a rod shall come forth from the root of Jesse and a flower will also spring up. He does not say that it is after the glorious ones have been shaken with might and the haughty ones have been humbled and Lebanon has fallen with them (cf. Is. 10:33, 34 LXX) that the rod will grow out of the root of Jesse. On the contrary, the meaning of the whole matter is revealed in summary form in the earlier chapters. We have learned in brief what was going to happen to the descendants of Israel as a result of their having impiously subjected our Lord Jesus Christ to drunken insults. Now the narrative returns to the same theme as if to the main argument of the book, by which I mean the Incarnation of the Only-begotten and his future birth from a woman according to the flesh in keeping with God's plan. For he called Christ, who was from the root of Jesse according to the flesh, a rod, and added to this the word 'flower'. By 'rod' he is probably alluding to the royal dignity. For the rod, or sceptre, is a sign of kingship. Indeed the divine David says somewhere to the same Son: 'Thy throne, O God, is for ever and ever; the sceptre of thy kingdom is a sceptre of righteousness' (Ps. 45:6). The word 'rod' also has a different meaning seeing that it controls all things, and maintains them in well being, and enables what is weak to stand up, that is to say, human nature, which is drunk with the passions and all but brought down by them. And so blessed David sings, assuming the role of the ordinary person: 'Thy rod and thy staff have comforted me' (Ps. 23:4). For the Lord will support the righteous according to Scripture. It is called by the prophets a mighty sceptre and a glorious staff (Jer. 48:17 (31:17 LXX)). The word 'rod' may be taken in yet another way, since it is the good shepherd who lays down his life for the sheep (cf. Jn 10:11). He is addressed by one of the prophets in the following words: 'Shepherd thy people with thy staff, thy tribe, the sheep of thy inheritance' (Mic. 7:14). If anyone forms the opinion, seeing that he is also a judge and renders to each according to his deeds, that he could very appropriately be called a rod, he will be interpreting the text correctly. For when Israel subjected him to drunken insults and

81

fell intemperately into disobedience, he was addressed in the following words: 'You shall rule them with a rod of iron, and dash them in pieces like a potter's vessel' (Ps. 2:9 LXX).

The law of the most wise Moses presents him to us in the same way. For the rod of Aaron which sprouted and put forth buds and was carried into the holy of holies (Num. 17:1–11) is interpreted as a type of Christ. For it put forth blossoms and produced almonds (Num. 17:8). What this passage is saying in a figurative manner needs to be explained. There are people who study natural phenomena who say that if an almond branch is laid by somebody's head, it naturally induces sleeplessness. Therefore since Christ was, by the grace of God, as blessed Paul says, destined to taste death for everyone (Heb. 2:9), and after a short while, as if shaking off drowsiness, to awake again, as it were from sleep, and return to life in a manner befitting God, having trampled on death, he is compared to an almond branch.[26] It is by this divine and spiritual rod that Moses worked his miracles and freed Israel from slavery in Egypt. He therefore called it the rod of God. For it became for him a rod of power, as Scripture says (Ps. 110:2 LXX). Therefore when the prophet hints at the mystery of Christ in riddles and says that a rod shall come forth for us from the root of Jesse, then, I say, he is contemplating with the eyes of the understanding the only-begotten Word of God himself, through whom and in whom all things exist, who became incarnate and was made man, and condescended to a voluntary self-emptying and endured a birth for us, a birth, I say, according to the flesh and from a woman which was in keeping with the dispensation of the Incarnation. And so he says with the prophet: 'O Lord, I have heard the report of thee and was afraid; I considered thy works and was amazed' (Hab. 3:2).

The rod, then, was called such for the reasons which I have just explained. We turn now to the flower. For human nature blossomed again in him, acquiring incorruption, and life, and a new evangelical mode of existence. The flower may also be understood in a different sense, as a spiritual fragrance. 'For I am a flower of the plain,' says Scripture, 'a lily of the valleys' (Song 2:1 LXX). For he became to us too a fragrance as if of the knowledge of God the Father. That is why the divine Paul says in one of his epistles: 'But thanks be to God who in Christ always leads us in triumph, and through us spreads the fragrance of the knowledge of him everywhere. For we are the aroma of Christ to God among those who are being saved and among those who are perishing, to one a fragrance from death to death, to another a fragrance from life to life' (2 Cor. 2:14–16). What he says is that from time to time the Spirit of God, who has many operations, rested upon this rod or upon the flower that has issued from the root of Jesse. He calls this a spirit of counsel and understanding, of knowledge and wisdom, of piety and the fear of God (cf. Is. 11:2 LXX).

B   We say that this carefully constructed prophetic proclamation does not present Jesus to us as a mere man who was then endowed with the Spirit and came to participate in divine graces as we do. We say instead that it clearly reveals to us the Word of God who became man, full of every good – a characteristic belonging to his nature – which he made his own along with his humanity and everything that pertains to it. For it is a property of human nature not to possess any trace of the heavenly graces of its own will or, as it were, by its own nature. 'For what have you that you did not receive?' it is asked (1 Cor. 4:7). Rather, it was enriched from outside and by acquisition, that is, from God, with that which transcends its own nature. It was therefore necessary that the only-begotten Word of God who brought himself down to the

C   level of self-emptying, should not repudiate the low estate arising from that self-emptying, but should accept what is full by nature on account of the humanity, not for his own sake, but for ours, who lack every good thing. If we say in consequence that he received the Spirit, even though he is himself the supplier of the Holy Spirit, and he does not give it in a measured way but distributes it to the worthy as if from his own fullness, let us take it that the receiving was proportionate to the self-emptying. In this way we shall arrive directly at the truth. But notice this: 'The Spirit of God,' says Isaiah, 'will rest upon him' (Is. 11:12). For in the beginning it was given to the first-fruits of our race, that is, to Adam. But he became careless about observing the commandment given to him, neglected what he had been instructed to do and sank into sin, with the result that the

D   Spirit found nowhere to rest among men. For 'all have turned aside, together they have gone wrong; no one does good, not even one' (Rom. 3:12). Then the only-begotten Word of God became man, even though he did not cease being God. Since he was not consumed by sin even though he became as we are, the Holy Spirit rested once again on human nature, first on him as the second first-fruits of our race, that it might also rest on us and remain henceforth dwelling in the minds of believers. It is thus that the divine John says that he saw the Spirit descend from heaven and remain on Christ (Jn 1:32). We have become fellow heirs to the evils experienced by our first parent. In a similar way we shall be partakers of those

316A things which have come to exist according to the dispensation through the second first-fruits of our race, that is to say, through Christ. That grace was not bestowed upon him as a particular gift, in the way that the Spirit is said to have rested on the saints, but that it was the fullness of the Godhead which took up residence in his own flesh as if in his own temple, and not flesh lacking a soul but rather flesh endowed with a spiritual soul, the prophet makes clear when he says, 'the spirit of the fear of the Lord shall fill him' (Is. 11:3). To the one Spirit he has given a multiplicity of operations. For there is not one Spirit of wisdom and another of understanding or of counsel or of might, and so on. On the contrary, just as the Word of God the Father is one but is called, according to his various operations, life, and light, and power, so it is too with regard to the Holy Spirit. He is one but is regarded as multiform because of the way in which he operates. That is

B why the most wise Paul lists for us the various kinds of gifts: 'All these,' he says, 'are inspired by one and the same Spirit, who apportions to each one individually as he wills' (1 Cor. 12:11).

THE LORD'S SERVANT

In Is. 3.5 (PG 70, 849B–852D)

42:1–4 Jacob is my servant; I will help him. Israel is my chosen one; my soul has accepted him. I have put my Spirit upon him; he will bring forth judgement to the Gentiles. He will not cry out or lift up his voice, or make it heard outside. A bruised reed he will not break, and smouldering flax he will not quench, but he will bring forth a true judgement. He will shine out and will not be broken until he has established judgement on the earth. And in his name shall nations and peoples place their hope.

He has just announced 'I will give dominion to Sion' (Is. 41:27) and now he clearly explains who this Sion is. For there has been appointed over the spiritual Sion, that is, over the Church, a prince and a teacher who was not promoted at the time when he is said to have acceded to that office. For the Word that was born from the Virgin was and is always king and Lord of all. But when he became man, he made the limitations of humanity his own. For in this way we could believe truly and without hesitation that he became as we are. Therefore although it might be said that he received dominion over all things, this refers to his accepting the dispensation of the flesh, not to his pre-eminence by which he is regarded as Master of all things. And he calls him Jacob and Israel, because by descent he was related to Jacob, who was given the name of Israel. For Scripture says that God will help him and calls him his chosen one (Is. 42:1). For the Father co-operates with the Son, and brings about his mighty works as if with the same power. And he is also chosen in reality, because 'he is fairer than the sons of men' (Ps. 45:2 LXX) and was accepted as beloved. For God the Father was pleased with him. He therefore said: 'This is my beloved Son, with whom I am well pleased' (Mt. 3:17).

That he was anointed in a human manner and is said to have received a share of the Holy Spirit, even though he was himself the giver of the Spirit, and the sanctifier of creation, is explained where it says: I gave him my Spirit to be upon him. For when he was baptized, the Spirit, says Scripture, descended upon him in the form of a dove and remained upon him (cf. Mt. 3:16). If at the time of his baptism he received the Spirit in accordance with the limitations of his humanity, this would be in keeping with other instances. Insofar as he is God he was not sanctified by receiving the Spirit. For he is the one, as I have said, who is doing the sanctifying. But insofar as he is human he is sanctified in accordance with the dispensation of the Incarnation. He was therefore anointed in order for him to bring forth judgement to the Gentiles. By judgement in this context he means righteous judgement. For he justified the Gentiles by condemning Satan who exercised tyrannical rule over them. And he taught us this

85

himself, saying: 'Now is the judgement of this world. Now shall the ruler of this world be cast out. And I, when I am lifted up from the earth, will draw all men to myself' (Jn. 12:31, 32). For he pronounced sentence for the destruction of him who exercised tyrannical rule, as I have said, over the whole earth, and with a holy judgement saved those who had been deceived.

B   'But he will not cry out,' the prophet says, 'or lift up his voice, or make it heard outside' (Is. 42:2). For the Saviour and Lord of all dwelt among us in great lowliness and humility and, as it were, noiselessly and without doing harm to anyone, and, moreover, in silence and tranquillity, so as not to break a bruised reed or put out smouldering flax. That is to say, he did not put his foot on even the most paltry things or on those heroically accustomed to bear injury. What, then, will he do, and what will he achieve for the Gentiles? He will bring forth a true judgement. Here the prophet seems to be referring to the law. For Scripture says concerning Israel and God who rules over all things that there he gave him ordinances

C   and judgement (cf. Num. 27:11). And again: 'Thou hast executed justice and righteousness in Jacob' (Ps. 99:4). Therefore the judgement, or the law that is in shadows and types, he will bring forth as the true judgement of the Gospel decrees, by which he indicated the path of the manner of life that was pleasing to him, and transformed the worship that was according to the letter of the law into a true worship. But the wretched Jews subjected him to abuse and dared to afflict him with the death of the flesh. Yet he shone out like a light and was not broken, that is, he was not vanquished by corruption nor did the madness of those who plotted against him prevail over him. For death has been dissolved and he has come back to life in a way befitting God, and has trampled over his enemies, and his suffering has become the occasion of the salvation of the whole world.

    He will therefore not be broken until he has established judgement on earth. And do not interpret this to mean that

D   he appoints a time at which he will in fact be broken, that is, after he has established judgement on earth. What he is saying, rather, is that he will triumph over his adversaries and will prevail to such an extent that he will establish his judgement throughout the entire world. For the Gospel has been proclaimed throughout the world and has, as it were, established his decrees. For it is written: 'Thy righteousness is for ever and thy law is truth' (Ps. 119:142 LXX). The Gentiles, it says, have placed their hope in his name. For having come to know that he was really God, even though he appeared in the flesh, they have made him their hope, and as the Psalmist says, 'they shall rejoice in his name all the day' (Ps. 89:16 LXX). For we have been called Christians and have placed our entire hope in him.

THE NEWNESS OF THE LIFE TO COME

In Is. 3.5 (PG 70, 856B–857A)

42:8,9 I am the Lord God, that is my name; my glory I will give to no other, nor my praise to graven images. Behold the former things have come to pass, and new things I will now declare; and before I declare them they have been made known to you.

If he is properly and truly the only God, he may be said by us to be the Creator of all things. As the most wise Paul says: 'Although there may be so-called gods in heaven or on earth – as indeed there are many "gods" and many "lords" – yet for us there is one God, the Father, from whom are all things and for whom we exist, and one Lord, Jesus Christ, through whom are all things and through whom we exist' (1 Cor. 8:5, 6). And since he has introduced himself to us as the author of great and marvellous things, he says that his glory, that is, the sum of virtues appropriate to God, is not to be given to lifeless idols or to any other created thing but is to be retained

856C for himself alone. It follows from this that the glory of the Godhead may not fittingly be attributed to any other being that differs from him in essence, but only to the ineffable and transcendent nature itself. Although he said that his own glory is to be given to nobody, however, he gave it to the Son. For the Son has been glorified in the same way, indeed, as the Father too who is worshipped in heaven and on earth.

How then did God give his glory to him, as to one who was not different from him in virtue of the consubstantiality, even though each was divided off into his own hypostasis?

D For the nature of the supreme deity is one in three distinct hypostases, conceived of and worshipped as such by those who hold orthodox views. When the prophet says: 'Behold the former things have come to pass, and new things I will now declare; and before I declare them they have been made known to you' (Is. 42:9), he does not allow the word of the Saviour to be disbelieved by us in any detail. For just as what was said from the beginning about his coming has come to fulfilment, he says, so too will what he calls the new things turn out to be true, and will be revealed before they appear. What are these things? They are the eternal life that is to come, which our Lord Jesus Christ promised us, that is, the life of

857A incorruption and holiness and righteousness, the kingdom of heaven, the glorious participation in spiritual good things, the fruits of forbearance, the rewards of piety, the crown of love for Christ. May we too attain them through his grace and loving kindness, through whom and with whom be glory to God the Father with the Holy Spirit for all eternity. Amen.

ISRAEL DELIVERED AND REDEEMED

In Is. 4.1 (PG 70, 909A–912B)

43:22–24 I have not now called you, O Jacob, nor have I made you weary, O Israel. You have not brought me your sheep for burnt offerings, nor have you glorified me with your sacrifices or served me with your sacrifices. I have not burdened you with sacrifices or wearied you with frankincense. You have not bought me incense with money, nor have I desired the fat of your sacrifices. But in your sins and iniquities and wrongdoing and suchlike I have protected you.

909B In the passage we have just studied, prophecies were made of the covenant of Christ and the graces bestowed by him. For he said that he would make a way in the wilderness and rivers in the dry land, and on account of this would be blessed by all the wild beasts of the field (Is. 43:19, 20 LXX). This may be understood as the praise of spiritual sacrifice and the fruit of the new covenant in Christ. In the present passage he attempts to assure Israel that they have been delivered from Egypt, and have been liberated from the slavery that they endured there, and have been freed from such distressing toil, not in order to offer him calves and win access to him by means of blood and smoke. For such things are eschewed by God, and are the shadow rather than the reality.

C He therefore says: 'I have not now called you, O Jacob' (Is. 43:22). The word 'now' should be taken to mean 'not when you were offering me sacrifice', that is, 'I have not called you while you were sacrificing oxen and slaughtering sheep, so that you should not conclude that you had received deliverance as some kind of reward for the offering. On the contrary, it was while you were in sin and guilty of defilement, for you had worshipped the gods of the Egyptians, that I deemed you worthy of mercy and love. Therefore the gift is one of gentleness, and the fruit of loving kindness is grace, and the liberation is as if out of love. The sheep of your burnt offerings are nothing to me, he says, nor indeed have you glorified me with your sacrifices. For how can that which is entirely unacceptable and offered in vain contribute to my glory? You

D have performed no service with your sacrifices. A person who pursues the good, he says, who achieves the moral character that leads to virtue, who submits to my will, who puts the teaching of the prophets into practice – that is the person who may be said to serve the God who rules over all. But a person who fills the holy tabernacle with the smoke of frankincense, who offers oxen or sheep, or who has put on a fine show, will not render any genuine glory. Such a person has done absolutely nothing that pleases me. Therefore service does not consist in offering sacrifice. It consists in the readiness to submit a tender neck, a neck that needs, as it were, not so much as a touch, to the will of God.[27]

912A The nearer you have come, he says, to that which pleases me, the less I have wearied you with frankincense. You have not bought me 'incense with money, nor have I desired the fat of your sacrifices' (Is. 43:24). This resembles something said by another prophet to them: 'Add your burnt offerings to your sacrifices and eat the flesh. For in the day I brought them out of the land of Egypt, I did not speak to your fathers concerning burnt offerings and sacrifices' (Jer. 7:21, 22). And the same prophet Jeremiah has said in another passage: 'To what purpose do you bring me frankincense from Sheba, and cinnamon from a distant land? Your burnt offerings are not acceptable, and your sacrifices have not pleased me' (Jer. 6:20). And indeed the Psalmist also says: 'I will accept no calves from your house, nor young he-goats from your flocks' (Ps. 50:9). Everywhere he represents worship in shadows as

B cast out and the things in types as taken away, drawing us to the righteousness that is in Christ and teaching us to be refashioned according to the evangelical way of life, which is the only way in which that which is pleasing to God can be brought about and in which we can arrive at the worship that is truly irreproachable and sincere, that is to say, the worship that is spiritual. 'For God is spirit, and those who worship him must worship in spirit and in truth' (Jn. 4:24).

In Is. 4.2 (PG 70, 960C–964B)

45:9,10   Will the ploughman plough the earth all day? Does the clay say to the potter, 'What are you making? Do you not work or have hands?' Does one say to one's father 'What are you begetting?' or to one's mother 'What are you giving birth to?'

960C   This is a deep saying, veiled in much obscurity, yet at the same time very useful and true. I think I ought to make a brief preliminary exposition of what it is driving at. In this way my readers will find it more accessible and easier to understand. Thus the God of all things freed Israel from Egypt, rescued them from the error of polytheism, and brought them by the law of Moses from the chicanery of the demons to the dawn of the true knowledge of God. He taught them to worship a single God and bow down before a single Lord. Then by means of types and shadows he wanted to raise

D   them up to what was still better and more perfect, that is, to the things that are in Christ. For the law was a preliminary instructor and was laid down until the time of setting aright. This came with the advent of our Saviour Jesus Christ, when he set aside the shadow of the commandments of the law and the types found in the letter, and introduced to those on earth the beauty of worship in spirit and in truth openly and without disguise.

But the Jews found this hard to bear, and as they were still

90

961A
complying with the types, took action against Christ and accused him of breaking the Mosaic commandments, saying, 'If this man was from God, he would not have broken the Sabbath' (cf. Jn 5:18, 9:16). Sometimes they sniped at him with harsher words. Therefore, since they found the benefit resulting from the preaching of the Gospel unacceptable, although it was advancing them from the unprofitable shadow to spiritual fruitfulness, the prophet says to them: 'Will the ploughman plough the earth all day?' 'O foolish people,' he is saying, 'a cultivator turns over the soil with the plough but he does not go on doing it for ever, nor is the whole business of cultivation taken up with ploughing. For he turns over the soil not simply for the sake of doing so but in order that it might be made ready to receive the seed when he sows it and prove to be productive. Therefore I gave the hearts of all of you,

B
which were once overgrown like wastelands, a preliminary working over, using the law of Moses as a plough, and turning them over like a farmer made them suitable for sowing with good seed. Therefore accept what he offers and do not remain permanently attached to your beloved plough, which is the law.' For he ploughed, as I have said, not so that you should hold fast to ploughing (for what would be the use of that?) but so that you should produce the fruits of truth. Since we have been spiritually refashioned in Christ, that is to say, we have been transformed, some of us from pagan error into the knowledge of the truth, and to a holy life through Christ the Saviour of us all, others from Judaism into the acquisition of evangelical teachings and into a newness of worship that no longer cleaves to the dreariness of the types but instead is

C
resplendent with the striking beauty of spiritual worship, both we and they have been enriched with rebirth in Christ through water and the Spirit.

Conversely, the grace that descended on these was rejected and not accepted by the Jewish people. For they resisted, as I have said, the teachings of Christ. Therefore the prophet says: 'Does the clay say to the potter, "What are you making? Do you not work or have hands?" Does one say to one's father, "What are you begetting?" or to one's mother, "What are you giving birth to?"' (Is. 45:9, 10). 'For I desire to refashion you,' he is saying, 'into something better, to remodel you into something finer through a spiritual birth, meaning, of

D
course, through water and the Spirit. But you resisted my

91

plans without understanding.' Therefore, the prophet says, does the clay reproach the potter for not having a craftman's hand, or for not knowing how to shape what was in his hands? Or does someone who is about to be begotten put the question to his own father, 'Why are you begetting?' How do you, then, who are like clay in the potter's hands, and have no knowledge at all of how your spiritual rebirth will take place, have the audacity to enter into argument? And why do you not rather understand that you should cede to the craftsman and father the knowledge of how to do these things?

964A It is not at all difficult to grasp the fact that the Jews contended with the words of the Saviour which was uttered by him on these matters. For he said to Nicodemus: 'Truly, truly I say to you, unless one is born of water and the Spirit, one cannot see the kingdom of God' (Jn. 3:5). But Nicodemus, grappling with transcendent matters in a foolish manner, argued with him, saying: 'How can a man be born when he is old? Can he enter a second time into his mother's womb and be born?' (Jn. 3:4). He added to this another spiritual teaching: 'How can this be?' (Jn. 3:9). What did Christ say to this? 'If I have told you earthly things and you do not believe, how can you believe if I tell you heavenly things?' (Jn. 3:12). It is therefore necessary to give way to what God says. He himself knows the way of his own works, and what he has fashioned is not to be curiously inquired into. It belongs to someone like ourselves to honour what transcends the human mind with an unquestioning faith.

B You should also know that the prophet Jeremiah was sent to the house of the potter to watch him at work. When the pot turned out badly and the potter refashioned the clay into a new vessel, God said to him: 'Can I not do with you as this potter has done, O house of Israel? Behold, like the clay in the potter's hand, so are you in my hand' (Jer. 18:6). That we are transformed spiritually and brought to a holy and utterly good life is explained by Paul when he says: 'And we all, with unveiled face, beholding the glory of the Lord, are being changed into his likeness from one degree of glory to another; for this comes from the Lord who is the Spirit' (2 Cor. 3:18). Through him we are also reborn, for we no longer contain a corruptible seed but that which is sown by the word of the living God who endures for ever.

PROMISE OF THE NEW
JERUSALEM

In Is. 5.6 (PG 70, 1417A–1420C)

65:16–18   But those who serve him will be called by a new name, which shall be blessed on earth; for they shall bless the true God. And those who take an oath on earth shall swear by the true God; for they shall forget their former affliction and it will not come into their minds. For there shall be a new heaven and a new earth, and they shall not remember the former things, nor will they come into mind. But they shall find in her joy and exultation.

1417B   All things have been made new in Christ: worship and life and legislation. For we do not adhere to shadows and useless types. Instead we offer adoration and worship to the God who is over all things in spirit and in truth (cf. Jn. 4:23). We do not take our name like the physical descendants of Israel from one of the original ancestors, or fathers, such as Ephraim, or Manasseh, or some other tribe, nor do we follow the path of the Scribes and Pharisees, who value the antiquity of the letter above every other thing. Instead, we accept Christ in the newness of life of the Gospel, and being given his name

C   like a crown, we are called Christians. This celebrated and blessed name has indeed spread throughout the world. Since we have been blessed by Christ, we in turn strive to gladden him with blessings and endless praises. Formerly, that is, before we believed in him, when we composed songs for gods that do not exist, we were rightly derided. But once we have come to know him who is God by nature, we sing hymns to him and offer him the fruit of our lips and tongues, commemorating his praises. And if any real need should arise to confirm our assurances with oaths in any matter, they swear

D   by the true God. For it is the custom with those who worship idols when they swear oaths to swear them by heaven or by one of the heavenly elements. Those who have accepted the Christian faith, have also in their youth abandoned their sins in this matter. For they swear oaths only by the God of all things, since they know that he is truly Lord by nature, and on no other god whatsoever. This was also decreed by the Mosaic law: 'You shall worship the Lord your God,' it says, 'and you shall serve him alone, and swear by his name' (cf. Deut. 6:13).

1420A   Then he says that 'they shall forget their former affliction and it will not come into their minds' (Is. 65:16). Here he apparently calls affliction the depravity they underwent when, not knowing the true God, they served the perversity of the demons. For they were ordered to sacrifice to them, not only sheep and oxen indeed, but also the fruit of their wombs. For it is written: 'They sacrificed their sons and daughters' (Ps. 106:37). Also depraved in a different way was their worship of innumerable gods and their eagerness to serve those which were unknown. It is likely that this was because people are attacked insidiously by those demons that are overlooked. For it is not unreasonable to suppose that the foul and bloodthirsty demons were able to dominate them and do them harm because they were not protected by God. 'They will forget this affliction of theirs,' the prophet says. 'For there shall be a new heaven and a new earth.' How or by what means will this be brought about? In former times people regarded heaven and earth as gods. When their minds have been illuminated by divine light through Christ, the Saviour of

B   us all, they will acquire new ideas about these things. For they will know that these are not gods but the works of the Maker and Creator of all things. With this new approach, the prophet says, 'they shall not remember the former things' (Is. 65:17). For along with Hellenism they will also repudiate the opinions they once held about these elements, and about the former deceivers, whether demons or human beings, who lent their own tongue as an advocate for error.

   Instead of their former affliction, the prophet says, 'they shall find in her joy and exultation' (Is. 65:18). In whom or in

C   what? In the Church of Christ, it may be said without any doubt. It should be noted that some commentators refer this not to the period of our earthly life but to the period that is to come after this present age.[28] For the prophet says that the just will find joy and exultation and will enjoy endless delight, that is, spiritual delight, when this creation has been transformed and renewed. For one of the holy apostles said: 'The day of the Lord will come like a thief, and then the heavens will pass away with a loud noise, and the elements will be dissolved with fire, and the earth and the works that are upon it will be burned up. But according to his promise we wait for new heavens and a new earth' (2 Pet. 3:10, 13). Choose, therefore, whichever of these interpretations appeals to you, the former or the latter. Whatever is useful to us is in no way to be rejected.

COMMENTARY ON JOHN

INTRODUCTION

The *Commentary on John* is an early work, antedating the outbreak of the Nestorian crisis in 429, for although the Antiochene tradition receives some adverse comment, Nestorius himself is not mentioned. The *terminus a quo* is less easy to determine. Reference is made, however, to two previously published works, the *Thesaurus* and the *Dialogues on the Holy Trinity*. As Cyril's works did not begin to circulate until after he had become archbishop, the most likely date for the *Commentary on John* is the years 425–8.[1]

St John's Gospel did not receive much attention from Christian exegetes before the fourth century.[2] In the second century John had been more popular with Gnostics than with Catholics. In fact the first commentary on John was by the Valentinian Gnostic, Heracleon. It was Origen who rescued John for the Church with a commentary answering Heracleon in some detail, which he completed at Caesarea in about 231.[3] There seem to have been no further commentaries on John until Cyril's own day when renewed interest was prompted by Arian appeals to the Johannine presentation of Christ. At Alexandria, Didymus the Blind, head of the Catechetical School at the time of Cyril's birth, wrote a commentary, which has not come down to us.[4] Among Cyril's nearer contemporaries, the Antiochenes Theodore of Mopsuestia and John Chrysostom both produced extensive commentaries, the latter in the form of a course of eighty-eight homilies delivered at Antioch in about 391.[5]

Cyril's own commentary, so far as we can tell, was not influenced by any of these.[6] He is neither a Hellenist like Origen, nor a philologist like Theodore. His intention, he says, is to write 'a commentary concerned rather with doctrinal matters' (*dogmatikotera exēgēsis*), which will attempt to cleave the spiritual wood of the Gospel, to lay bare its heart, to reveal its doctrinal and theological purpose and refute those who express erroneous opinions about the nature of the second and third persons of the Trinity.[7] His interests are not so much scholarly as pastoral and soteriological. Although he refers to the inadequacy (*pachytēs*) of language when it comes to dealing with divine realities,[8] and on one occasion notes a textual variant at John 12:27,[9] his main concern is with the practical consequences of biblical teaching for the Christian life.

Cyril's opponents are neo-Arians who would make the Word of God subject to passion and therefore, in his view, incapable of raising the believer to participation in the divine life. He had already made a systematic study of their opinions for his *Thesaurus*. This research was to stand him in good stead for the *Commentary on John*, though he did supplement it from time to time on an *ad hoc* basis. At the beginning of Book 9, for example, he mentions how he came across an Arian work and looked up what it had to say on the point he was considering at the time.[10]

In his arguments against the Arians, Cyril takes up a firmly Athanasian stance. At the Incarnation the eternal Word united himself with human nature in a way that implied not simply a moral union on the one hand, or any change in the Word on the other, but a drawing up of humanity into the divine life itself. The *Commentary on John*, however, does mark an advance in some respects on the christology of the *Thesaurus* and the *Dialogues on the Holy Trinity*. The exigencies of the Johannine text lead Cyril to consider seriously for the first time certain aspects of the humanity of Christ that seemed to entail the inferiority of the Son in relation to the Father. These are the gifts the Son has received, his susceptibility to *pathē*, or emotions, his shrinking from death, his sanctification by the Holy Spirit and his glorification by the Father.[11] Cyril argues that these do not detract from the power of the Word because they represent an accommodation by the Word, for economic reasons, to life in the flesh. It has long been held that Cyril did not regard the human soul of Christ as theologically significant until he was forced to do so by the challenge of the Nestorian controversy.[12] Recent research, however, has shown that even in this early period Cyril was aware of the problem of consciousness in Christ and without working out all the implications had nevertheless made the soul the active principle of Christ's human action.[13]

Cyril's vast work is arranged in twelve books, each divided into a number of chapters. Books 7 and 8 (on Jn 10:18–12:48) have not survived in their original form but have been reconstructed to some extent from the *catenae*, the biblical commentaries in the form of chains of excerpts from various fathers which were compiled in the Byzantine period.

The text I have used is the critical edition published by P.E. Pusey in 1872.[14] The headings are my own.

TEXT

THE DISPENSATION OF THE INCARNATION

In Jo. 1.9 (Pusey I, 130.8–144.9)

89a   1:11   He came unto his own, and his own received him not

The Evangelist intensifies his plea that the world did not recognize who it was that was bringing it light, that is, the Only-begotten, and beginning with the more serious sin of the people of Israel not only firmly establishes the crimes
b   of the Gentiles but also demonstrates the disease of ignorance and unbelief that had come to affect the whole world. Having prepared the ground very carefully, he embarks on his account of the Incarnation and gradually works his way down from pure theology to an exposition of the dispensation in the flesh which the Son brought about for our sake.

It was no wonder, he says, that the world did not recognize the Only-begotten, seeing that it had abandoned the under-
c   standing that befits human beings, and 'not knowing that it is and was made in honour, had become like the dumb beasts', as the divine Psalmist said (Ps. 48:13). The very people supposed by all to belong to him in a special way repudiated him when he was present in the flesh and did not want to receive him when he lived among them for the salvation of all, rewarding faith with the kingdom of heaven. Notice how persuasive the Evangelist's argument is on these matters. He accuses the world of not recognizing at all the one who was bringing it light, as if he is working to bring about a just pardon on these grounds, and is preparing in advance sufficient reasons for the grace that has been given it. But to the people of Israel, who for their part were reckoned

d amongst those who belonged to him in a special way, he assigns the phrase 'received him not'. For it would not have been true to say 'knew him not', when the older law had proclaimed him and the prophets had used it to guide them into an understanding of the truth. The severity of the sentence passed upon them was therefore just, as indeed was the kindness shown towards the Gentiles (cf. Rom. 11:22). For the world, that is, the Gentiles, having lost their intimacy with God through their recourse to wickedness, were also penalized by losing the knowledge of the one who was enlightening them. Those on the other hand who had been enriched with knowledge through the law, and had been recalled to the

e pleasant régime of God, henceforward sinned voluntarily, for they did not receive the Word of God whom they already knew and who was living among them as among his own people. For with God the whole world is his own, in virtue of its having been made by him and its having been brought into being from him and through him. But Israel will rather

90a more appropriately be called God's 'own', and will inherit the glory that accompanies this title both through the election of the holy patriarchs and through being named the beginning and the first-born of God's children. 'For Israel is my first-born son,' says God somewhere to Moses (Ex. 4:22). And indeed setting Israel apart for himself as a unique and distinctive people, he pronounced it his own, saying to Pharaoh, the Egyptian tyrant, 'Let my people go' (Ex. 8:1). The true teaching of the Mosaic books shows that Israel belonged to

b God in a special way. 'For when the Most High,' it says, 'gave to the nations their inheritance, when he separated the sons of Adam, he fixed the bounds of the people according to the number of angels of God, and his people Jacob became the Lord's portion; Israel was the line of his inheritance' (Deut. 32:8, 9). And he dwelt among them as among his own portion and line, saying, 'I was sent only to the lost sheep of the house of Israel' (Mt. 15:24). But because he was not received he transferred his grace to the Gentiles and the world is enlightened through repentance and faith although

c it was originally ignorant of him, while Israel returns to the darkness from which it emerged, which is why the Saviour said, 'For judgement I came into this world, that those who do not see may see, and that those who see may become blind' (Jn 9:39).[15]

1:12 But to all who received him, who believed in his
name, he gave power to become children of God

d
Truly a just judgement and one befitting God. Israel the
first-born Son is cast out. For Israel did not wish to remain in
a relationship of intimacy with God. Nor did it receive the Son,
when he came to live among his own people. It rejected the
bestower of nobility. It thrust away the giver of grace. But the
Gentiles received him by faith. Therefore Israel will rightly
receive the just deserts of its folly. It will bewail the loss of the
blessings of God. It will receive the bitter fruit of its own ill
counsel, for it has been stripped of its sonship. Instead, the
e
Gentiles will delight in the blessings that come through
faith. They will receive the brilliant rewards of obedience and
will supplant Israel. They will be cut 'from what is by nature
a wild olive tree and grafted, contrary to nature, into a cul-
tivated olive tree' (Rom. 11:24), and Israel will hear: 'Ah,
sinful nation, a people laden with iniquity, offspring of
evildoers, sons who deal corruptly! You have forsaken the
Lord and despised the Holy One of Israel' (Is. 1:4).

One of Christ's disciples, however, will say to the Gentiles:
91a
'But you are a chosen race, a royal priesthood, a holy nation,
a people for his possession, that you may declare the
wonderful deeds of him who called you out of darkness into
his marvellous light' (1 Pet. 2:9). Since they received the Son
through faith, they receive the privilege of being counted
among the children of God. For the Son gives what belongs
properly to him alone and exists by nature within him as a
right, setting it out in common, as if making the matter
an image of the loving kindness inherent within and of his
love for the world. There was no other way for us who have
borne the image of the man of dust to escape corruption,
b
unless the beauty of the image of the man of heaven is
imprinted upon us through our having been called to sonship
(cf. 1 Cor. 15:49). For having become partakers of him
through the Spirit (cf. Heb. 3:14; 6:4), we were sealed into
likeness to him and mount up to the archetypal form of the
image, in accordance with which divine Scripture says we
were also made (cf. Gen. 1:27). For scarcely do we thus
recover the ancient beauty of our nature, and are conformed
to that divine nature, than we become superior to the evils
that arose from the Fall.

c   We, therefore, ascend to a dignity that transcends our nature on account of Christ, but we shall not also be sons of God ourselves in exactly the same way as he is, only in relation to him through grace by imitation. For he is a true Son who has his existence from the Father, while we are sons who have been adopted out of his love for us, and are recipients by grace of the text 'I have said, you are gods and all of you sons of the most high' (Ps. 82:6). Beings of a created and

d   dependent nature are called to a transcendent status by the mere nod and will of the Father. But he who is Son and God and Lord does not acquire his being God the Son because God the Father has decreed it, or in virtue of the divine will alone, but because he has shone forth from the very essence of the Father and thus procures for himself by nature the distinctive good of that essence.[16] Once again the Son is seen to be a true Son when contrasted with ourselves. Since the status of 'by nature' is different from that of 'by adoption', and the status

e   of 'in reality' different from that of 'by imitation', and since we are called sons by adoption and by imitation, it follows that what he is by nature and in reality we who have attained these things become in a relative sense, for we have acquired this blessing by grace rather than by natural status.[17]

> 1:13 Who were born, not of blood nor of the will of the flesh, nor of the will of man, but of God

Those, he says, who through faith in Christ have been called

92a to the sonship of God, have put off the inferiority of their own nature. Radiant with the grace of him who is honouring them, as if dressed in brilliant white clothing, they advance to a status that transcends nature. For they are no longer called children of the flesh but rather offspring of God by adoption (cf. Rom. 8:14–15; 9:8).

Note how cautious the blessed Evangelist is in his choice of words. His caution was necessary, for he was intending to say that those who have believed have been born of God, and he did not want anyone to think that they were literally produced from the essence of God the Father, thereby making them indistinguishable from the Only-begotten one, or to say that the verse 'I have begotten you from the womb before the morning' (Ps. 110:3) applied to him only loosely, bringing him down in this way to the nature of creatures, even though he is said to have been born of God. For once the Evangelist had said that power was given to them to become children of God by him who is Son by nature, and had therefore implied that they became children of God 'by adoption and grace', he could then proceed without danger to add that they were 'born of God'. He did this in order to demonstrate the magnitude of the grace bestowed upon them, which was such that it gathered that which was alien to God the Father into a natural kinship with him and raised that which was servile to the noble status of a master, through his ardent love for it.

What more, then, should one say, or what is remarkable about those who believe in Christ compared with Israel, since the latter too are said to have been begotten by God, according to the text, 'Sons have I begotten and brought up, but they have rejected me' (Is. 1:2)? To this I think one should reply as follows: First, that since 'the law has but a shadow of the good things to come instead of the true form of these realities' (Heb. 10:1), even this was not given to the descendants of Israel for them to have in a literal sense but was depicted in them typologically and figuratively 'until the time of reformation' (Heb. 9:10), as Scripture says, when it would become apparent who those were who more appropriately and more accurately called God their Father because of the Spirit of the Only-begotten one dwelling within them. For the descendants of Israel had 'a spirit of slavery inducing fear', while Christians have 'a spirit of sonship' eliciting freedom, 'which enables us to cry "Abba! Father!"' (Rom. 8:15). Therefore the people who were destined to attain adoption as sons through faith in Christ were depicted beforehand in Israel in symbolic form, so that, for example, we understand our spiritual circumcision to have been prefigured originally in their physical version. To put it briefly, everything concerning us was already present in them typologically. Moreover, we can also say that Israel was called to attain sonship typologically through the mediation of Moses, with the result that they were baptized into him, as Paul says, 'in the cloud and in the sea' (1 Cor. 10:2) and were restored from idolatry to the law of slavery, the written commandment being supplied by angels (cf. Gal. 3:19). But those who have attained adoption as sons of God through faith in Christ are baptized not into anything belonging to the created order but into the Holy Trinity itself, through the mediation of the Word, who on the one hand joined what is human to himself by means of the flesh that was united to him, and on the other was joined by nature to him who had begotten him, since he was by nature God. Thus what is servile rises up to the level of sonship through participation in him who is Son in reality, called and, as it were, promoted to the rank which the Son possesses by nature. That is why we are called offspring of God and are such, for we have experienced a rebirth by faith through the Spirit.

Since there are some who venture in a dangerous fashion to allege falsely with regard to the Holy Spirit, as they do with regard to the Only-begotten one, that he too has been originated and created and to exclude him completely from consubstantiality with God the Father, let us mobilize the word of the true faith against their unbridled tongues and provide both for ourselves and for our readers opportunities for spiritual benefit.[18] For if the Spirit is neither God by nature – I am addressing these objectors – nor a distinctive property of God deriving from him and therefore existing within him by virtue of essence, but is something different from him and not set apart from the common nature of created things, how are we who are born through him said to be born of God? We must admit that either the Evangelist is totally mistaken, or if he is right and the matter is precisely as he says, that the Spirit is God and from God by nature, and indeed that we who are deemed worthy to participate in Christ through faith are made 'partakers of the divine nature' (2 Pet. 1:4) and are said to be born of God.[19] We are therefore called gods, not simply by grace because we are winging our way towards the glory that transcends us, but because we already have God dwelling and abiding within us, in accordance with the prophetic text 'I will live in them and move among them'.[20] In what way do those who are so lacking in learning explain how we can be temples of God, as Paul says,[21] because we have the Spirit dwelling within us, if the Spirit is not God by nature? If he belongs to the created order that has come into being in time, why is it that God destroys us, on the grounds that we are destroying the temple of God, when we pollute the body, in which the Spirit dwells (cf. 1 Cor. 3:17), who on the level of nature possesses the specific character of God the Father in all its fullness, and similarly the specific character of the Only-begotten one? How is the Saviour speaking the truth when he says, 'If anyone loves me, he will keep my word, and my Father will love him, and we will come to him and make our home with him' (Jn 14:23) and abide in him? It is indeed the Spirit that dwells within us and we believe that through him we also have the Father and the Son, as John again himself tells us in his epistles: 'By this we know that we abide in him and he in us, because he has given us of his own Spirit' (1 Jn 4:13). And how will he be said to be the Spirit of God at all unless he is from him and in him by nature and for that reason God? If, as our opponents say, he is the Spirit of God even though created, there is nothing to hinder the other creatures too from being called spirits of God. For every creature will possess this potentiality if it is conceded at all that a created essence can be Spirit of God.

It would be entirely appropriate at this juncture to develop a long discourse on these topics discussing them more fully and refuting the ill-considered opinions of the unholy heretics, but I have already dealt with the Holy Spirit in sufficient detail in my book on the Holy Trinity,[22] so I shall refrain from saying any more.

1:14a And the Word became flesh

With this verse the Evangelist enters explicitly upon his discourse on the Incarnation. For he explains clearly that the Only-begotten one both became and was called a son of man. For the statement that the Word became flesh means that and nothing else: it is like saying that the Word became a human being, but even more starkly. Now to speak in this way should not appear strange or unusual to us, since sacred Scripture often refers to the entire living creature by the word 'flesh' alone, as in the verse of the prophet Joel, 'I will pour out my Spirit on all flesh' (Joel 2:28). Doubtless we should not suppose that the prophet is saying that the divine Spirit is to be supplied to human flesh alone unendowed with a soul, for that would be totally absurd. On the contrary, understanding the whole by the part, he names man by the flesh. And that is perfectly right and proper. Why this should be so, it is probably necessary to explain.

Now man is a rational but at the same time a composite animal, made up, that is to say, of soul and this perishable and earthly flesh.[23] When he was created by God and brought into being, since he did not possess incorruptibility and immortality of his own nature (these attributes belong essentially only to God), he was sealed with the spirit of life, thus acquiring a relationship with the divine good that transcends nature. For Scripture says, 'he breathed upon his face the breath of life, and the man became a living soul' (Gen. 2:7 LXX). But when he was punished for his transgression, he rightly heard the words, 'You are earth and to earth you shall return' (Gen. 3:19 LXX) and was stripped of the grace. The breath of life, that is, the Spirit who says 'I am the life', departed from the earthly flesh and the living being succumbed to death through the flesh alone, since the soul was preserved in its immortality, with the result that it was to the flesh alone that the words 'You are earth and to earth you shall return' were addressed.

It was therefore necessary that that which was most endangered in us should be the more urgently restored and by interacting again with that which has life by nature should be recalled to immortality. It was necessary for the affected part to obtain a release from evil. It was necessary, then, for the phrase 'You are earth and to earth you shall return' to be relaxed through having the fallen body united in an ineffable manner with the Word that endows all things with life. And it was necessary that when the flesh had become his own flesh it should partake of his own immortality. Considering that fire has the power to transfer to wood the physical quality of the energy naturally present within it and all but transform into itself whatever it comes to be in by participation,[24] it would be quite absurd if we did not take it for granted that the Word of God who transcends all things could make his own proper good, which is life, operative in the flesh. That, in my opinion, is the most probable reason why the holy Evangelist, indicating the whole living being by the part affected, says that the Word of God became flesh. It is so that we might see side by side the wound together with the remedy, the patient together with the physician, that which had sunk towards death together with him who raised it up towards life, that which had been overcome by corruption together with him who drove out corruption, that which had been mastered by death together with him who was superior to death, that which was bereft of life together with him who

95a

b

c

d

105

is the provider of life. He does not say that the Word came into flesh; he says that he became flesh in order to exclude any idea

e   of a relative indwelling, as in the case of the prophets and the other saints. He really did become flesh, that is to say, a human being, as I have just explained.

That is why the Word is God by nature both in the flesh and with the flesh, since he has it as his own property,[25] yet is conceived of as something separate from it, and is worshipped in it and with it, in accordance with the saying of the prophet Isaiah: 'Men of stature shall come over to you and be

96a   your slaves; they shall follow you bound in chains and bow down to you; they will make supplication to you, saying: "God is with you only, and there is no other, no god besides him"' (Is. 45:14). Observe how they say that God is in him, without separating the Word from the flesh. Moreover, they maintain that there is no God besides him, uniting with the Word that which he wore, as his own particular property, that is to say, the temple he took from the Virgin. For Christ is one from both.[26]

b   1:14b And dwelt in us[27]

The Evangelist rephrases in a useful way what he has just said, and brings the significance of his doctrine into sharper focus. Having stated that the Word of God became flesh, he is anxious in case anyone out of profound ignorance should assume that the Word has abandoned his own proper nature and has in reality been transformed into flesh and has suffered, which is impossible, for with regard to its mode of being the divine is far removed from any kind of change or alteration into something else. The Theologian therefore

c   very aptly added at once: 'and dwelt in us', so that realising that he was referring to two things, the subject of the dwelling and that in which the dwelling was taking place, you should not think that the Word was transformed into flesh but rather that he dwelt in flesh, using as his own particular body the temple that is from the holy Virgin. 'For in him the whole fullness of deity dwells bodily', as Paul says (Col. 2:9).

Nevertheless, the assertion that the Word dwelt in us is a

d   useful one because it also reveals to us a very deep mystery. For we were all in Christ. The common element of humanity is summed up in his person, which is also why he was called the last Adam: he enriched our common nature with everything conducive to joy and glory just as the first Adam impoverished it with everything bringing corruption and gloom. This is precisely why the Word dwelt in all of us by dwelling in a single human being, so that through that one being who was 'designated Son of God in power according to the Spirit of holiness' (Rom. 1:4) the whole of humanity might

e   be raised up to his status so that the verse, 'I said, you are gods and all of you sons of the Most High' (Ps. 82:6) might through applying to one of us come to apply to us all. Therefore 'in Christ' that which is enslaved is liberated in a real sense and ascends to a mystical union with him who put on the form of a servant, while 'in us' it is liberated by an imitation of the union with the One through our kinship according to the flesh. For why is it 'not with angels that he is concerned but with the descendants of Abraham, whence he had to be made like his brethren in every respect' (Heb.

97a   2:16–17) and become a real human being? Is it therefore not clear to everyone that he descended to the level of a servant, not providing anything for himself by this, but giving us himself as a gift, 'so that we by his poverty might become rich' (cf. 2 Cor. 8:9), soaring through the attainment of likeness to him to his own proper and superlative good, and might prove to be by faith gods and children of God? For he who is by nature Son and God dwelt 'in us'; wherefore we also in his Spirit 'cry Abba! Father!' (Rom. 8:15). The Word

b   dwells as if in all in the one temple taken for us and from us, that containing us all in himself 'he might reconcile us all in one body to the Father', as Paul says (Eph. 2:16, 18).

> 1:15 And we have beheld his glory, glory as of the only
> Son from the Father, full of grace and truth

Having said that the Word became flesh, that is, a human

c   being, and having brought him down to brotherhood with things created and in bondage, he preserves intact with this verse the dignity befitting the divine and shows him again full of the distinctive property of the Father that is present within him. For the divine nature is truly immutable in itself, not susceptible of change into anything else, but rather always remaining the same, and retains its own prerogatives.

107

Therefore even though the Evangelist says that the Word became flesh, he is not asserting that he was overcome by the infirmities of the flesh, or that he fell away from his original power and glory when he clothed himself in our frail and inglorious body. For we have seen his glory, he says, a glory surpassing that of others, and which one should confess befits the Only-begotten Son of God the Father. For he was full of grace and truth. Now if one turns one's attention to the choir of the saints, and examines the marvellous things done by each of them, one will probably be amazed and will exult at the good things that belong to each, and will surely say that they are filled with glory from God. The theologians and martyrs, however, say that in their experience the glory and grace of the Only-begotten cannot be compared with that of the others but surpasses it by far, and ascends by unparalleled excellences, since its grace is not measured out, as if given by another, but is as perfect and true as it is in him who is Perfect. That is to say, it is not added on or brought in from outside by way of appendage, but inheres within essentially, and is the fruit of the characteristic property of the Father passing over on the level of nature from him to the Son.[28]

If anyone wishes to check what has been said against a broader body of evidence, he should examine for himself the miracles of the saints one by one and compare them with those of Christ our Saviour, and he will find that the difference is as great as we have already just said. Moreover, I would add the following: the former are like devoted domestic servants about the house; the latter is 'over God's house as a son' (Heb. 3:6). And concerning the Only-begotten, divine Scripture says, 'Blessed is he who comes in the name of the Lord' (Ps. 117:26), whereas concerning the saints God the Father says, 'I have sent you all my servants the prophets' (Jer. 7:25). And the latter were lent power from above, whereas the former, since he is the Lord of the powers, said: 'If I am not doing the works of my Father, then do not believe me; but if I do them, even though you do not believe me, believe the works' (Jn 10:37–8). Therefore if the Only-begotten is seen by the works themselves to have the same power as the Father, he should accordingly be glorified with equal honours, seeing that he performs equal works. For indeed even in the flesh he transcended those called to be his brothers in the same degree as he who is God by nature transcends human beings and he

108

who is the Son in reality transcends those who are sons by adoption. Since it has been written by blessed Luke that 'Jesus increased in wisdom and grace' (Lk. 2:52), it should be noted that in this text our divinely inspired author says that the Son's glory is full of grace. How then can that which is full increase, or in what possible way can it receive addition, when there is nothing beyond it? Therefore he is not said to increase in his being Word and God, but because, being ever wondered at more greatly, he was declared more full of grace by those who saw him on account of his works. What was increasing, to put it more accurately, was the disposition of those who marvelled, rather than he who in virtue of being God was perfect with regard to grace. I hope this will be found to be useful, even though I digress.

THE EFFICACY OF THE EUCHARIST

In Jo. 3.6 (Pusey I, 473.26–476.27)

[323b] 6:35 He who comes to me shall not hunger, and he who believes in me shall never thirst

Something again is hidden in these words which calls for explanation. For it was the custom with Christ the Saviour not to disparage the glories of the saints but on the contrary to crown them with remarkable honours. But when some of the less well-informed, not knowing how much he excelled the saints, attributed to them the greater glory, he persuades them, very much to their advantage, to adopt a more fitting attitude and consider who the Only-begotten is, and how he most certainly surpasses them in an incomparable manner. But he does not make his discourse on this theme at all clear, veiling it somewhat and keeping it free from any self-advertisement. Yet from a consideration of the facts themselves, that is, from a comparison of them, his discourse easily wins the day every time.

Let us take an example. Once he was engaged in conversation with the Samaritan woman, to whom he promised to give the living water. Understanding nothing of what was said, the woman replied: 'Are you greater than our father Jacob, who gave us the well?' (Jn 4:12). But then when the Saviour wished to persuade her that he was indeed greater than Jacob, and worthy of considerably greater belief, he goes on to discuss the difference between the two kinds of water, saying, 'Whoever drinks of the water that I shall give him will never thirst; the water that I shall give him will become in him a spring of water welling up to eternal life' (Jn 4:14). And what does he mean here? Surely this, that the giver of the better gifts must necessarily be better than the person to whom he is compared.

A similar method of instruction and teaching is also deliberately used at this juncture. Since the Jews felt somewhat superior to him, and arrogantly used to put forward Moses the lawgiver in a topsy-turvy fashion, often maintaining that one should follow his teaching rather than that of Christ, thinking that the provision of the manna and the flow of water from the rock were an incontrovertible proof of his superiority in all things, our Saviour Jesus Christ was himself forced to fall back on his usual method and not state plainly that he was superior to Moses, because of the unbridled insolence of his hearers and their ready proneness to anger. Instead, he turns the discussion to the event which was the source of such wonder, and by comparing it to what was greater, proves it to be of lesser importance. 'He who comes to me,' he says, 'will not hunger, and he who believes in me shall never thirst.' Yes indeed, he says. I will myself agree with you that the manna was given through Moses, but those who ate of it grew hungry. I will concede that from the travail of the rocks water was given to you, but those who drank grew thirsty, and the gift described brought only a temporary relief to them. But he who comes to me shall never be hungry, and he who believes in me shall never thirst.

What, then, does Christ promise? Nothing corruptible, but rather the eucharistic reception of the holy flesh and blood, which restores man wholly to incorruption, so that he has no further need of those things that keep death away from the flesh, by which I mean food and drink.[29] He appears to call water here the sanctification brought about by the Spirit, or else the divine and holy Spirit himself, as he is so often named by the divine Scriptures. Accordingly, the holy body of Christ endows those who receive it with life and keeps us incorrupt when it is mingled with our bodies. For it is not the body of anyone else, but is thought of as the body of him who

110

is Life by nature, since it has within itself the entire power of
the Word that is united with it,[30] and is endowed with his
qualities, or rather is filled with his energy, through which all
things are given life and maintained in being. This being the
case, those who have been baptized and have tasted divine
grace should know that if they go reluctantly or scarcely at all
to church, and cease to receive communion for years on end,
yet feign a pernicious reverence as a pretext for not wishing
to participate in him sacramentally, they cut themselves off
from eternal life, for they have refused to be given life. And
this refusal, even if they make it seem to be in some way
the fruit of reverence, becomes a snare and a stumbling-
block. They ought instead to make every effort to realize the
power and willingness that is within them, that they might
become eager to clear away sin and attempt in its place to
follow a more spiritual regime, and thus run all the more
courageously to participate in life.

But since Satan deceives in a variety of ways, he never
allows them to think that they ought to discipline themselves. On the contrary, having defiled them with evil, he
persuades them to shrink back from the very grace by which
in all likelihood, once they have returned to their senses from
the pleasure that leads to vice as if having woken up from
wine and drunkenness (cf. Joel 1:5), they would see and
consider what is to their advantage. Having therefore burst his
bonds, and having shaken off the yoke which he has thrown
over us in order to oppress us, let us serve the Lord with
fear, as Scripture says (Ps. 2:2, 11), and prove ourselves to be
already superior to the pleasures of the flesh through self-
control. Let us approach the divine and heavenly grace, and
go up to the holy partaking of Christ. For that is precisely
the way in which we shall overcome the deceits of the devil,
and having become partakers of the divine nature (2 Pet.
1:4), shall ascend to life and incorruption.

THE DIVINE AND HUMAN
WILLS OF CHRIST

In Jo. 4.1 (Pusey II, 485.9–488.15)

[330a] 6:38-9 For I have come down from heaven, not to do my
own will, but the will of him who sent me; and this

111

is the will of him who sent me, that I should lose nothing of all that he has given me, but raise it up at the last day

b   To anyone who approaches it in a hasty manner this passage will seem difficult and something of a trap with regard to the faith. Consequently, at this juncture there are already those who expect us to get bogged down in insuperable difficulties thrown up by our opponents. But there is nothing at all difficult here. 'For all things are straightforward to those who understand,' as Scripture says, 'and plain to those who find knowledge' (Prov. 8:9), that is to those who devoutly study to interpret and understand the mysteries contained in the divine Scriptures.[31]

331a   In these words, then, Christ gives us, as it were, clear proof and assurance that anyone who comes to him will not be rejected. That is precisely the reason, he says, why I came down from heaven, that is, why I became man according to the good pleasure of God the Father, and virtually begged not to be occupied with anything he did not desire until I should overcome the power of death and obtain for those who believe in me eternal life and the resurrection of the dead.

b   What was it then that was both willed and not willed by Christ? The treatment he bore at the hands of the Jews – the dishonour, the revilings and insults, the tortures and scourgings and spittings, and moreover the false charges, and last of all the death of the flesh. Christ bore these things willingly for our sake, but if it had been possible for him to achieve what he earnestly desired for us without suffering, he would not have wished to suffer. But since the Jews were undoubtedly utterly intent on inflicting these things upon him, c   he accepts that he has to suffer and turns what he does not will into what he wills, for the sake of the good that would ensue from his suffering. God the Father concurred with him and consented that he should willingly undergo all things for the salvation of all. In this we see very clearly the infinite goodness of the divine nature, for it did not refuse to make that which was undesirable the object of its will for our sake.

That the suffering on the Cross was in a sense not willed by Christ the Saviour, yet at the same time was willed for our sake and the good pleasure of God the Father is something d   you will in consequence understand. For when he was about to ascend to him and addressed his discourses to God, he said clearly in the form of a prayer, 'Father, if it be possible, let this cup pass from me; nevertheless, not as I will, but as thou wilt' (Mt. 26:39). That the Word was God, immortal and incorruptible, and by nature Life in itself who could not cower before death, is I think abundantly clear to all. Nevertheless, having come to be in the flesh, he allows himself to experience the things proper to the flesh, and consequently, when death is at the door, to cower before it, that he might appear to be a real human being. That is why he says, 'If it be possible, let this cup pass from me'. What he means is this: 'If it be possible, Father, that without suffering death I should win life for those who have fallen under its power, if death could die without my dying, that is to say, with regard to the flesh, let the cup pass from me. But since this cannot take place in any other way, not as I will but as thou wilt.' Do you see how weak human nature is, even in Christ himself, when it relies on its own powers? Through the Word that is united with it, the flesh is brought back to a courage befitting God and is retrained in order to have a more valiant spirit, so as not to rely upon what seems right to its own will, but rather to follow the aim of the divine will and eagerly to run towards whatever the law of the Creator calls us.

That we are right in saying this you may also learn from the text that follows, for 'the spirit is willing,' it says, 'but the flesh is weak' (Mt. 26:41). Christ, of course, was not unaware that to seem to be defeated by death and to experience fear as a result of this fell very short of the dignity appropriate to God. That is why he added a most spirited defence to what he had just said, declaring that the flesh is weak because of what is proper to it and belongs to it by nature, whereas the spirit, by contrast, is willing because it knows that it can suffer nothing that can harm it. Do you see how death was not willed by Christ on account of the flesh and the ignominy of suffering, and yet at the same time was willed by him until he should bring to a happy conclusion for the sake of the whole world that which was the object of the Father's good pleasure, namely, the salvation and the life of all? For is it not certainly true that he is presented as indicating something of this kind to us when he says that this is the will of the Father, that nothing that has been brought to him will perish, but he will raise it up on the last day (cf. Jn 6:40)? For as we have already taught, God the Father, in his compassion for humanity, brings those lacking life and salvation to Christ, who is Life and Saviour.

In Jo. 4.2 (Pusey I, 528.12–536.18)

[360b]   6:53 Truly, truly, I say to you, unless you eat the flesh of the Son of man and drink his blood, you have no life in you

c   Christ is truly long-suffering and full of mercy, as one may see from the words now before us. For he does not reproach the small-mindedness of the unbelievers in any way but freely bestows on them again the life-giving knowledge of the mystery. Overcoming as God the arrogance of those who grieved him, he enunciates that by which they will mount up to eternal life. He does not yet teach them by what means he will give them his flesh to eat. For he knew that they were in darkness and in no way able to understand the ineffable. But he indicates to them in a profitable manner how much good would result from their eating, that by persuading them to desire to live in a state of greater preparation for lasting joys,

d   he might perhaps teach them to believe. For when people have come to believe, the power of learning naturally follows. That is why the prophet Isaiah says, 'If you do not believe, neither will you understand' (Is. 7:9 LXX). It was therefore right that the understanding of that of which they were ignorant should be introduced once faith had taken root in them, rather than that the investigation should precede faith.

   This, in my opinion, is the reason why the Lord rightly refrained from telling them how he would give them his flesh

e   to eat and calls them to the necessity of believing before inquiring. It was for those who had already believed that he broke the bread and gave it to them, saying, 'Take, eat; this is my body' (Mt. 26:26). And similarly he passed the cup round to them all, saying, 'Take, drink of it, all of you; for this is my blood of the covenant, which is poured out for many for the forgiveness of sins' (Mt. 26:27, 28). Do you see how he does not explain the mode of the mystery to those who were still

361a   devoid of understanding and rejected faith without investigating it, but to those who already had faith we find him expounding it with great clarity? Let those who from lack of understanding have not yet accepted faith in Christ therefore take heed of the saying: 'Unless you eat the flesh of the Son of man and drink his blood, you do not have eternal life in you' (Jn 6:53). For those who do not receive Jesus through the sacrament will continue to remain utterly bereft of any share in the life of holiness and blessedness and without any taste of it whatsoever. For he is Life by nature, seeing that he was born of a living Father. And his holy body is no less life-giving, for it has been constituted in some way and ineffably united with the Word that gives life to all things.

Therefore it is reckoned to be his and is thought of as one with him. For after the Incarnation they are not divisible, except insofar as one knows that the Word that came from the Father and the temple that came from the Virgin are not identical in nature. For the body is not consubstantial with the Word that is from God. But they are one in their coming together and in the ineffable way in which they are combined.[32] And if the flesh of the Saviour became life-giving, seeing that it was united with that which is Life by nature, i.e. the Word that is from God, when we taste of it we have that life within ourselves, since we too are united with the flesh of the Saviour in the same way as that flesh is united with the Word that dwells within it.

That is also why when he raises the dead the Saviour is seen to be operating not by word alone, nor by commands such as befit God, but he firmly insisted on using his holy flesh as a kind of co-worker, that he might show it to be capable of giving life and already made one with him. For it really was his own body and not that of another. Thus when he raised the daughter of the ruler of the synagogue, saying, 'Child, arise' (Lk. 8:54), he took her by the hand, as Scripture records. While giving life as God by his all-powerful command, he also gives life by the touch of his holy flesh, demonstrating through both that the operation was a single and cognate one. On another occasion as he approached a city called Nain, 'a man who had died was being carried out, the only son of his mother' (Lk. 7:12). Again he 'touched the bier' and said, 'Young man, I say to you, arise' (Lk. 7:14). He does not simply leave it to the word[33] to effect the raising of the dead, but in order to show that his own body was life-giving, as we have already said, he touches the corpses, and by this act puts life into those who had already decayed. And if by the touch

362a

alone of his holy flesh he gives life to that which has decayed, how shall we not profit more richly from the life-giving Eucharist when we taste it? For it will certainly transform those who partake of it and endow them with its own proper good, that is, immortality.

Do not be astonished at this, or ask yourself in a Jewish manner about the 'how'. Instead, reflect on the fact that water is cold by nature, but when it is poured into a kettle and put on the fire, it all but forgets its own nature and moves across to the energy of that which has dominated it.[34] In the same way, although we are corruptible because of the nature of the flesh, we too through our mingling with Life abandon

b

our own weakness and are transformed into its property, that is to say, into life. For it was absolutely necessary, not only that our soul should be re-created into newness of life by the Holy Spirit, but also that this coarse and earthly body should be sanctified by a coarser but analogous participation and called to incorruption.

Our Jewish opponents, slow as they are of understanding, should not suppose that we have invented some kind of new

c

mystery. For in the older writings, by which I mean those of Moses, they can see it already recorded and bearing the force of truth in that it was accomplished in the outward forms alone. For what, tell me, put the destroyer out of countenance? And what arranged that their ancestors should not perish with the Egyptians, when death, the conqueror of all, was arming himself against the first-born? Is it not obvious to everyone that when in obedience to the divine law they sacrificed the lamb, and having tasted of its flesh anointed the doorposts with blood, death was forced to pass them by

d

as a sanctified people (cf. Ex. 12:7)? For the destroyer, that is the death of the flesh, was arrayed against the whole of humanity on account of the transgression of our original ancestor. For it was then that we first heard, 'You are earth and to earth you shall return' (Gen. 3:19). But since Christ was going to overthrow this terrible tyrant, by coming to be in us as Life through his holy flesh, the mystery was prefigured to those who lived long ago, and they tasted of the flesh of the

e

lamb, and sanctified by the blood were saved, for he who was set to destroy them passed them by, in accordance with the will of God, since they were partakers of the lamb. Why do you Jews become angry at being called from types to the reality, when

Christ says, 'Unless you eat the flesh of the Son of man and drink his blood, you have no life in you' (Jn. 6:54)? Indeed, you should have been able to grasp the sense of the mysteries somewhat more easily, seeing that you had been instructed in advance by the Mosaic books and guided unequivocally by the most ancient types towards what you ought to believe.

363a

> 6:54 He who eats my flesh and drinks my blood has eternal life and I will raise him up at the last day.

At this point too it is right to marvel at the holy Evangelist who has openly proclaimed: 'And the Word became flesh'. He was not content to claim that he came to be *in* the flesh but went so far as to say that he *became* flesh, in order to represent the union. We do not, of course, say that God the Word who is from the Father was transformed into the nature of flesh, or that the flesh changed into the Word. For each remains what it is by nature and Christ is one from both. The Word was united with his own flesh in a transcendent manner that is beyond human understanding, and having, as it were, transferred the flesh wholly to himself by that energy by which it lies in his power to give life to those things that lack life, he drove corruption out of our nature and also rid it of that which through sin has prevailed from of old, namely, death. Therefore he who eats the holy flesh of Christ has eternal life.[35] For the flesh contains the Word who is by nature Life. That is why he says, 'I will raise him up at the last day'. Instead of saying, 'My body will raise him up,' that is, will raise up the person who eats it, he has put in the word 'I', since he is not other than his own flesh – a view that is naturally unacceptable, for he utterly refuses to be divided into a pair of sons after the union. Therefore what he is saying is that I who have come to be in him, that is, through my flesh, will raise up him who eats of it at the last day. For it was surely impossible that he who is Life by nature did not defeat corruption and overcome death absolutely. Therefore although death, which sprang upon us because of the Fall (cf. 1 Pet. 5:8), forces the human body towards unavoidable decay, nevertheless if Christ comes to be in us through his own flesh, we shall certainly rise. For it is not credible, or rather, it is impossible that he should not endow with life those in whom he comes to dwell. It is as if one took a glowing ember and

b

c

d

e

thrust it into a large pile of straw in order to preserve the vital nucleus of the fire. In the same way our Lord Jesus Christ hides away life within us by means of his own flesh, and inserts immortality into us, like some vital nucleus that destroys every trace of corruption in us.[36]

[364d]   6:56 He who eats my flesh and drinks my blood abides
            in me, and I in him.

In these passages Christ unfolds his meaning in a variety
e   of ways. Since his discourse is somewhat difficult of access to
the less well instructed, demanding the insight that comes
from faith rather than from investigation, he makes it easier
in a number of ways by going over the same ground again and
again and sheds light from all directions for us on whatever is
useful in the matter, planting a powerful desire for it by faith
as if putting down a foundation and laying the preliminary
courses. For 'he who eats my flesh', he says, 'and drinks my
blood abides in me, and I in him.' For if someone were to fuse
365a   together two pieces of wax, he would no doubt be able to see
that each had come to be in the other. In the same way, I
think, anyone who receives the flesh of our Lord Jesus Christ
and drinks his precious blood, as he himself says, comes to be
one with him, mixed and mingled with him, as it were,
through partaking of him, so that he comes to be in Christ, as
Christ in turn is in him. This is rather similar to what Christ
b   taught us in the Gospel according to Matthew, where he
says, 'The kingdom of heaven is like leaven which a woman
took and hid in three measures (*sata*) of meal, till it was all
leavened' (Mt. 13:33). Who the woman is, what the number
three of the so-called *sata* stands for, and what the *saton* itself
actually means, will be discussed at the appropriate place.
Here we shall speak only of the leaven. Paul says, 'that a little
leaven leavens the whole lump' (1 Cor. 5:6). In the same way
c   the smallest portion of the sacrament mingles our whole
body with itself and fills it with its own energy. And thus
Christ comes to be in us and we in turn come to be in him. For
one may say with perfect accuracy that the leaven is in the
whole lump, and by the same principle that the lump is in
the whole leaven. Here you have in a nutshell the sense of the
passage.

Now if we really yearn for eternal life, if we long to have the provider of immortality within ourselves, let us not abstain from the Eucharist like some of the more negligent, nor let us provide the devil in the depths of his cunning with a trap and a snare for us in the form of a pernicious kind of reverence. 'Yes, indeed,' someone might say. 'But it is written: "Anyone who eats of the bread and drinks of the cup unworthily, eats and drinks judgement upon himself" (cf. 1 Cor. 11:29). I have examined myself and I see that I am not worthy.' But then when will you be worthy? My response would be: 'When will you present yourself to Christ? If you are always going to be afraid of falling, you will never cease falling – "For who can discern his faults," as the holy Psalmist says (Ps. 18:12 LXX) – and you will end up totally bereft of a share in saving sanctification.' Make up your mind, then, to lead a more devout life in conformity with the law, and so partake of the Eucharist in the conviction that it dispels not only death but even the diseases that are in us (cf. 1 Cor. 11:30). For when Christ has come to be within us he lulls to sleep the law that rages in the members of flesh. He rekindles our reverence towards God, while simultaneously causing the passions to atrophy. He does not reckon our faults against us. Instead, he tends us as a doctor would his patients. For he binds up that which has been wounded, he raises that which has fallen, as a good shepherd who has laid down his life for his sheep (cf. Ez. 34:16; Jn 10:11).

e

366a

THE HUMANITY OF CHRIST

In Jo. 8 (Pusey II, 315.15–320.12)

[703d]   12:27 Now is my soul troubled. And what shall I say? Father, save me from this hour? No, for this purpose I have come to this hour. Father, glorify thy Son.

'Now,' he says, 'is my soul troubled. And what shall I say? Father, save me from this hour? No, for this purpose I have come to this hour.' Notice here again how easy it is to produce confusion and fear in human nature, whereas by contrast the divine and ineffable power is in all respects indestructible and invulnerable and orientated only towards the courage that befits it. For the thought of death that has slipped in attempts to agitate Jesus, while the power of the divinity at once masters the emotion that has been aroused and immediately transforms that which has been conquered by fear into an incomparable courage.[37]

e

We may therefore suppose that even in the Saviour Christ himself that which belonged to his humanity was moved in two necessary ways. For it was absolutely essential that even in this manner he should show himself to be a human being, not in mere appearance or by some fiction, but rather a natural and true human being born of a woman and bearing every human characteristic except sin alone. Now fear and timidity, being natural emotions in us, are not to be classified among the sins. Moreover, the human qualities were active in Christ in a profitable way, not that having been set in motion they should prevail and develop further, as is the case with us,

704a

but that having been set in motion they should be brought up short by the power of the Word, nature having first been transformed in Christ into a better and more divine state. For it was in this way and in no other that the mode of healing passed over into ourselves too.

In Christ as the first-fruits human nature was restored to newness of life. And in him we have gained also that which transcends nature. That is also why he was called a second Adam in the divine Scriptures (cf. 1 Cor. 15:45). Just as he experienced hunger and weariness as a man, so too he accepts

b

the disturbance that comes from the emotions as a human characteristic. He is not, however, disturbed in the way that we are, but only insofar as he needs in order to experience the perception of the thing, and then immediately he reverts to the courageous attitude that is appropriate to him.

[705a]

[. . . .][38] He puts a request to the Father, and expresses this in the form of a prayer, not because he who had the power to do all things was weak, but because as a man he assigns to the divine nature those things that transcend the human – even

b

though he is not outside this divine nature – when he addresses his own Father, and because he knows that the power and glory that is to be in everything will come through the Father and the Son. Whether the Gospel has 'glorify thy Son' or 'glorify thy name' makes no difference to the interpretation of its precise meaning.[39] Christ, however, despising death and the

shame that comes from suffering, focused only on the achieve-
ments resulting from the suffering. And immediately seeing
the death of all of us departing from our midst as a result of
the death of his own flesh, and the power of decay about to be
completely destroyed, and human nature already formed
anew in anticipation of newness of life (cf. Rom. 6:4), he all
but says to God the Father something on the following lines:
'The body, O Father, shrinks from suffering and is afraid of a
death that violates nature. Indeed it seems scarcely endurable
that he who is enthroned with thee and has power over all
things should be subjected to the outrageous treatment of
the Jews. But since I have come for this purpose, glorify thy
Son, that is, do not hinder him from going to his death
but give thy consent to thine offspring for the good of all.'
That the Evangelist also calls the cross 'glory' elsewhere
you may learn when he says: 'For as yet the Holy Spirit had not
been given, because Jesus was not yet glorified' (Jn 7:39). It
is clear that in this passage 'glorified' means 'crucified'.
'Glory' is equivalent to 'the cross'. For if at the time of his
passion he willingly endured many insults with forbearance,
and accepted suffering voluntarily for our sake when it was
in his power to avoid it, this acceptance of suffering for the
good of others is a sign of extraordinary compassion and the
highest glory. The glorification of the Son also took place in
another way. Through his victory over death we recognize
him to be life and Son of the living God. The Father is
glorified when he is shown to have such a Son begotten from
himself and with the same attributes as himself. He is goodness, light and life; he is superior to death and whatever he wills
he brings about. When he says, 'Glorify thy Son', he means,
'Allow me to suffer in a voluntary fashion.' For the Father did
not give up his Son to death without premeditation, but
advisedly for the life of the world. Therefore the consent of the
Father is described as a bestowal of blessings. For instead of
mentioning suffering he referred to glory. He said this also in
order to set an example for us, namely, that we should pray not
to fall into temptation, but if we do fall into it to bear it
courageously and not to side-step it but to pray to God to be
saved. But 'Glorify thy name'. For if it is the case that God is
glorified through the dangers that threaten us, let all things
be considered secondary to that end.[40]

121

THE MISSION OF THE SPIRIT

In Jo. 9.1 (Pusey II, 466.4–470.7)

[808e]   14:16–17 And I will pray to the Father, and he will give
you another advocate, to be with you forever,
even the Spirit of truth, whom the world
cannot receive, because it neither sees him nor
knows him; you know him, for he dwells with
you, and will be in you.

He mingles again the human with the divine and neither
returns to the pure glory of the Godhead nor indeed dwells
wholly on the human dimension, but in a manner which
809a   transcends reason yet at the same time is consistent with the
union of the natures operates through both, seeing that he is
simultaneously both God and man. For he was God by
nature, in virtue of being the fruit of the Father and the
reflection of his essence. On the other hand he was man in
virtue of having become flesh. He therefore speaks both as
God and as man at the same time, for in this way it was
possible to observe properly the form of words appropriate to
the dispensation of the flesh. Only we shall say this while we
are exploring the meaning of the passage before us, that our
Lord has now necessarily made mention of God the Father
b   in order to build up faith and bring enormous benefit to his
hearers, as our discussion will show as it develops. For when
he commanded us to ask in his name (cf. Jn 14:13–14) – and
amongst other things instituted a way of praying to which
the ancients were unaccustomed – promising to give us, and
very readily too, whatever we wished to receive, he said
c   that he would be an effective co-provider and would join in
bestowing the counsellor upon us. This was so that the
person of God the Father should not seem to be thrust aside
by these words, that is to say, that the authority of him who
had begotten him should not be diminished – I mean with
regard to satisfying the aspirations of the saints. The phrase 'I
will pray', moreover, he added in his human capacity
attributing properly to the divine and ineffable nature as a
whole, as if represented in the person of God the Father, that
which was most appropriate to it. For this was his custom, as
we have often already said.

Nevertheless he calls the Spirit, who is of the essence of God the Father, or of his own essence, another advocate.[41] For the principle of the essence is one with regard to both; it does not exclude the Spirit but allows the principle of the difference to be conceived of solely in his being and subsisting in his own person.[42] For the Spirit is not a Son, but we accept by faith that he exists and subsists truly and individually as that which he is. For he is the Spirit of the Father and the Son. But since the Son knew that he himself was in truth an advocate, and is named as such in the sacred Scriptures, he calls the Spirit 'another advocate', not that the Spirit, who is and is said to be the Spirit of the Son, can by any chance bring about anything of a different kind in the saints than he can himself. That the Son is himself an advocate, both in name and in reality, John will witness in his own writings, where he says, 'I am writing this to you so that you may not sin; but if anyone does sin, we have an advocate with the Father, Jesus Christ the righteous, and he is the expiation for our sins' (1 Jn 2:1–2). He therefore calls the Spirit 'another advocate', intending that he should be conceived of as a separate hypostasis, yet possessing such a close likeness to himself and with the power to operate in a manner identical to that in which he himself might perhaps do, that he appears to be the Son himself and not at all different. For he is his Spirit. And indeed he called him the very Spirit of truth, also calling himself the truth in the passage we are considering (Jn 14:6).

Now one may reasonably object to those who hold that the Son is alien to the essence of God the Father: 'Tell me, how is it that the Spirit of truth, that is, of the Son, is given by the Father not as something foreign or alien but as his own Spirit, when in your view the principle of his essence is distinct from that of the Son, yet the Spirit is of the Son – for this last point is not disputed. Moreover, how is it that if the Son is indeed of a different essence, he gives the Spirit of the Father as his own Spirit? For it is written that "he breathed on his disciples and said to them, 'Receive the Holy Spirit'" (Jn 20:22). Therefore will not one suppose, and very rightly too, or rather will not one be strongly disposed to believe, that since the Son is a partaker in an essential manner of the natural excellences of God the Father, he possesses the Spirit in the same way as one would conceive of the Father possessing him, that

123

is, not as something added on, or of external origin? For it is foolish, or rather mad, to think in this way. A suitable analogy is how each of us has his own breath inside himself and sends it forth from the depths of his being. That is why Christ also breathed on the disciples physically (Jn 20:22), demonstrating that just as breath issues from the human mouth in a physical way, so the Spirit of God pours forth from the divine essence in a manner befitting God. Since the Spirit of God the Father is indeed the same as that of the Son, how will they not necessarily possess a single authority subsisting simultaneously both in a separate and in a unified mode? For the Father is the Father and not the Son, and the Son is the Son and not the Father, albeit that the Father is in the Son and the Son in the Father. Nevertheless when they give the Advocate, that is, the Holy Spirit, the Father and the Son do not each give him separately. Rather he is supplied to the saints from the Father through the Son. That is why when the Father is said to give, the Son 'through whom are all things' gives; and when the Son is said to give, the Father 'from whom are all things' gives (1 Cor. 8:6).

That the Spirit is divine and not of a different essence – I mean with respect to the Father and the Son – will not I think be doubted by any right-minded person. The following argument also necessarily convinces us of this. For if someone should say that the Spirit is not from the essence of God, how could a creature, when it receives the Spirit, be a partaker of God? In what way do we become temples of God in fact and name if we receive a created or alien spirit and not that which is from God? How do we become 'partakers of the divine nature' (2 Pet. 1:4), as the saints declare, in virtue of our being partakers of the Spirit (Heb. 6:4) if he is reckoned amongst created beings and has not rather proceeded for us from the divine nature itself? He does not pass through it into us as something alien to it but, in a manner of speaking, becomes in us some quality as it were of the Godhead. He dwells in the saints and remains with them for ever, if they cleanse the eye of their understanding by cleaving to every sound doctrine and by resolutely pursuing every virtue, and thus maintain the grace within themselves. For Christ says that those who are in the world, that is, those who are preoccupied with the things of this world and choose to love earthly things, are unable to contain or to behold the Spirit.

b The saints, on the other hand, can contain him and can behold him with ease. For what reason? Since the impurity of the former is difficult to cleanse but fills up their mind like some mucous discharge, they cannot examine closely the beauty of the divine nature, nor can they receive the law of the Spirit, dominated as they are in every way by the passions of the flesh. But those who are good and sober-minded, who keep their heart free of the evils that are in the world, willingly open themselves to the Advocate, and having received him

c keep him, and so far as is humanly possible, behold him spiritually, thereby winning a wonderful reward worthy of emulation. For he will sanctify them and prove them to be accomplishers of every good thing, and will release them from the shameful state of the slavery that belongs to the human condition and bestow upon them the dignity of adoption as sons. Paul, too, witnesses to this, when he says 'Because you are sons, God has sent the Spirit of his Son into your hearts, crying, "Abba! Father!"' (Gal. 4:6).

THE UNITY OF CHRISTIANS

In Jo. 11.9 (Pusey II, 694.5–698.18)

[969d] 17:11 Holy Father, keep them in thy name, which thou hast given me, that they may be one, even as we are one.

In every respect he upholds the blending of the two elements into a single reality, I mean the human element, which in our case possesses a humble status, and the divine element, which brings forth the highest of all glories. For this text represents a mingling of both, and as we were saying earlier in our

970a commentary, the divine element neither soars wholly to the heights nor indeed does it detach itself completely from our level. For he is God who has become man, occupying, as it were, a middle position by an ineffable and indescribable union, since he has neither left the sphere of the truly divine nor has he entirely abandoned that of the human. For his ineffable generation from God the Father raises him up, in that he is Word and Only-begotten, to the divine essence and to the glory that naturally accompanies it, while his self-emptying draws him down somewhat to our world. Not that this self-emptying is sufficient to overwhelm by force, so to speak, him who with the Father is king of the universe, for the Only-begotten is never forced against his will. Rather, it was of his own accord, out of his love for us, that he accepted the self-emptying and persevered with it. That is to say, he humiliated himself voluntarily, not as a result of any compulsion. For he would have been convicted of not having undergone the suffering of his humiliation willingly, if there had been anyone at all powerful enough to have had an advantage over him and with the ability to order him to undergo this against his will. Therefore he humbled himself willingly for our sake. For we ourselves would never have been called sons by grace and gods (cf. Ps. 82:6) if the Only-begotten had not undergone humiliation for us and on our behalf. Having been conformed to Christ through participation in the Spirit, we are described as children of God and gods. Therefore when he says something that combines in some way the human with the divine, do not on this account take offence and foolishly cease admiring as one ought the incomparably skilful way in which he has chosen his words, elegantly preserving for us in every way his dual character, so that we see him who is by nature truly both God and man speaking as such at one and the same time, brilliantly combining the humble element of the humanity with the glory of the ineffable divine nature, and maintaining a proportionality of expression with regard to both, in a way that is entirely blameless and free from any reproach.

Yet when we say this, how is it that we are not affirming that the nature of the Word is reduced to a lower status than that which it had originally? To think in such a way would be to betray the most profound ignorance, since the divine is wholly impassible in every way and not susceptible of any change whatsoever, but rather maintains its own position with the utmost stability. No, we say this because the manner of the voluntary self-emptying, since it necessarily implies the form of the humiliation, makes God the Only-begotten, who is equal to the Father and naturally of the same form as he is, and is in him and from him, appear because of the human element to be somewhat inferior in some respects to him. And do not be perplexed at hearing that on account of

126

his human element the Son appears to fall short of the majesty of the Father, seeing that Paul himself asserted that for this very reason the Son was inferior even to the angels themselves, when he writes, 'Jesus, who for a little while was made lower than the angels, crowned with glory and honor because of the suffering of death' (Heb. 2:9), even though the angels were commanded to worship him, for 'when he brings the first-born into the world, he says, "Let all God's angels worship him"' (Heb. 1:6), and indeed the holy Seraphim also stood in a circle round him and fulfilled the office of house-

b   hold servants, when, seated 'on a high and exalted throne', he appeared to the prophets (Is. 6:1). Therefore with regard to whatever concerns the real birth and generation from God the Father, the humanity is not a property of the Son. On the other hand, it is a property of the Son, in that he became a man yet remains what he always was and is and for ever will be, even though he brought himself down to that which he was not for our sake.

Therefore he says, 'Holy Father, keep them in thy name, which thou hast given me, that they may be one even as we are one.' He wishes the disciples to be preserved by the power and authority of his ineffable nature, attributing rightly and

c   fittingly to him who is truly and by nature God, and very readily too, the power of saving whomsoever he wills. By this means he glorifies not something different from himself but his own nature as existing in the person of the Father by whom he was begotten as God. That is why he says, 'keep them in thy name, which thou hast given me,' that is, in the divine name. He says, moreover, that the name of divinity was given to him, though this does not imply that not having previously been God by nature he was called to the additional dignity of divinity. For he would then be adopted as we are, and have a spurious and allotted glory and a fraudulent

d   nature, a thought which we should not even entertain, for this would also be detrimental to his being Son by nature. But since, as the divine Scriptures proclaim, the Word became flesh, that is, a human being, he says that he received what he already had in his capacity as God. For the name and reality of the divine glory could not naturally appear to be a human attribute. Moreover, you should consider and understand exactly how he showed himself to be the living and enhypostatic power of God the Father, through which he

127

accomplishes all things. For when in addressing the Father he says, 'keep them', he was not content with these words alone, but skilfully brought in himself as well, since it was he who was to effect the keeping and was for that purpose the power and executive action of him who had begotten him. For he says, 'keep them in thy name, which thou hast given me.' Do you see how carefully expressed this is? For by assigning and as it were attributing our supervision and providential care to the nature of the divinity as something appropriate to it alone, he immediately asserts that the glory of the divinity was given to him, saying on account of the form of the humanity that what was an attribute of his by nature, that is, 'the name which is above every name' (Phil. 2:9), was something granted to him. Consequently, we say that those things which he receives as man are in one sense natural attributes of the Son, in virtue of his being from the Father, but in another sense are received in a human way in the form of a gift, so far as our own human speech is concerned. For man is not by nature God, but Christ is God by nature, even though we conceive of him in terms of our own make-up.[43]

Nevertheless he wishes the disciples to be kept in a state of unity by maintaining a likemindedness and an identity of will, being mingled together as it were in soul and spirit and in the law of peace and love for one another. He wishes them to be bound together tightly with an unbreakable bond of love, that they may advance to such a degree of unity that their freely chosen association might even become an image of the natural unity that is conceived to exist between the Father and the Son. That is to say, he wishes them to enjoy a unity which is inseparable and indestructible, which may not be enticed away into a dissimilarity of wills by anything at all that exists in the world or any pursuit of pleasure, but rather preserves the power of love in the unity of devotion and holiness, which is what actually happened. For as we read in the Acts of the Apostles, 'the company of those who believed were of one heart and soul' (Acts 4:32), that is, in the unity of the Spirit. This is also what Paul himself meant when he said, 'one body and one spirit' (Eph. 4:4), 'we who are many are one body in Christ, for we all partake of the one bread' (1 Cor. 10:17; cf. Rom. 12:5), and we have all been anointed in the one Spirit, the Spirit of Christ (cf. 1 Cor. 12:13). Therefore since they were to be members of the same body and fellow d participants in one and the same Spirit, he wishes his disciples to be kept in a unity of spirit that can never be prised apart and in a oneness of mind that cannot be broken. If anyone should suppose that the disciples were united in the same way as the Father and the Son are one, not only according to essence but also according to will, for there is a single will in the divine nature and an identical purpose in every respect, let him think that. For he will not stray outside the bounds of orthodoxy since identity of will may be observed amongst those who are true Christians, even if identity of substance in our case is not of the same kind as that which exists in the case of the Father and of God the Word who is from him and in him.

AGAINST NESTORIUS

INTRODUCTION

The Five Tomes Against Nestorius were composed during the spring of
430 in response to a series of public lectures which Nestorius had given
twelve months earlier in the great church of Constantinople.[1] By
now the positions of the two archbishops had become polarized.
When reports had begun to circulate in Egypt of Nestorius'
opposition to the title *Theotokos*, 'Mother of God', Cyril's initial
response, early in 429, was to issue a firm statement on Alexandrian
christological teaching in his annual letter to the churches of Egypt
announcing the date of Easter.[2] He followed this up shortly
afterwards with a pastoral letter to the monks of Egypt in which he
expresses his amazement that anyone should hesitate to call the holy
Virgin *Theotokos*.[3] When he was informed that Nestorius had been
upset by the *Letter to the Monks*,[4] Cyril wrote to him to say that he had
been in touch with Celestine, bishop of Rome, and that the Romans
had been greatly scandalized by Nestorius' teaching.[5] Nestorius
responded with a curt letter protesting at Cyril's aggression, which
was 'not according to brotherly love, to put it mildly'.[6] Cyril's
celebrated Second Letter to Nestorius, dated February 430, was his
response to Nestorius' protest.[7] In it he gives a brief summary of
the Alexandrian christological position, a summary which was
subsequently to receive conciliar endorsement.

Meanwhile, Cyril was preparing a detailed refutation of the views
which Nestorius had expressed in his lectures of the previous year.
He had before him a copy of the lectures, sent to him by his agents
in Constantinople, which he was working through systematically,
setting down the more significant passages verbatim and discussing
each in turn. The importance of the *Five Tomes* lies in their showing
Cyril working out at some length and with considerable dialectical
skill the position which he was to sum up succinctly in his dogmatic

letters.[8] The first book discusses the christological implications of the title *Theotokos*, the remaining four the way in which deity and humanity are united in the person of the Word made flesh.

The *Five Tomes* do not appear to have been widely circulated.[9] Copies were evidently kept to hand, however, to send to suitable recipients as the occasion demanded. Cyril himself tells us of two such recipients, the imperial chamberlain, Chryseros, and an Isaurian bishop called Successus. In the months following the Council of June 431 Cyril feared the possibility that the emperor Theodosius II might fail to impose the decisions of the council on those bishops who normally took their lead from Antioch. Accordingly, he wrote to his agent Eulogius, an Alexandrian priest resident in Constantinople, instructing him to forward to the 'venerable Chamberlain' (an important but hostile palace official) a dossier which was to include the *Five Tomes*.[10] We know from the letter from Epiphanius, archdeacon and syncellus of Alexandria, to Archbishop Maximian of Constantinople, that theological persuasion was not the only kind to which Cyril resorted in order to achieve his aims. Chryseros was to receive rich gifts of tapestries, carpets and inlaid furniture, and, if he joined the Cyrillian camp, two hundred pounds of gold.[11] Bishop Successus of Diocaesarea, by contrast, was a fervent admirer of Cyril, even though his diocese lay within Antioch's sphere of influence. He wrote to Cyril, probably shortly after April 433, when John of Antioch and Cyril were reconciled, asking Cyril to set down his convictions in writing for him.[12] In response Cyril sent him a copy of Athanasius' letter to Epictetus of Corinth together with his own five-volume work against Nestorius and his defence of the Twelve Chapters.[13] In Successus' case the gift of books alone was enough to ensure his support.

The following passages have been translated from Schwartz's critical edition in ACO I, 1, 6, pp. 13–106. The marginal references in italic are to chapters. The other marginal references are to the page numbers in Schwartz.

TEXT

MARY, MOTHER OF GOD

I Prooem. 1 – I, 2, 2 (ACO I, 1, 6, pp. 16.1–21.14)

16   I do not know how they can bring themselves to do it, but there are those who besmirch the most sacred beauty of the

teachings of the Church and calumniate the holy and most pure Virgin,[14] reducing her to the meagre level of their own flimsy ideas and planting in our midst a host of novel inventions. For they brand the word '*Theotokos*', which the holy fathers who preceded us devised and applied to the holy Virgin, an illegitimate and inept term, or rather one that goes beyond all reasonable language.[15] They bisect the one Lord Jesus Christ, dividing him into two separate sons, and remove from God the Word the sufferings of the flesh, even though we have certainly not said that he suffered in his own nature, by which we conceive of him as God, but rather have attributed to him along with the flesh the sufferings that befell the flesh, so that he too should be acknowledged as Saviour.[16] For 'with his stripes we were healed', as Scripture says, 'and he was bruised for our sins' (Is. 53:5), even though he was incapable of experiencing bruising. We have been saved by his taking death upon himself for our sake through his own body.

I shall attempt to demonstrate clearly what I have said. For I shall now quote the author of this book verbatim, first of all a passage in which he mounts a strong attack on the term '*Theotokos*'. Because he repeats himself frequently, and we consequently need to go through the same ideas a number of times, I earnestly ask your forgiveness for a repetitiveness which is not of my choosing.[17] For we have decided that whatever the thrust of his argument, that is where we should oppose him. This is what he said then, when he pronounced the term '*Theotokos*' unsound as applied to the holy Virgin:

1 I often asked them (that is, those who contradict him), 'Do you say that the Godhead has been born of the holy Virgin?' At once they pounce on the phrase, 'And who,' they say, 'is so sick with such a blasphemy as to say that in her who gave birth to the temple, in her was God conceived by the Spirit?' Then when I reply to this, 'What is wrong, then, about our advising the avoidance of this expression and the acceptance of the common meaning of the two natures?' then it seems to them that what we have said is blasphemy. Either admit clearly that the Godhead has been born from the blessed Mary, or if you avoid this expression as blasphemous, why do you say the same things as I do, yet pretend that you are not saying them?[18]

Those who hold the opposite view to what you yourself have said and consider – I do not know how – to be right are therefore clearly proved by your own words to hold a correct and unerring opinion with regard to Christ the Saviour of us all and to profess a faith which was delivered to the churches 'by those who from the beginning were eyewitnesses and ministers of the word' (Lk. 1:2) and priests and faithful stewards of our divine mysteries. For they shake off, and rightly too, as clear evidence of ignorance and at the same time of extreme impiety, the merest thought that the Word who is from God the Father was called to a second beginning of being or took flesh from the holy Virgin as if it were some root of his own existence. Nevertheless, they call her *Theotokos* since she has given birth to Emmanuel who is clearly God by nature, for the Word who is God by nature and above us came to be 'God with us' (Mt. 1:23). Do they therefore say the opposite to what they think? I suppose that someone who thinks as you do will say, 'If you do not claim that the nature of the Word is a product of the flesh, and free yourself from this charge, how do you assert that the holy Virgin brought forth God?' And he will hear from us in reply: 'The inspired Scriptures say that the Word who is from God the Father became flesh (cf. Jn 1:14), that is to say was hypostatically and without confusion united with the flesh. For the body which was united to him was not alien to him, even though it was born from a woman, but as our own bodies are proper to each of us, so in the same way the body of the Only-begotten was proper to him and not to anyone else. For that is how he was born according to the flesh.'

Tell me, then, how could he have become flesh, if he had not received birth from a woman, since the laws of human existence demand this and corporeal existence could not have been initiated in any other way? For we shall not pay any attention to the claptrap of the Greeks and come out ourselves with some rigmarole about human bodies being born from an oak tree or a rock. Nature framed the laws that govern us, or rather the Creator of nature. Every being produces offspring of the same species as itself. It is the same with us. How could it be otherwise? Nothing at all is impossible, of course, that the divine and ineffable power wishes to accomplish. But God works through what is appropriate to the nature of beings; He does not violate the laws which he himself has established.

133

It would not have been impossible for the Word who can do all things, since he had decided to become one of us for our sake, if he had declined to be born from a woman and had fashioned a body for himself by his own power from something external to himself. Indeed, we say that this is what happened in the case of our ancestor Adam, for the Lord took dust from the ground, says Scripture, and formed man (cf. Gen. 2:7). But this would have offered a pretext to those unbelievers who wish to misrepresent the mystery of the Incarnation, and above all to the unholy Manichaeans, whom you say repeatedly that you fear, lest they should spring upon those who call the holy Virgin '*Theotokos*', as people who assert that the incarnation of the Word took place only in appearance.[19] He therefore necessarily observed the laws of human nature, and since his aim was to assure everybody that he had truly become man, he took to himself the seed of Abraham (cf. Heb. 2:16) and with the blessed Virgin acting as a mediator to this end, partook of flesh and blood in the way that we do (cf. Heb. 2:14). For this was the only way in which he could become 'God with us'.

There is another very necessary reason as far as those on earth are concerned why the Word of God took flesh or became man. If he had not been born like us according to the flesh, if he had not partaken of the same elements as we do, he would not have delivered human nature from the fault we incurred in Adam, nor would he have warded off the decay from our bodies, nor would he have brought to an end the power of the curse which we say came upon the first woman.[20] For it was said to her, 'in pain you shall bring forth children' (Gen. 3:16). But human nature, which fell sick through the disobedience of Adam, now became glorious in Christ through his utter obedience. For it is written that as by one man's disobedience many were made sinners, so by one man's obedience many will be made righteous' (Rom. 5:19). In Adam it suffered the penalty: 'You are earth and to earth you shall return' (Gen. 3:19 LXX). In Christ it was enriched by being able to overcome the snares of death and, as it were, exult in triumph over decay, repeating the prophetic text, 'O death, where is thy victory? O Hades, where is thy sting?' (Hos. 13:14 LXX; 1 Cor. 15:55). It came under a curse, as I have said, but this too was abolished in Christ. And indeed it has been said somewhere to the holy Virgin, when Elizabeth prophesied in the spirit, 'Blessed are you among women and blessed is the fruit of your womb' (Lk. 1:42). Sin has reigned over us and the inventor and father of sin has lorded it over all who dwell under the sky, provoking the transgression of the divine laws. But in Christ we see human nature, as if experiencing a new beginning of the human race, enjoying freedom of access to God. For he said clearly, 'the ruler of this world is coming and he has no power over me' (Jn 14:30).

Now it would be reasonable to say, my distinguished friend, that unless the Only-begotten had become like us, and he could not have become like us except by physical birth from a woman, we would not have been enriched with what belongs to him. For as Paul writes in his great wisdom, Emmanuel, the second Adam, did not come forth for us from the earth like the first, but from heaven (cf. 1 Cor. 15:47). For the Word that is from above and from the Father came down not into the flesh of any particular person nor into a flesh alien to humanity, as we have already said. Moreover, he did not descend on a particular individual like ourselves, in order to dwell within him, as doubtless happened in the case of the prophets. On the contrary, having made his own the body which was from a woman, and having been born from her according to the flesh, he recapitulated human birth in himself, he who was with the Father before all ages having come to be with us according to the flesh.

This is the confession of faith that the divine Scriptures have transmitted to us. But you pretend to be concerned in case anyone of our way of thinking should suppose that the Word brought forth from God had the beginning of his existence from earthly flesh and you destroy utterly the mystery of the economy of the flesh by saying that the holy Virgin should not be called *Theotokos* by us and you misrepresent those who apply to her the term *Theotokos* as an inevitable and indispensable title as necessarily supposing that the Word who is from God became the fruit of the flesh.

But this is not so. Indeed, it is far from the case. For he who has his existence from God the Father, an existence that is before all time (for he is the creator of the aeons), in the last days of this age, seeing that he became flesh, is said to have been begotten after the flesh. For if his body is conceived of as his own, how will he not necessarily make the birth of his body completely his own? You yourself would approve of the correct and blameless faith of those who think in this way if you would let yourself be persuaded to consider the matter and confess that Christ is truly God, the one and only Son of God the Father, not divided separately as man and similarly as God, but the same existing both as Word from God the Father and as a human being from a woman, who is like us while at the same time remaining God. That you calumniate the birth of the Word according to the flesh, maintaining consistently that there are two sons and bisecting the one Lord Jesus Christ, will be demonstrated not by my arguments but by your own words.

2,1 Look what follows, heretic. I do not begrudge you the expression 'Virgin *Christotokos*'.[21] I know that she who received God is venerable, she through whom the Lord of all things passed, through whom the sun of righteousness shone forth. Again I am suspicious of your applause.[22] How do you understand 'passed through'? I did not use 'passed through' as a synonym for 'was born'. I have not forgotten my own words as quickly as that. That God passed through from the Virgin as *Christotokos* I have been taught by the divine Scriptures, but that God was born from her I have not been taught anywhere.[23]

2 And a little further on:

Nowhere do the divine Scriptures say that God was born from the Mother of Christ, but Jesus Christ, Son and Lord.[24]

3 And then he adds that Christ was not truly God but rather a God-bearing man, as he supposes, offering as proof the message of the angel who said to blessed Joseph, 'Rise, take the child' (Mt. 2:13). Even the angels, he says, knew that he was a child, and they are wiser than we are.

Here he calls a heretic someone who holds the right and admirable faith concerning Christ and who calls she who bore him *Theotokos*. But it will not be a matter of doubt to any who think correctly that it is himself who, fastening the accusation of heresy on those who choose to think correctly, condemns the ugliness of his own words and has all but confessed plainly that he has left the main road and has taken a perverse path.

19   Tell me, therefore, why do you begrudge such a title to the holy Virgin, and moreover deprive her of the dignity of divine birth and say that she is not *Theotokos?* When you condemn the term as unsound and declare that it is full of blasphemy, how is it that you allow those who wish to do so to attribute it to the holy Virgin? Furthermore, I hear you calling her venerable. How then do you consider this term which is so blasphemous (as it seems to you alone) fit to adorn the most venerable one and you pretend to crown her, presenting this calumny against the Word of God as if dedicating some choice gift to her? For if it is utterly detestable to the Word that has come from God to undergo physical birth, and yet you allow her who did not give birth to God to be called *Theotokos,* is it not true to say that you have manifestly despised the Lord's will? Will you not be caught insulting the venerable one rather than, as you yourself think and say, choosing to honour her by assigning her a title detestible to God? For if we give names to those we intend to honour through which the glory of the supreme nature is denigrated, first we shall involve ourselves unintentionally in such impious crime, and secondly with regard to them we shall do them no small disservice, glorifying those who are praised, as if by the bestowal of honour, with what does not praise them, and weaving for them a eulogy hateful to God.

One may also marvel at this too. Although you repeatedly rebuke the terms used by unholy heretics, and allow them in no way to prevail, because they strip away the truth from the divine doctrines, then subject the term *Theotokos* to a stream of invective and amongst other things accuse it of being untrue and blasphemous, you nevertheless say that you will allow it and not begrudge it to the Virgin, even if one should choose to call her *Theotokos.* Would you therefore also allow those who are sick with the madness of Arius to say that the Son is inferior to the Father, or those others who bring down the nature of the Holy Spirit from its divine pre-eminence? No, you would not choose to do this, and if anyone should wish to know the reason, you would no doubt say 'I cannot tolerate impious language'. Therefore, if she is not *Theotokos,* yet you permit this to be said, know that you have forsaken the truth and are little concerned to appear to be wise.

For do you not say that Elizabeth or any other of the holy women is worthy of all reverence? Does it not follow that you would not object if anyone were to choose to call these too *Theotokoi*? But I think you would totally disagree with this and say, 'That is not so. For they gave birth to sanctified human beings and nobody among them was God by nature.' Therefore take away this term from every woman, or if you allow of all of them only the holy Virgin to have this, what words will you use in your defence? For if the saying is true with regard to her and she really did give birth to God, confess with us that the Word who is from God has become flesh and you will deliver yourself from the charge of impiety. But if she did not give birth to God, to allow anyone to call her *Theotokos* is to participate in their impiety. But she is *Theotokos*, because the Only-begotten became a man like us, having been united with flesh and undergone physical birth and not having despised the laws of our own nature, as I have already said.

But since he says that he knows she is venerable, that is to say, that the holy Virgin is venerable, come, let us examine the cause of the reverence that has been shown to her. For 'I know,' he says, 'that she is venerable, through whom the Lord of all things passed, through whom the sun of righteousness shone forth.' How then do you say that she received God? Or in what way did the Lord of all things pass through her? Or how did the sun of righteousness shine forth? For if she did not give birth to God, I mean according to the flesh, how did she receive God? How did he pass through her? Perhaps you will reply with your clever saying, at least as you think it and even dare to utter it: 'God the Word was united to a man and dwelling within him.' But the tradition of the faith contradicts your words. For we have been taught to worship not a God-bearing man but an incarnate God, but this is not what you say. How then do you not perceive that you are talking nonsense and debasing the truth that is in the divine dogmas? For the Word became flesh. How do you say that she received God unless you believe that she has given birth to Emmanuel who is God by nature? How did the Lord of all things pass through her and the sun of righteousness shine forth, and who is it that you deem worthy to adorn with such titles? Is he an ordinary man like one of us, only sanctified because he has the Word of God dwelling within him? Then

20

how will such a person be Lord of all things and the sun of righteousness? For the power of ruling and holding sway over all things and of illuminating creatures endowed with intelligence belongs not to beings on our level but to the supreme and transcendent nature alone.

But since you have taken 'passed through' from I know not where and have applied it to God, explain the word clearly.[25] What is the meaning of this so-called 'passage'? Tell those who do not know what you have in mind. For if the Word of God passed through her in the sense of transferring from one place to another, this will knock you down. For you will hear him saying by the voice of the saints: 'Do I not fill heaven and earth? says the Lord' (Jer. 23:24). The divine does not occupy a place and does not experience physical transfers of location, for it fills all things. But if while awaiting the appropriate time for the birth, he dwelt incidentally in a human being, and that is why you say that God was in transit in the holy Virgin, or 'passed through' her (for on every occasion I shall use your own sacred terms[26]), it follows that we see nothing more in the holy Virgin than in other women. For Elizabeth gave birth to the blessed Baptist who was sanctified by the Holy Spirit, the same Spirit through whom the Son himself makes his home in us. The wise John testifies to this when he says: 'By this we know that we abide in him and he in us, because he has given us of his own Spirit' (1 Jn 4:13). Therefore the Word of God also passed through Elizabeth herself, dwelling in the infant through the Spirit even before his birth.

So you are suspicious of the applause, when it came to you from the people for having chosen to say what was right. For you called him who was born from the holy Virgin sun of righteousness and Lord of all things. Moreover, you pretend to be using precise terminology and you find fault with the applause and accuse those who rejoice over you of not having understood. Oh what power there is in your words! You were no sluggard in finding just what was needed to upset them. You immediately turned their joy into mourning, you tore off their gladness and girded them with sackcloth (cf. Ps. 30:11) when you added:

> Again I am suspicious of your applause. How do you understand 'passed through'? I did not use 'passed through' as a synonym for 'was born'. I have not

139

forgotten my own words as quickly as that. That God passed through from the Virgin Mother of Christ I have been taught by the divine Scriptures, but that God was born from her I have not been taught anywhere.

These, then, are your perverse words. The applause was out of love, in that your mind had gained some glimpse of ortho-doxy. But I will object now no less and say: What is this 'passed through' if it does not indicate the birth? Or do you say that the Word of God passed through the Virgin on his own without the flesh? Is this not complete nonsense? For it would be necessary to conceive of the divine as endowed with quantity and be capable of movement that transposes it from one place to another. If the divine is incorporeal, infinite and omnipresent and is not localized or circumscribed, how will it pass through an individual body? But whatever it is that you are saying, how is it not necessary to clarify it and speak more plainly, if you are confident in your own opinions on this matter and are able to testify to their irreproachable orthodoxy? Where have you heard the inspired Scriptures saying that the Word of God passed through the holy Virgin? That life on earth is brief and transient blessed David taught, when he said: 'As for man, his days are like grass; he flourishes like a flower of the field, for the wind passes over it, and it is no more' (Ps. 103:15–16).[27] But what text do you have that speaks of the holy Virgin in a similar vein? That God was born from her, I mean according to the flesh, the inspired Scriptures have clearly indicated.

THE UNITY OF CHRIST

II Prooem (ACO I, 1, 6, pp. 32.6–34.9)

[32] 'The tongue is a fire – a restless evil', as Scripture says (Jas 3:6, 8). Rejecting the harm of which it is capable, the divine David sings: 'Set a guard over my mouth, O Lord, keep watch over the door of my lips? Incline not my heart to any evil words' (Ps. 141:3–4). For to be able to keep silent and to maintain a tight control over the tongue as to what it should say and what it should not is truly a gift from God. It is no small accomplishment in those who are pursuing a not unadmirable

way of life. But rashness in speech and an unbridled propensity towards nitpicking are full of danger and carry those who are given to them down to 'a snare of hell' (Prov. 9:18 LXX). For it is written that 'death and life are in the power of the tongue, and those who master it will eat of its fruits' (Prov. 18:21 LXX). Another of our sages has uttered: 'If you have understanding, answer; but if not, put your hand on your mouth' (Sir. 5:12). For how is not silence better than ignorant speech? The spouting of bitter words is also accursed in another way, as is the pouring of wicked words over the ineffable glory when instead we should be honouring it with unending praises. 'In sinning against our brethren and wounding their conscience when it is weak, we sin against Christ', for that is what the divine Paul said (1 Cor. 8:12).

I say these things having read Nestorius' words and observed that he not only disapproves of our custom of saying that the holy Virgin is *Theotokos* and that she has given birth to Emmanuel who is God, but in addition to this he is determined to oppose the glory of Christ in other ways too. For he attempts to show us that he is a God-bearing man and not truly God, a man conjoined with God as if possessing an equal status. For that is how he alone, in contrast to everyone else, has thought fit to think and to write, even though the catholic Church, which Christ presented to himself, is without any wrinkle (cf. Eph. 5:27), unlike the person who has written such things, but instead is blameless, and possesses a knowledge of Christ that is utterly irreproachable, and has formed her tradition of faith in an excellent manner. For we believe in one God, Father almighty, maker of all things both visible and invisible, and in one Lord Jesus Christ, and in the Holy Spirit; and following the professions of faith of the holy fathers that supplement this, we say that the Word begotten essentially from God the Father became as we are and took flesh and became man, that is, he took for himself a body from the holy Virgin and made it his own. For that is how he will truly be one Lord Jesus Christ, that is how we worship him as one, not separating man and God, but believing that he is one and the same in his divinity and his humanity, that is to say, simultaneously both God and man.

But the inventor of this latest impiety, even though he purports to say that Christ is one, divides the natures completely and sets each apart, saying that they did not truly come together. He employs pretexts for sins, as Scripture says (cf. Ps. 141:4 LXX), and devises some kind of conjunction referring only, as I have said, to an equality of status, as indeed will be shown from his own words. And he has the Word of God dwelling in Christ by participation as in an ordinary man, and he divides up the sayings in the Gospels assigning them sometimes exclusively to the Word alone and sometimes exclusively to the man born from a woman.[28] But how is it not beyond dispute by anyone that the Only-begotten, being God by nature, became man, not simply by a conjunction, as he himself says, that is conceived of as external or incidental, but by a true union that is ineffable and transcends understanding?[29] In this way he is conceived of as one and only and every word befits him and everything will be said as from one person. For the incarnate nature of the Word is immediately conceived of as one after the union.[30] It is not unreasonable to see something similar in our own case too. For a human being is truly one compounded of dissimilar elements, by which I mean soul and body. But it is necessary to note here that we say that the body united to God the Word is endowed with a rational soul. And it will also be useful to add the following: the flesh, by the principle of its own nature, is different from the Word of God, and conversely the nature of the Word is essentially different from the flesh. Yet even though the elements just named are conceived of as different and separated into a dissimilarity of natures, Christ is nevertheless conceived of as one from both, the divinity and humanity having come together in a true union.

The inspired Scriptures support us in this view with countless deeds and sayings, using images which one may penetrate clearly without the least effort so as to be able to discern the mystery of Christ. The blessed prophet Isaiah said accordingly: 'And there was sent to me one of the seraphim, and he had in his hand a coal which he had taken with tongs from the altar. And he touched my mouth and said: "Behold, this has touched your lips and will take away your iniquities and will cleanse you of your sins"' (Is. 6:6, 7 LXX). When we investigate, so far as is possible, the deepest meaning of the vision, we say that it is none other than our Lord Jesus Christ who is the spiritual coal lying on the altar, from whom the incense we offer ascends as a sweet fragrance to God the

Father, for through him we have had access (cf. Eph. 2:18) and are acceptable as we perform our spiritual worship (cf. Heb. 9:6). Accordingly, when this divine coal touches the lips of a person who approaches it, it immediately renders him cleansed and utterly free from participation in any sin. The manner in which it touches our lips is revealed by blessed Paul, when he says: 'The word is near you, on your lips and in your heart... because if you confess with your lips that Jesus is Lord and believe in your heart that God raised him from the dead, you will be saved. For man believes with his heart and so is justified, and he confesses with his lips and so is saved' (Rom. 10:8–10). He is compared to a coal because he is conceived of as being from two things which are unlike each other and yet by a real combination are all but bound together into a unity. For when fire has entered into wood, it transforms it by some means into its own glory and power, while remaining what it was.[31]

Again, our Lord Jesus Christ likens himself to a pearl, saying: 'the kingdom of heaven is like a merchant in search of fine pearls, who, on finding one pearl of great value, went and sold all that he had and bought it' (Mt. 13:45, 46). I also hear him presenting himself to us in a different way, when he says: 'I am a flower of the plain, a lily of the valleys' (Song 2:1 LXX). For he possesses in his own nature the divine brilliance of God the Father, and moreover gives forth his fragrance – I mean, of course, a spiritual fragrance. In the case of the pearl and indeed of the lily the physical object is thought of as the underlying reality. The brilliance or the fragrance that are in it are properly distinct from those things in which they reside, yet equally belong properly to them and are not alien from those things in which they inhere in an indissoluble manner.[32] In my view we should reason and conceptualize and think in the same way with regard to Emmanuel too. For Godhead and flesh are different in their nature, yet the body was the Word's own; the Word that was united to it was not separated from the body. For this is the only way in which we can conceive of Emmanuel, which means 'God with us' (Mt. 1:23). There is no other way. That is precisely why on one occasion, having made himself manifest to us as man from the point of view of his self-emptying, he says, 'No one takes my life from me' (Jn 10:18), while on another occasion, conceived of as God from a heavenly point of view and one

143

with his own flesh, he says, 'No one has ascended into heaven but he who has descended from heaven, the Son of Man' (Jn 3:13).

II, 3–10 (ACO I, 1, 6, 39.4–48.31)

[39] Failing utterly to follow a correct line, this man [Nestorius] sinks to such a level of impious thought and arrives at such a pitch of perversity as a result of dividing the one Lord Jesus Christ into two that he says quite frankly that Emmanuel is neither truly God nor Son by nature but is named 'Christ' and 'holy' in the way that no doubt others are like ourselves or like those who worship the impure demons. For further on he says:

4
> Just as we call the creator of the universe 'God' and Moses 'god' (for 'I have made you a god to pharaoh' (Ex. 7:1)), and Israel 'son of God' (for 'Israel is my first-born son' (Ex. 4:22)), and just as we call Saul 'Christ' (I will 'not stretch forth my hand against him, seeing he is the Lord's Christ' (1 Sam. 24:6)) and also Cyrus ('thus says the Lord to his Christ, to Cyrus' (Is. 45.1)) and the holy one of Babylon ('for I will marshall them, they are made holy and I will lead them' (Is. 13:3 LXX)), so we call the Lord 'Christ' and 'God' and 'son' and 'holy'. But although they share the same names, their rank is not the same.[33]

What are you saying? What word are you blurting out from your own heart and not from the mouth of the Lord, as Scripture says (Jer. 23:16 LXX)? No one says 'Jesus be cursed' except by Beelzebub (cf. 1 Cor. 12:3). Tell me, should Moses be thought of as God or be called 'God' by us in the same sense as Christ? Is Christ to be a son in the same way as Israel? Oh what impiety! Oh what words that recklessly disparage the glory of our Saviour! Oh what extreme idiocy that overcomes all restraint, I mean with regard to wanting to treat the doctrines of the Church so profanely! Let the blessed David now sing: 'The Lord's enemies have lied to him' (Ps. 81:15 LXX). For the divine Moses was by nature a man like ourselves and nothing else. But when God said, 'Come, I will send you to Pharaoh, king of Egypt, and you shall bring forth the sons of

Israel out of Egypt' (Ex. 3:10), and Moses was putting forward as an excuse for not going his slowness of speech and lack of eloquence 'in former times' (Ex. 4:10 LXX), he heard God saying, 'See, I have made you a god to Pharaoh and Aaron your brother shall be your interpreter' (Ex. 7:1). For the law was too weak to be able to deliver anyone from slavery to the devil, but when Christ acted as mediator this too was achieved. In a similar way, in this instance too, when Aaron accompanied the divine Moses, Israel was delivered from slavery in Egypt. Since it was intended that in due course Christ too would be under the law, seeing that he was to be a man like us, Aaron was in a sense appointed Moses' deputy. That is the spiritual meaning. But if one should choose to say the following, that even that great man Moses was honoured by the call of God in the sense in which God in his grace and generosity says to us in common: 'I said, you are gods and all of you sons of the Most High' (Ps. 82:6), does it follow that Christ is a god in this fashion? How is this not indeed madness and the empty froth of an ignorant mind? For the one, as I have said, being a man by nature has been honoured by the mere title alone. But the other is truly God, for the Word was God in human form, who kept the superiority of his own nature over all others unimpaired. For the divine nature's descending in order to participate in flesh and blood would not have involved it in any change for the worse. At any rate he was recognized as God when he appeared as man.

Clear proof of this is furnished by the things written about him in the Gospels. For the divine John said: 'Now when he was in Jerusalem at the Passover feast, many believed in his name when they saw the signs which he did; but Jesus did not trust himself to them, because he knew all men and needed no one to bear witness of man; for he himself knew what was in man' (Jn 2:23–25). And indeed to be able to see into the heart of a man and to know the things that are hidden does not belong to any one of us – why should it? – nor to any other creature, but rather to him alone who is said to fashion our hearts individually (cf. Ps. 33:15 LXX). Then how is Emmanuel honoured by being called 'god' simply as a mere title in the manner of Moses, rather than by being in actual fact that which he is and is said to be? John thus writes again of him: 'For he whom God has sent utters the words of God, for it is not by measure that he gives the Spirit' (Jn

3:34). Do you understand then how although he was seen as a man like us he utters the words of God? For it is something exceptional and beyond the powers of creation that belongs to him alone who is by nature and in reality God to be able to achieve by the spoken word that which is in accordance with his will, and to make those who have been justified by faith partakers of the Holy Spirit. In this matter one may see that we are referring to Christ. For he said to the leper: 'I will; be clean' (Mt. 8:3), and to the widow's son: 'Young man, I say to you, arise' (Lk. 7:14). He showed his own disciples to be partakers of the Holy Spirit, for he breathed on them, saying: 'Receive the Holy Spirit' (Jn 20:22). In what way will he who has arrived at this level and been crowned with divine glory be a god in the same sense that Moses no doubt was? Whose heart did Moses know? Who has believed in his name? Whom has he justified through faith in himself? Where has he spoken the words of God as a son – although indeed he is seen crying to the people of Israel, 'Thus says the Lord' (Ex. 32:27), and he does have the status of a household servant, for he became 'faithful in God's house as a servant' (Heb. 3:5, cf. Num. 12:7)?

Moreover, if Emmanuel was a son in the same way as Israel, who became so according to the flesh, you have reduced him who is free in his essential nature to the level of a slave, even though he did take on the form of a slave because of the flesh and everything connected with it. You have placed on the same level as those who are sons by grace the one on whose account they have been enriched by the grace of adoption. For he has been called first-born among us on account of his humanity, but even so he remained only-begotten in his capacity as God. Therefore, as the most wise Paul says, when the first-born was brought into the world by the Father, the powers above were ordered to worship him (cf. Heb. 1:6), and on learning the mystery concerning him they worship him who is by nature the one real Son with ceaseless praises. For if he gives to those who receive him power to become children of God, as John says (cf. Jn 1:12), and if it is true that we ourselves receive adoption as sons through his Spirit (for 'God has sent the Spirit of his Son into our hearts crying, "Abba! Father!"' (Gal. 4:6)), no one who is accustomed to think in an orthodox way would tolerate this man saying that Christ is a son in the same way as Israel.

Furthermore, how was he Christ and holy in the same way as Cyrus who was king of the Persians was Christ and holy and indeed the Persians and Medes themselves?[34] For now is the time to say that Christ was not made holy in a human fashion, even though the Holy Spirit came down upon him in the form of a dove. For Cyrus, son of Cambyses, mounted an expedition against the land of the Babylonians in his time, but he was in error and used to offer worship to the impure demons. But when he was stirred up by God and aroused to anger and took the land of the Babylonians, he was called Christ in the sense of a common noun, even though he had not been anointed by the Holy Spirit, and the Medes and Persians who accompanied him were called holy in a similar way. They too served the creature rather than the Creator and worshipped the work of their own hands (cf. Rom. 1:25). But since according to the words of the Mosaic law, once something was set aside as a sacrifice to God, whether a calf or a sheep, it was called holy, they too were called holy through the voice of the prophet because they were set aside by the divine will for the capture of the land of the Babylonians. Therefore if Emmanuel was Christ in the same way as Cyrus and holy in the same way as the Medes and the Persians, one could reasonably say from the absurdity of the notion that he was neither anointed by the Holy Spirit nor indeed is he holy at all. Our divine David would therefore be lying when he says to him somewhere: 'You have loved righteousness and hated wickedness. Therefore God, your God, has anointed you with the oil of gladness above your fellows' (Ps. 45:7).

He has thus conducted a campaign of gossip against the majesty and glory of our Saviour and thinks that he can rebut the charge of impiety by setting forth some childish nonsense, saying: 'they share the same names but their rank is not the same'. How? Tell me, for I do not understand. For if he is God in the same way as Moses, and a son in the same way as Israel, and a Christ in the same way as Cyrus, and indeed holy like the Medes, how can one avoid the conclusion that his rank is the same as theirs? You will therefore be caught treating the very nature of the Word irreverently, for you go on to state:

Say of him who did the assuming that he is God. Add with respect to that which was assumed that it has the

147

form of a servant. Next bring in the dignity of the conjunction, in that the sovereign power is common to both. Confess the unity of the rank, in that the dignity of the two is the same, for the natures remain.[35]

He therefore again makes a twofold division. With extraordinary stupidity he assigns to 'rank' the significance of union, probably, I suppose, because he does not understand what the union is or what is the meaning of 'rank'. But we can say this much: he describes the sovereign power of the two natures as one and the dignity as one. Accordingly, seeing that he who is on a level of glory equal to that of the Word will not surpass Moses with regard to being a god, it would seem to be clear that the Word who is from God will have a status equal to that of Moses, with respect, I presume, to nature and glory. For if the middle term is like the first and third terms, and is indistinguishable from them in every detail, the principle of their nature will not be differentiated.[36] But perhaps he will say that the way in which the rank is expressed does not equate to nature. How then do you expect to gather, as you yourself say, into a single sovereign power elements that are essentially so different with regard to communion with each other and indeed equality, and crown them with equal honours? For where one nature is so entirely inferior to the other, how will it acquire not only an equal share of privileges but also the same dignity and a degree of esteem which does not differ?

That by defining '*synapheia*' presumably as a conjunction merely of proximity and juxtaposition, or indeed as one which is thought of as accidental, he contradicts his own words, rebuilding what he has demolished and setting up what he has overthrown, will become clear in the passage that follows, for he said:

42

6   That is why I wish you to applaud secure in the knowledge of what you are applauding. There is no division in the conjunction, or in the dignity, or in the sonship. There is no division in his being Christ, but there is division between the divinity and the humanity. Christ insofar as he is Christ is indivisible; the Son insofar as he is Son is indivisible; for we do not have two Christs or two Sons. Nor do we accept a

first Christ and a second one, or two different Christs, or two different Sons. On the contrary, the Son himself is twofold, not in rank but in nature.[37]

Tell me again, what do you mean by 'indivisible conjunction'?[38] Is it the union, by which I mean the hypostatic union, which we on our side advocate in our joint labour for doctrines expressive of the truth? Or is it that which is conceived of in terms of the juxtaposition and proximity of one thing to another? For that is the sense of the word in the inspired Scriptures. For God said to the most holy Moses in his discourses concerning the ancient tabernacle: 'You should make fifty golden rings and you shall join (*synapseis*) the curtains to each other with the rings' (Ex. 26:6 LXX). For since there were five curtains and each was a separate item in relation to the others, they were joined together by the rings. We for our part do not say that with regard to Christ the union was accomplished in such a way. For in Christ's case the union does not resemble the casual joining of one thing to another, whether understood in terms of spiritual concord or of physical proximity. On the contrary, as I have frequently said, he made the body taken from the holy Virgin his own; the Word of God, we say, was united in a true sense with flesh endowed with a soul.

Therefore if the expression 'conjunction', as he puts it, signifies the union as we conceive of it, by which I mean the hypostatic union, he will rightly be saying that there is no division in Christ in the sense of his being Christ. For he is not two different beings or two sons, or one and then another, or a first and a second, but clearly one both before the flesh and along with the flesh. For that is how he will be with regard to rank, as you call it, and indeed with regard to power: indivisible, or rather, the same. How is it then that you say that the one and indivisible being is twofold, and not simply in respect of rank but in respect of nature? For it is surely not because the Word of God the Father took flesh and came forth as a man like us that he was called twofold. For he who in his proper nature is foreign to flesh and blood is a single being yet not without flesh. By way of example, if one were to kill an ordinary human being one would not reasonably be accused of having wronged two people, but only one, even though that one person is perhaps conceived of as being from

soul and body and the nature of the component parts is not the
same but different. We should think about Christ in the same
way. For he is certainly not twofold. On the contrary, the
Word of God the Father, together with his flesh, is the one and
only Lord and Son. That the difference between the humanity
and the divinity or indeed the distance separating them is
vast I too will concede. For these elements I have mentioned
are clearly different in their mode of being and nothing like
each other. But when the mystery of Christ is set before us,
our discussion of the union does not ignore the difference
but nevertheless puts the division aside, not because we are
confusing the natures or mixing them together, but because
the Word of God, having partaken of flesh and blood, is still
thought of as a single Son and is called such.[39] But you, while
saying that one should not speak of two Christs, or say that there
are two Sons – and here you are stealing the appearance of
doctrinal orthodoxy – are caught speaking of two Christs and
dividing man and God into their own separate identities.
And you attempt to demonstrate that one is the object of
action and the other the subject. Here is what you say:

7   The glory of the Only-begotten is sometimes attributed
      to the Father (for Scripture says 'it is my Father who
      glorifies me' (Jn 8:54)), sometimes to the Spirit (for
      'the Spirit of truth will glorify me' (Jn 16:13, 14)) and
      sometimes to the authority of Christ (for 'they went
      forth and preached everywhere, while the Lord worked
      with them and confirmed the message by the signs that
      attended it' (Mk 16:20)).[40]

If he is saying that the Only-begotten Word of God,
conceived of as the Word in himself and not yet incarnate, is
glorified by the Father and the Holy Spirit, I shall leave aside
for the moment the fact that he has blundered and missed the
truth. For the occasion leads us to another point. He seems to
me to have forgotten what he has just now considered and
discussed. For he said, 'we do not have one Christ and another
Christ, or one Son and another Son, nor do we have two
Christs and two Sons.' But I would say, my astute friend, that
if you affirm that the glory of the Only-begotten is to be
attributed to the authority of Christ, how will he not be one
subject and another subject, or how will he not necessarily be

150

really two, if he who gives and he who receives are not the same, or if he ascribes to someone other than himself the attributes which by nature belong to him? In that case he would have operated under the control of another, as if there were another Christ apart from the Only-begotten. For if, as you say, the glory of the Only-begotten is to be attributed to him, and the divine disciples, using the authority that came from him, proclaimed the word and worked wonders, how is it that what I have said is not true? For he would have operated using an external authority, so that he who was the operator rather than himself should have been glorified by those who are in the world. What then, tell me, would there appear to be in him more than in the holy apostles? For they worked wonders by a power that was not their own and themselves acknowledged the fact openly. They were remarkable in that they knew this and glorified him who was operating through them. How, then, was it not necessary that Christ, who in your view was operated upon by another, and received the glory of the Only-begotten as an external thing, should not have proclaimed to those who approached him as God and sought help from him: 'May this blessing come upon you in the name of the Only-begotten or through his power'? For that is what the most wise disciples used to do, naming Jesus of Nazareth at every opportunity. But he never spoke to anyone in this way. On the contrary, he attributed what he accomplished to his own power, on one occasion saying to the blind, 'Do you believe that I am able to do this?' (Mt. 9:28), and demanding their assent, and on another saying with authority, 'I will; be clean' (Mt. 8:3). Why do you not put away these old wives' tales which you yourself have dreamed up on your own and apply yourself intelligently to the profundity of the mystery?[41]

But one can see that he does not have much to say at all even about the essentials. It is as if he is afraid that he will let slip something expressing the truth or will be caught thinking something laudable. He thinks of whatever jars the most and contradicts the doctrines of the Church in an utterly bizarre fashion. Yet he should have remembered God's words by the mouth of Ezekiel to those who have charge of spiritual flocks: 'You fed on the good pasture, and drank the clear water, and disturbed the residue with your feet, and my sheep eat what you have trodden with your feet,

44 and drink the water disturbed by your feet' (Ez. 34:18–19 LXX). For when we apply our minds to the inspired Scriptures we feed on the good pasture, as the Bible says, and we drink the clear water, that is to say, the word of the Spirit that is utterly pure and translucent and uncontaminated with falsehood. But when we defile it and mix in the dreariness of our own speculations, as if muddying the water, we conspire against the flocks of the Saviour.

That this also is true will be demonstrated by the ideas concerning Christ that he has pondered and carelessly expressed. This is what he says:

8 For even before becoming man God the Word was Son and God and coexistent with the Father, but in these latter days he assumed the form of a servant. Yet because he was Son prior to this, and was recognized as such, after the assumption he cannot be called a separate Son, otherwise we would be maintaining a doctrine of two Sons. But since he is conjoined with him who in the beginning was Son and was conjoined with him, with regard to the dignity he cannot admit of a division of sonship – I mean with regard to the dignity of sonship, not with regard to the natures. That is why God the Word is also called 'Christ', seeing that he has an unbroken conjunction with Christ and it is not possible for God the Word to do anything without the humanity. For the latter has been made to conform exactly to a perfect conjunction, not to an apotheosis, as our learned purveyors of novel doctrines maintain.[42]

He who has dared to say that the glory of the Only-begotten is to be attributed to the authority of Christ and has shattered the bond of unity draws it together again into a union and then once more separates the natures from each other. For the most part he babbles on about it to us, setting forth his fantastic theories, with the result that even if he seems to say something that tends towards orthodoxy, he is clearly proved not to know what he is saying. For he says in this passage that the Word of God is both Son and God 'even before becoming man' and that 'in these latter days he assumed the form of a servant'. Tell me therefore, if I do not seem to you to be speaking sensibly, who is it that is said to have become man and what do you say becoming man means? Who was it who assumed the form of a servant? And in what way was this form assumed by him? How could anyone doubt that when you say a man became man you are exposing yourself to ridicule? For since he was man by nature, how could he become again what he already was and pass over, as it were, into something different, I mean with respect to nature? In what way will that which by its own nature is not free be said to have become a servant, as though it were not a servant from the beginning? Therefore becoming man cannot apply to someone who is already man – far from it – and taking up the form of a servant cannot go with someone who even in the beginning had the status of a servant. On the contrary, it goes with one who was not man by nature but is believed to have become so, and who in spite of being Lord of all in that he is God, entered into our situation by uniting what was human to himself in a concrete and personal manner and assuming the form of a servant. For thus will what you said be true, that 'after assuming the form of a servant he cannot be called a separate Son, otherwise we would be maintaining a doctrine of two Sons'.

The correct doctrinal path that does not deviate but runs in a straight line is this and no other. But now the same man who spoke to us explicitly about the incarnation of the Word of God straightaway all but becomes oblivious of what he said, and again divides the One into two, buoyed up inanely by the foolishness of his ideas and constantly using untested expressions. For he said:

45   But since he is conjoined with him who in the beginning was Son and who was conjoined with him, with regard to the dignity he cannot admit of a division of sonship – with regard, he says, to the dignity of sonship, not with regard to the natures.

You are right, my friend, to reject as useless that which seems to be uncertain. You are always earnestly concerned to express yourself in a vigilant manner. For here you are, while dividing the natures, bringing them together into a union on the level of the dignity of the sonship. Is sharing the same name, or homonymy, and a dignity arising from this sufficient to establish a true union between things which are by nature disparate? For that is what you seem to be saying. It would therefore follow that since the name of Christ and indeed of son and lord have also been shared by others in common (for most of those who have become Christs have also been called sons and lords), these too on the level of the dignity of sonship would be indivisible from each other and all of them one with regard to the union which you yourself think was brought about in the case of Christ. But a man like us will be wholly distinct from the Word of God. I cannot conceive of how they are not divided, or how the Son is a single being, unless we say that the human element and the Word have come together in a true union.

But since it is necessary on account of these expressions of his to reduce the discussion to the absurd, that the error of his reasoning may be demonstrated from every angle, we venture to add the following. For if the dignity of sonship is sufficient for the union, since the Word that comes from God the Father is and is called his Son, and this title is common to many others, then tell me what is there to prevent all these others from also being said to be united to him, with the result that Emmanuel has nothing more than they have? For the significance given to the same names will naturally enough contend with him and strive for equality and the mode of conjunction for us will lie in the mere appellation alone, or in homonymy. What then is the Incarnation understood to mean? Furthermore, what is the descent to the form of a servant? For if, as he maintains, the manner in which the Incarnation takes place is by a mere conjunction and only on the level of the dignity of sonship, what is there to prevent our saying that the same has been effected with regard to all the others too? Surely my learned friend sees the unseemliness of such a statement. No, demented of course as he is, what perverse line will he follow next? We shall say to him what was uttered by the mouth of Jeremiah: 'You were wearied with your many ways' (Is. 57:10 LXX), for he is 'tossed to and fro and carried about with every wind of doctrine' (Eph. 4:14), as Paul in his great wisdom says. Therefore accept the 'sure and steadfast anchor of the soul' (Heb. 6:19). Set your feet upon a rock (cf. Ps. 40:2). If you say that the Word of God became man, this will suffice as an indication that he who is above all creation became what we are. He assumed the form of a servant, although as God he possessed freedom. For he was in a position of equality with the Father who possesses dominion over all things. Cease dividing the natures after the union. That the divine and the human natures are two different things must be obvious, I maintain, to everyone of sound mind, for they are separated from each other by vast differences. But in the case of Christ, the Saviour of us all, bring them together into a true and hypostatic union, and abandon the division. For thus you will confess one Christ and Son and Lord.

For some reason, however, our inventor of foolish doctrines minimizes the fact of the union and apparently rejecting both this and the power of the truth, resorts again to his own fancies and says:

> That is why God the Word is also called 'Christ', seeing that he has an unbroken conjunction with Christ and it is not possible for God the Word to do anything without the humanity. For the latter has been made to conform exactly to a perfect conjunction, not to an apotheosis, as our learned purveyors of novel doctrines maintain.

46 When therefore he says that the Word of God the Father has been named 'Christ' in a proper manner because he has a conjunction with Christ – clearly with a separate entity – how is he not talking nonsense when he says that 'after the assumption he cannot be called a separate Son' given that that which is said to be conjoined to something else by an external relationship is not regarded by us as something that is a unity? For two parties that make a pact with each other will rightly be regarded as two and not as a single entity joined to itself. What he tells us is a lie and utter rubbish. As for ourselves, if after the union one should call the Word God, we do not think of him without his own flesh, and if one should call him Christ, we recognize the incarnate Word.

How, then, is what you call 'conjunction' to be understood? For if you say that the human element was united hypostatically with the Word begotten by God, why, tell me, do you insult the divine flesh – though indeed you do not refuse to worship it – saying that one should fittingly worship only the divine and ineffable nature? But if you do not think that a true union has taken place, but prefer to apply the term 'conjunction' to that which is in accordance with the identity of names and with the rank that derives solely from a merely titular equality, why do you talk high-sounding nonsense, claiming that he who has been born of a woman 'has been made to conform exactly to a perfect conjunction', that is, to the conjunction with the Word? For they have a nominal identity with each other, one son with another and one lord with another, but the names are not in the least inferior to each other and to inquire further into them is pointless in my opinion. For a son simply as a son has nothing more or less than any other son. You are therefore very clearly wasting words when you state that 'he has been made to conform exactly to a perfect conjunction'. It would seem to me more appropriate to say not that the homonyms were made to conform to each other but rather to those things which appear to be responsible for equality and likeness in anything whatsoever that we believe to constitute a unity. For example, we say that with regard to so-and-so what is made to conform exactly to his perfect likeness is either the son begotten by him or perhaps his portrait. But with regard to the manner of the conjunction, how can anything be said or be conceived to be made to conform exactly to it?

He himself, however, has interpreted for us the significance of the conjunction. 'It is not possible,' he says, 'for God the Word to do anything without the humanity.' Of one mind, then, with each other and of the same will, in your view, and proceeding to carry out every action on the basis of a common purpose – that is what we are to believe of the pair of sons described by you. How then are there not two Christs and Sons and Lords? It seems, however, that you maintain that the Word used his body as an instrument. But if you speak of one son and one hypostasis, the incarnate hypostasis of the Word,[43] he will not himself be an instrument of the Godhead but rather will use his own body as an instrument, as indeed the human soul does. Therefore confess that he is one, not dividing the natures, and at the same time you should know and hold that the principle of the flesh is one thing and that of the Godhead, which belongs appropriately to it alone, is another. For we deny that the flesh of the Word became the Godhead, but we do say that it became divine in virtue of its being his own. For if the flesh of a man is called human, what is wrong with saying that that of the Word of God is divine?

Why do you mock the beauty of the truth and call the deification of the sacred flesh an apotheosis, all but scolding those who have chosen to hold an orthodox view for professing this?[44] Furthermore, you yourself say:

9

In order, then, that it might be shown to the Magi who this was who was worshipped by them and to whom the grace of the Holy Spirit had led them, because it was not an ordinary baby that was viewed by them in a normal way but a body conjoined ineffably with God.[45]

Seeing, then, that he says that the body was conjoined ineffably with God, and that that which is ineffable is truly beyond mind and speech, it follows that the union, or at any

47   rate what he calls the conjunction, is necessarily true. For such things are ineffable and nobody I suppose can know the manner in which they thus come together. But if you know you can express it, and are able to state clearly the significance of the conjunction, how is the matter still ineffable? It is striking that although he says that a body is conjoined with God, and ineffably at that, he does not also say that it is his own and proper to him, so that it may be regarded as one with him. Instead he divides the one Christ and Lord Jesus into man and God separately and individually and pretends that he is expressing an orthodox opinion, saying:

10

No, Christ is not a mere man, slanderer, but simultaneously man and God. If he had been God alone, he should have said, Apollinarius, 'Why do you seek to kill me, a God who has told you the truth?' In fact he says, 'Why do you seek to kill me, a man who has told you the truth?' (Jn 8:40). This is he on whom was set the crown of thorns. This is he who said 'My God, my God, why hast thou forsaken me?' (Mt. 26:47). This is he who endured the three-day death. Him do I worship along with the Godhead as an advocate of the divine sovereign power.[46]

Observe again how he grabs the semblance of truth and wraps it round his own words (for 'Christ is not a mere man,' he says, 'but simultaneously man and God') but then he separates him, and says that he is not one, and ignorantly accepts

157

something that is without foundation, and constructs what pleases his fancy. It is as though someone were saying that the Word was seen on earth by us unclothed and without the flesh and that is how he delivered his discourses to us or worked his miracles, or else that he was in fact an ordinary man and that the Word himself did not become flesh, for Christ is not a mere man, he says, but also God. We ourselves, however, my distinguished friend, at least in my view, even though we call him simultaneously man and God, do not separate these elements when we speak about him, but instead know that the same subject who before the Incarnation was Son and God and Word of the Father became after it a man like us endowed with flesh. But he, in maintaining that he ought not to be regarded as a mere man but as God and man, assigns the crown of thorns and the other marks of the Passion separately and peculiarly to the man and confesses that he worships him together with the Godhead and – more impious still – as apparently not really God and Son but as having become an advocate of the sovereign power of the Word. The fact that he clearly makes a separation will be made evident, moreover, by his professing that he ought to be worshipped 'along with' the Godhead. For that which is worshipped along with something else must necessarily be different from that with which it is said to be worshipped. We for our part are accustomed to honouring Emmanuel with a single worship, not separating from the Word the body that was hypostatically united to him.

It is worth investigating what the phrase 'advocate of the divine sovereign power' might mean.[47] For did our Lord Jesus Christ himself, like one of the holy apostles and evangelists, proclaim another Christ to the world, or Son and Lord, as possessing divine sovereign power or authority over all things, and did he himself speak as an advocate for the glory of another? Furthermore, the choir of theologians proclaims to the world Jesus Christ 'who was descended from David according to the flesh' (Rom. 1:3), and the form of our faith comes from our confession of him, and we are justified by believing not simply in a man like ourselves but in him who is naturally and truly God. Indeed the Gentiles were living 'without God in the world', at one time not knowing Christ, as blessed Paul says (Eph. 2:11, 12). But since they have come to know him, they have not remained in ignorance of him

48 who is by nature God. Let him therefore teach us whose glory
and sovereign power it was that Christ acted as an advocate for,
even though he demanded from those who came to him faith
in his own person, and referred this faith to the Father
himself. Indeed he said: 'Believe in me, believe also in God'
(Jn 14:1), and again: 'He who believes in me, believes not in
me, but in him who sent me. And he who sees me sees him who
sent me' (Jn 12:44, 56).

But perhaps to be an advocate for someone is equivalent in
his view to speaking as an equal to him. For indeed I concede
that the word has different meanings. Then how would a
human being speak as an equal to God, as you hold, especially when he is enduring the insulting behaviour of the Jews?
Come, let us examine the speech appropriate to each. It will
be appropriate for him who is truly God by nature to say: 'I
am invisible, impalpable and superior to suffering, and
moreover incorporeal, life and life-giving and over all things
as God.' The other, explaining the character of his own nature
to us, is likely to say: 'I am visible and palpable, passible and
subject to decay and to God.' Will he who says such things be
speaking as an equal to him who excels and transcends all
things by the principles of his own nature? How is this not
an ignorant thing to say? For one or the other will necessarily
be mistaken. In saying of 'advocacy' or 'pleading' that ultimately it is nothing other than speaking in harmony with
another, are you not admitting in spite of yourself – you who
talk about 'connection' and 'one Christ and Lord' yet divide
him in two to worship him, or rather co-worship him, and
think you are delivering the Church from the accusation of
manufacturing gods – that you yourself are deifying a man
and not speaking of one Son, even though he is not regarded
as separate from his own flesh? For you will then worship in
a blameless fashion, and 'will know where you were,' as
Scripture says (Is. 30:15 LXX), when you were departing
from true doctrine.

Yes certainly, he declares, he said to the leper, 'I will; be
clean' (Mt. 8:3), and to the daughter of the ruler of the
synagogue, 'Child, arise' (Lk. 8:54), and to the sea, 'Peace, be
still' (Mk 4:39). In this he was an advocate, for he uttered the
divine words through which he was able to accomplish all
things easily. Those who give the commands are therefore
two and we shall grant that the words in each of these cases

are from both. Therefore when he says: 'Why do you seek to kill me, a man who has told you the truth?' (Jn 8:40), tell me, whose words do you say that these are? Or do you assign the earlier expressions to the Word and these to the man born of a woman as if to someone other than the Word? Where then will you place the most holy Paul when he says plainly: 'for us there is one God, the Father, from whom are all things and for whom we exist, and one Lord, Jesus Christ, through whom are all things and through whom we exist' (1 Cor. 8:6)? But he says in an incongruous fashion that there is one Son and not two different Sons, nor is there Christ and a second Christ, and then contradicts his own words, assigning the expressions of Christ and the Evangelists to two *prosōpa* and distinct hypostases.[48]

THE DISPENSATION OF
THE INCARNATION

III, 1–2 (ACO I, 1, 6, pp. 58.14–62.16)

[58] *(1)* That he ignorantly refers the import of his own words and innovations and indeed the very name of high priesthood simply to the man born of a woman, detaching it from the only-begotten Word of the Father, he will make plain in the passage that follows. For he has gone on to write:

2   'It is not angels he takes to himself but the seed of Abraham' (Heb. 2:16). Is the seed of Abraham the deity? And listen to the next verse: 'Therefore he had to be made like his brethren in every respect' (Heb. 2:17). Did God the Word have any brothers resembling the deity? And note what he immediately appends to this: 'so that he might become a merciful high priest in the service of God. For because he himself has suffered and been tempted, he is able to help those who are tempted' (Heb. 2:17, 18). Therefore he who suffers is a merciful high priest. It is the temple that is capable of suffering, not the life-giving God of him who suffered. It is the seed of Abraham who is yesterday and today, according to Paul's saying (Heb. 13:8), not he who says, 'Before Abraham was, I am' (Jn 8:58). It is he who assumed

brotherhood of a human soul and human flesh who is
like his brethren, not he who says, 'Anyone who has
seen me has seen the Father' (Jn 14:9).[49]

Since he was God, the Word therefore took to himself, as he
himself has just admitted, the seed of Abraham. How then is
the descendant of Abraham still seen to be the possessor of
deity if he was assumed by God and did not himself assume
deity? The seed of Abraham would not then be confused in the
least with the nature of deity, but rather has become the body
of God the Word, according to the Scriptures, and his own
distinctive property. And when he who in his capacity as God
is not to be classified with creation as regards his own nature
became man, who *is* a part of creation, then and only then he
very appropriately deigns to call us brothers, saying, 'I will
proclaim thy name to my brethren' (Heb. 2:12). That it was
by reason of the measure of his self-emptying that the Word
of God the Father descended even to the point of having to call
those on earth his brothers, the most wise Paul will make
clear, for he has written about both him and us as follows:
'For he who sanctifies and those who are sanctified have
all one origin. That is why he is not ashamed to call them
brethren, saying, "I will proclaim thy name to my brethren"'
(Heb. 2:11, 12). For before the Incarnation the name of
brotherhood with us was an extremely small thing to the Word
begotten by God. When he had descended to his voluntary self-
emptying, it was still a small thing, but it has slipped in
excusably. For he has partaken of flesh and blood and has been
called a brother to those who are also of flesh and blood (cf. Heb.
2:14). For if he is sanctified with us, in that he became man,
even though he was God by nature and himself the giver of the
Spirit, how if he should also be called a brother will this not
be perfectly reasonable? For it was on account of this reason
that he became as we are, that he might make us brothers and
free men. 'To all who received him,' Scripture says, 'he gave
power to become children of God; who were born, not of
blood nor of the will of the flesh nor of the will of man, but of
God' (Jn 1:12, 13). For the Word of God the Father was born
according to the flesh in the same way as ourselves, so that we
too might be enriched with a birth which is from God
through the Spirit, no longer being called children of flesh
but rather, having been transformed into something that

transcends nature, being called sons of God by grace. For the Word, by nature and in reality the only-begotten and true Son, became like one of us. Of this the divine Paul will convince us, where he says: 'And because you are sons, God has sent the Spirit of his Son into your hearts, crying, "Abba! Father!"' (Gal. 4:6).

Why then do you deal violently with the wisdom of the dispensation of the Incarnation and make it appear that it was not brought about in a proper fashion by saying, 'Is the seed of Abraham the deity? Did he have any brothers resembling the deity?' Is this not sheer madness? To make an absurd analysis and draw a blasphemous conclusion from things which are so correct and irreproachable with regard to how we conceive of the dispensation of the Incarnation in Christ, what else is this but proof of the most utter insanity? For we acknowledge that, according to the nature of the body or to the principle of the humanity that is perfect in itself, the Word of God the Father put himself alongside us and became like us in every respect except sin. I shall ask him who said, 'Did God the Word have any brothers resembling the deity?' the following question. What did the most holy Paul have in mind when he wrote to certain people: 'My little children, with whom I am again in travail until Christ be formed in you!' (Gal. 4:19), and indeed in another passage to those who through faith had attained perfection in the Spirit: 'And we all, with unveiled face, beholding the glory of the Lord, are being changed into his likeness from one degree of glory to another, for this comes from the Lord who is the Spirit; now the Lord is the Spirit, and where the Spirit of the Lord is, there is freedom' (2 Cor. 3:18, 17)? Does he say this to the Galatians as if they did not have the qualities of bodily freedom with regard to what is of the seed of David according to the flesh, but is in travail with them that Christ may somehow be engraved in them and formed according to the flesh? Indeed how will not everybody, I suppose, say unequivocally that all who are on earth are conformed to one another, and to Christ himself insofar as he is conceived of as being a man like us and with us? What kind of formation in the likeness of Christ is he looking for in them? Or in what way are we changed from glory to glory? What form do we leave behind and into what are we transformed? Let our divine spiritual leader come forward, the priest of the sacred mysteries, the 'teacher of the Gentiles in faith and truth' (1 Tim. 2:7) and let him instruct us. 'For those whom he foreknew,' he said, 'and predestined to be conformed to the image of his Son, he also called' (Rom. 8:29, 30). Therefore, as I have just said, insofar as he became man and was of the seed of Abraham, we are all conformed to him.

All those, then, on earth whom the Father foreknew and predestined, once he had called them he sanctified them and glorified them. But not all were predestined; not all were sanctified and glorified. Therefore the phrase 'conformity to the Son' is not to be understood only in a physical sense or as referring to the humanity, but in a different manner. And this the blessed Paul sets before us when he says: 'Just as we have borne the image of the man of dust, we shall also bear the image of the man of heaven' (1 Cor. 15:49), signifying by the man of dust Adam and by the man of heaven Christ. What then is the image of our first ancestor? It is to be prone to sin and subject to death and decay. And what is the image of the heavenly man? It is not to be conquered by passions in any way; it is to be ignorant of transgression and free from subjection to death and decay; it is holiness, righteousness and whatever is brother to these and like them. In my view these qualities are appropriately possessed by that nature which is divine and undefiled. For holiness and righteousness are superior to both sin and decay. The Word of God includes us in this, for he makes us partakers of his divine nature through the Spirit (cf. 2 Pet. 1:4).

He therefore has brothers like him who bear the image of his divine nature in the sense of having been made holy. For this is how Christ is formed in us, the Holy Spirit as it were transforming us from what belongs to the human to what belongs to him. On this point the blessed Paul said to us: 'You are not in the flesh, but in the Spirit' (Rom. 8:9). Therefore the Son does not change the least thing belonging to the created order into the nature of his own deity (for that would be impossible) but there is imprinted in some way in those who have become partakers of the divine nature, through participating in the Holy Spirit, a spiritual likeness to him, and the beauty of the ineffable deity illuminates the souls of the saints. How is it that you do not blush in attributing the likeness merely and solely to the flesh, ignoring the divine and spiritual formation, or rather obliterating it utterly? No, the Only-begotten, the Lord and God of all things, reduced himself to a self-emptying for our sake, that he might bestow on us the dignity of brotherhood with him and the loveable beauty of his innate nobility. But he [Nestorius], depriving us of all that is most beautiful, says that an ordinary man has become our brother, and thinking that he has demonstrated this by a solid argument, adds: 'And note what he immediately appends to this: "so that he might become a merciful high priest in the service of God. For because he himself has suffered and been tempted, he is able to help those who are tempted" (Heb. 2:17, 18). Therefore he who suffers is a merciful high priest. It is the temple that is capable of suffering, not the life-giving God of him who suffered.'

No one, I suppose, will have the least doubt that by choosing to think in this way, and moreover by expressing it, he separates the Word of God again into two distinct hypostases and indeed two persons. And this is the Word whom he has just presented to us as a God-bearing man, seeing that he who suffers is a separate subject, and he who is life-giving is another.

He has also lost his wits in a different way, for he has drunk deeply of the wine from the vine of Sodom (cf. Deut. 32:32) and has become intoxicated with error and perhaps does not even know what he is saying. For where is the Word of God (I shudder to say this) named as the God of Christ? There is one Lord Jesus Christ and there is one faith in him. We do not believe in two separately, but through one baptism we believe in one Son and God and Lord who is the Word of God the Father even after he had become man. He will not lose his being God because he became as we are. Why should that follow? Nor because he is God by nature will he be incapable of enjoying a likeness with us and have to reject being a man. Just as he remained God in his humanity, so too in the nature and pre-eminence of deity he was nonetheless man. Therefore in both these Emmanuel was at the same time both one God and man.

This worthy fellow, however, rejecting the way in which the dispensation of the Incarnation took place as something unattractive, strips the Word of God of the human element, with the result that he then appears not to have benefited our condition in any way at all. For he does not say that it is he who

61

became a merciful and faithful high priest, but attributes this title to him who suffered as if to someone else. Yet if he wished to be a wise spiritual teacher, how is it that he did not regard it as necessary to make a careful collection of the expressions and concepts used in the inspired Scriptures and understand that the title is truly appropriate to God and not inconsistent with what is appropriate and suitable to the self-emptying? And how is this so? We shall explain as briefly as we can.

The God of all things delivered the law to the ancients in an oracular manner through the mediation of Moses. But the power of attaining the good in a blameless fashion by those who wished to do so did not lie in the law. For it 'made nothing perfect' (Heb. 7:19). Nor was the first covenant faultless, for the most wise Paul called it a 'dispensation of condemnation' (2 Cor. 3:9). And I hear him say: 'We know that whatever the law says it speaks to those who are under the law, so that every mouth may be stopped, and that the whole world may be held accountable to God. For no human being will be justified in his sight by works of the law' (Rom. 3:19, 20). 'For the law brings wrath' (Rom. 4:15) and 'the written code kills' (2 Cor. 3:6). And as he says somewhere, 'A man who has violated the law of Moses dies without mercy at the testimony of two or three witnesses' (Heb. 10:28). Seeing then that the law condemned sinners and sometimes imposed the supreme penalty on those who disregarded it and was in no way merciful, how was the appointment of a truly compassionate and merciful high priest not necessary for those on earth – one who would abrogate the curse, check the legal process, and free the sinners with forgiving grace and commands based on gentleness? 'I,' says the text, 'I am he who blots out your transgressions for my own sake, and I will not remember your sins' (Is. 43:25). For we are justified by faith, not by works of the law, as Scripture says (Gal. 2:16).

By faith in whom, then, are we justified? Is it not in him who suffered death according to the flesh for our sake? Is it not in one Lord Jesus Christ? Have we not been redeemed by proclaiming his death and confessing his resurrection? If we had believed in a man like one of us rather than in God, this would then have been dubbed anthropolatry and it could not have been claimed that it was anything else. But if we believe that he who 'suffered in the flesh' (1 Pet. 4:1) is God, and that it is he who became our high priest, we have not erred in any way. We acknowledge the Word of God as having become man, and thus there is engendered in us faith in a God who sets aside the penalty and delivers from sins those who have succumbed to them. For 'the Son of man has authority on earth to forgive sins,' as he himself says somewhere (Mt. 9:6). Therefore contrasting the harshness, so to speak, of the severity of the law with the salvation and grace that comes through Christ, we say that Christ has become a merciful high priest. For he was and is a God who is by nature good and compassionate and merciful, and he did not become this in time but has been shown to us to have always been such. And he is called 'faithful' because he remains what he is, always in accordance with the saying relating to the Father: 'God is faithful, and he will not let you be tempted beyond your strength' (1 Cor. 10:13). Therefore Emmanuel became for us a merciful and at the same time a faithful high priest. As Paul says, 'The former priests were many in number, because they were prevented by death from continuing in office; but he holds his priesthood permanently, because he continues for ever. Consequently, he is able for all time to save those who draw near to God through him, since he always lives to make intercession for them' (Heb. 7:23–25). That the Word of the Father remained God, even though he became a priest, as Scripture says, in the form and measure that befitted the dispensation of the Incarnation, the word of blessed Paul will suffice to assure us. For he goes on to say: 'Now the point in what we are saying is this: we have such a high priest, one who is seated at the right hand of the throne of the Majesty in heaven, a minister in the sanctuary and the true tabernacle which is set up not by man but by the Lord' (Heb. 8:1, 2). Observe, then, the Word begotten of the Father, magnificent as God in his supreme glory and seated on the thrones of deity, and the same Word as man officiating as a priest and offering to the Father not an earthly sacrifice but rather a divine and spiritual one, and observe how he has heaven as his holy tabernacle. For he 'has become a high priest, not according to a legal requirement concerning bodily descent but by the power of an indestructible life,' as Scripture says (Heb. 7:16). He is therefore faithful in this too and able to give a pledge to those who approach him that he can save them, and very easily at that. For by his own blood and 'by a single

62

166

offering has he perfected for all time those who are sanctified'
(Heb. 10:14). For this I think is what holy Paul reveals to us
when he says: 'because he himself has suffered and been
tempted, he is able to help those who are tempted' (Heb.
2:18).

THE BODY OF CHRIST

IV, 3–7 (ACO I, 1, 6, pp. 83.30–85.27; 88.35–91.8)

[83] {3} The expressions that are appropriate to the degree of self-
emptying will in no way disturb those who are wise and
knowledgeable and firmly grounded in faith. From these,
and equally from the expressions appropriate to the divine
nature, they acknowledge the same Son as being both God
and man. But he [Nestorius] does not come forward to speak
with sound words (cf. 1 Tim. 6:13). Inclining very much
towards wilfulness, he busies himself without understanding, and sees fit to hold opinions which seem good and well-
founded interpretations to himself alone. And he destroys
others in whose presence he has spoken, dividing the one
Lord Jesus Christ into two and calumniating our divine
mystery itself by not bringing himself to confess with us that
Christ was not a God-bearing man like one of the holy
prophets or one of the apostles and evangelists but rather was
God who became man and really did participate in blood and
flesh. For he goes on to say, presenting the saying as coming
from the person of Christ:

4   'He who eats my flesh and drinks my blood abides in
me and I in him' (Jn 6:56). Notice that the saying is
84   about the flesh. 'As the living Father sent me' (Jn 6:57),
me who am visible. But sometimes I misinterpret. Let
us hear what follows: 'As the living Father sent me.' He
[Cyril] says the Godhead, I say the manhood. Let us see
who is misinterpreting. The heretic at this point says
the Godhead, i.e. he sent me, God the Word. 'As the
living Father sent me, and I – God the Word – live
because of the Father.' Then after this: 'so he who eats me
will live'. What do we eat? The Godhead or the flesh?[50]

167

You say then that it was only the flesh that was sent, and you assert that this is the visible element. This alone is therefore sufficiently able to give life to that which is subject to the tyranny of death. What then? Do the inspired Scriptures rhapsodize in vain, asserting repeatedly that the Word of God the Father became flesh? What need would there be for the Word at all if the human nature is sufficiently able, even when conceived of alone and in itself, to abolish death for us and dissolve the power of corruption? And if indeed it is as you suppose and deem right to think that it was not God the Word who has been sent through becoming like us, but it was only, as you say, the visible flesh which has been sent by the Father, how is it not obvious to everybody that we have come to participate in a human body that does not differ from our own in any way at all? How is it then that in other passages you laugh at those who hold that view? For you say further on:

5   I will even utter offensive words. The Lord Christ was speaking to them about his own flesh. 'Unless you eat the flesh of the Son of man and drink his blood, you have no life in you' (Jn 6:53). His hearers did not grasp the sublime significance of what he was saying. For in their ignorance they thought he was introducing cannibalism.[51]

How, then, is the matter not one of plain cannibalism? And in what way can we still claim that the mystery is sublime, if we do not say that the Word of God the Father was sent and confess that the manner of the sending was the Incarnation? Only then shall we observe that it is the flesh united to him and not someone else's flesh that has the power to endow with life, in the sense that it became the peculiar property of him who has the power to endow all things with life. For if ordinary fire transmits the power of the natural energy inherent within it to the material with which it appears to come into contact, and changes water itself, in spite of its being cold by nature, into something contrary to its nature, and makes it hot, what is strange or somehow impossible to believe about the Word of God the Father, who is Life by nature, rendering the flesh united to him capable of endowing with life? For it is his own flesh and not that of another

168

conceived of as separate from him and as the flesh of someone like ourselves. If you detach the life-giving Word of God from the mystical and true union with the body and separate them entirely, how can you prove that it is still life-giving? Who was it who said, 'He who eats my flesh and drinks my blood abides in me, and I in him' (Jn 6:56)? If it was a particular human being, and not rather the Word of God who became as we are, the act of eating would be cannibalism and participation in it wholly without benefit. For I hear Christ saying, 'The flesh is of no avail. It is the Spirit that gives life' (Jn. 6:63). For as far as its own nature is concerned, the flesh is subject to decay and can in no way endow others with life, since the sickness of decay is endemic to it. But if you say that the body is the personal property of the Word himself, why do you devise fantastic theories and talk gibberish, contending that it was not the Word of God the Father who was sent, but someone other than him, 'the visible one' or his flesh, even though the inspired Scriptures everywhere proclaim that Christ is one and assert very clearly that the Word became a man like us, thereby defining the tradition of the true faith?

But out of his excessive piety he blushes, apparently, at the degree of the self-emptying and cannot bear to see the Son who is co-eternal with God the Father, the one who in every possible respect is of the same form as him who begot him and equal to him, descend to such a humble level. He brings an indictment against the dispensation of the Incarnation and perhaps does not even allow the divine will and plan to escape censure. He pretends to be closely investigating the significance of the sayings of Christ and to be probing, as it were, the profundity of the concepts and then tries, as he thinks, to reduce our own line of argument to an absurd and ignorant conclusion. 'Let us see who is misinterpreting,' he says. 'As the living Father sent me, and I – God the Word – live because of the Father. So he who eats me will live. What do we eat? The Godhead or the flesh?'

Can you really be aware of where your argument is leading you? The Word of God says that he has been sent and then adds: 'he who eats me will live'. When we eat, we are not consuming the Godhead – perish the awful thought – but the Word's own flesh, which has been made life-giving because it has become the flesh of him who lives because of the Father. We do not say that the Word has been endowed with life by the Father by means of an external participation or in an accidental manner. We maintain, on the contrary, that he is Life by nature. For he has been begotten as if from the life of the Father. Take as an analogy the bright light emitted by the sun. Although it may perhaps be said to be bright on account of its sender, or its source, it does not possess this quality of brightness by participation. It bears the distinction of that which emits it or flashes it forth as if through its own natural excellence.[52] In a similar way, I think, and by the same principle, although the Son says that he lives because of the Father, he witnesses to the excellence of the Father in himself and professes not to possess life as something acquired and external, as is the case with the rest of creation in general.

[. . . .]

[88] {6}   Not at all abashed, he comes out with an even more loathsome blasphemy, adding to what he has said:

> Listen not to my own words but to the words of the blessed Paul: 'As often as you eat this bread,' of which the body is the antitype. Let us see from this whose death it is. 'As often as you eat this bread and drink this cup you proclaim the Lord's death.' And listen to it stated even more clearly in what follows: 'until he comes' (1 Cor. 11:26). Who is it who is coming? 'They will see the Son of man coming on the clouds of heaven with great glory' (Mt. 24:30). And what is more, before the apostles the prophet portrayed him who was
> 89   coming more clearly and cried out with respect to the Jews: 'They shall look on him whom they have pierced' (Jn 19:37; cf. Zech. 12:10). Who is it, then, who has been pierced? The side. The side of the body or the side of the deity?[53]

The benefit conferred by the bloodless sacrifice is therefore, as I have said, extremely small, because it is probably not feasible for the nature of the divinity to be consumed along with the flesh, for we do not have control over impossibilities, so as to make the purely incorporeal something consumable. You seem to me to forget that it is by no means the nature of the divinity that lies upon the altars of the churches, even though it is the body proper to the Word begotten of God the

Father, and the Word is by nature and in reality God. Why then do you throw all things into confusion and jumble them up in a senseless manner, all but mocking our heavenly bread which gives life to the world, because it has not been called deity in the inspired Scriptures, but rather the body of him who was made man for us, that is, the Word of God the Father? Why, tell me, do you call it the Lord's body at all, if you do not believe it to be divine and belonging to God? For all things are servants of him who made them (cf. Ps. 119:91). No, the ideas you hold are not correct, for you believe Emmanuel to be simply a God-bearing man. Then, with total disregard of the thoughts and expressions consonant with piety, you expect the priest of truth (cf. Rom. 15:16), the skilled master builder and teacher of the Gentiles (1 Cor. 3:10, 1 Tim. 2:7), the truly holy and all-wise Paul to be your accomplice in your calumnies, twisting the sense of his orthodox and sound teaching and diverting it from the straight and thoroughly approved path:

> Let us see then from this, he says, whose death it is: 'until he comes'. Who is it who is coming? 'They will see the Son of man coming on the clouds of heaven with great glory.' And what is more, before the apostles the prophet portrayed him who was coming more clearly and cried out with respect to the Jews: 'They shall look on him whom they have pierced.'

He who will come is therefore he who suffered death in human fashion, who rose from the dead in divine fashion, who ascended into heaven, who glories in the thrones of the ineffable Godhead and is seated with the Father, with the seraphim and the higher powers, who are not ignorant of the degree of their subjection to him, standing in a circle around him, and with every authority and power and dominion worshipping him, for 'at the name of Jesus every knee shall bow and every tongue confess that Jesus Christ is Lord to the glory of God the Father' (Phil. 2: 10, 11). He will come, as I said, appearing not in a low estate like ours but rather in the glory most appropriate to God, escorted by heaven and with the higher spirits attending him as God and King and Lord of all. Therefore if it was not the Word of God the Father in the flesh or made man, but instead a God-bearing man, who possessed the bodily side and endured the piercing, how is he seen on the thrones of the supreme deity, as if he were a new god revealed to us as a fourth after the Holy Trinity? Did you not shudder at deifying an ordinary man and devising worship for a creature?[54] Are we then trapped in the ancient snares? Have we then insulted God and has the holy multitude of the spirits above fallen into error with us? If we have been set free from the ancient deceit, and have abandoned the worship of creatures as an impious practice, why do you make us liable again to the ancient charges and represent us as worshippers of human beings? As for us, we know and believe that the Word of God the Father assumed flesh and blood, but since he remained the same, that is to say, God, he preserved the dignity of his innate pre-eminence over all things even though he was embodied like ourselves. But since he is now no less divine than he was formerly, even though he became man, he has heaven as his servant and earth as his worshipper. For it is written that 'the earth is full of thy praise; thy virtue covered the heavens, O Lord' (Hab. 3:3 LXX).

90   But you in your extreme stupidity do not see him who possesses such a nature and such glory. For you say, 'Who is it who is coming? "They will see the Son of man coming on the clouds of heaven"', as if you are afraid that no one will believe that you are saying that it is the Son of man who is coming. And you confirm the proof with a testimony from the prophets, for it is written, you say: 'They shall look on him whom they have pierced.' And then, as if supposing that you are supplying a stronger proof, you append to this most foolishly: 'Who is it, then, who has been pierced? The side. The side of the body or the side of the deity?' If there were some who said that the Word of God did not become a man like ourselves but came to dwell amongst those on earth in his unveiled Godhead, or in appearance and as if in shadow, as some of the impious heretics were pleased to think, a case could be made for saying that the framing of such arguments is not altogether unreasonable. But since the true teaching of the Gospel says clearly and plainly that the Word of God became flesh, and was called like us a son of man, and suffered for us in the flesh, and will come back in the same way as he went up into heaven, according to the angel's message (cf. Acts 1:11), against whom, tell me, are you directing your

172

argument and whose opinion are you denigrating as ignorant and foolish as you strive to prove to us that the one who is coming is a man with a physical side which has been pierced through with a spear? But your aim, as you have said, is to bring Emmanuel into our midst as a God-bearing man and not rather as an incarnate God. For the Word of God has become man and this faith is in harmony with the sacred and divine Scriptures, and the aim of the apostolic and evangelical tradition is entirely concentrated on this same goal.

But you are also promoting a strange theory in another way too. For you allege that you are censuring those who mingle the nature of the flesh with that of the divinity to produce a single essence, even though nobody, so far as I know, confuses them or mixes them up with each other.[55] In fact you say:

7
> And why, as we have just heard, when both are in your view mixed together, does the Lord in teaching the disciples the significance of the Mystery say the following? 'And he took the bread, and when he had given thanks he broke it and gave it to his disciples, saying, "Take, eat, all of you; for this is my body."' Why did he not say: 'This is my divinity which is broken for you'? And again when he gave them the cup of the Mysteries, he did not say: 'This is my divinity which is poured out for you'; but 'This is my blood which is poured out for you for the forgiveness of sins' (Lk. 22:19, 20; Mt. 26:27, 28).[56]

Is it not obvious to everybody that it is quite absurd to be determined to take up an offensive position against an enemy who is not in the least inclined to come out and fight, or to take as opposition that which no one has a mind to think or to say? For if someone should choose to argue that the ox is not by nature a horse or that man is not a horse, which no one would dream of thinking or saying, would he not surely be making a fool of himself, and a ranter into the bargain, beating the air and boxing at shadows (cf. 1 Cor. 9:26), and devising for himself hardships and labours in respect of something that does not exist? For my own part I say that whatever it is that is held as a conviction should first be established, so that our own arguments may then be advanced against it in due order. Let me show what I mean. If there is anyone, as you seem to

91 think, who would dare to say that the Word of God has been transformed into the nature of the body, one could very reasonably object that when he gave his body he did not say, 'Take, eat; this is my Godhead which is broken for you, and this is not my blood but rather the Godhead which is poured out for you.' Since the Word, being God, made the body born from a woman his own body without undergoing change or alteration in any way, how could he not say to us without any dissimulation, 'take, eat; this is my body'? For being life in virtue of being God, he rendered the body life and life-giving.

Having opened your eyes a little to the truth, you will yourself, I think, condemn yourself for the emptiness of your arguments, as you drivel on, foolishly opposing the doctrines of piety with this counterfeit and joyless discourse of yours.

AN EXPLANATION OF THE TWELVE CHAPTERS

INTRODUCTION

The Twelve Chapters are twelve propositions which Cyril had drawn up and appended to his Third Letter to Nestorius.[1] The letter was handed to Nestorius by an Egyptian delegation at his residence in Constantinople after the liturgy on Sunday, 30 November 430, and immediately provoked a furore. The propositions were deliberately phrased in uncompromising terms. Cyril's intention was to force Nestorius to abandon the provisos and nuances he had expressed hitherto and either accept the christological position set out in the chapters and thus bring an end to the controversy or else reject it and prove himself a heretic.

The plan misfired badly. Nestorius, outraged by what he read, at once sent the letter to John of Antioch, who reacted with similar indignation. The Easterners closed ranks, perceiving Cyril's démarche as an attack on the Antiochene christological tradition as such. What had begun as an exchange of letters between Cyril and Nestorius now became a pamphlet war between Antioch and Alexandria. Responses to the Twelve Chapters were written by Andrew of Samosata and Theodoret of Cyrrhus, to each of which Cyril replied in detail.[2] Accusations of heresy flew backwards and forwards with the result that it was two deeply divided sides to the dispute that met at Ephesus in June 431.

The late arrival at Ephesus of the delegation from Antioch enabled Cyril to have the Twelve Chapters minuted and then rush through the condemnation of Nestorius with very little opposition. When John of Antioch's party finally arrived, they immediately held a rival session with the minority of bishops who sympathized with Nestorius and pronounced Cyril deposed. In consequence, both Cyril and Nestorius were put under house arrest by the authorities.[3]

It was at this juncture that Cyril composed his *Explanation of the Twelve Chapters*. While intense lobbying was being conducted on his behalf in government circles at Constantinople, Cyril used his enforced leisure to compose a clarification for the bishops, apparently at their request, of precisely what errors he meant to exclude by the Twelve Chapters. The Eastern bishops wanted the chapters rescinded. Cyril could not do this without destroying the basis upon which Nestorius had been condemned, but he needed as much support among the Eastern bishops as he could muster. Although he does not shift his theological position, he is more conciliatory than in his previous two commentaries on the Twelve Chapters in that he tries to restrict the scope of the anathemas to positions which the Antiochenes could more readily concede to be heretical.[4] The essential points for Cyril were first that there was only a single subject of all the words and actions attributed to Christ, namely, the Word made flesh, and secondly that in relation to the inspired figures of sacred history Christ was different in kind, not merely in degree, otherwise he could not have effected our salvation.

Cyril carried the day at Ephesus yet he could not dispel the impression that his chapters propounded an Apollinarian Christ who was neither God nor man but a hybrid being. The Council of Chalcedon, whilst approving Cyril's Third Letter to Nestorius, did not include the Twelve Chapters in its list of documents which were to be regarded as providing a standard of orthodoxy. Their christology was not compatible with that of the Tome of Leo, which made them a potential source of embarrassment. It was not until the Fifth Ecumenical Council of 553, when Theodore of Mopsuestia's writings were condemned, that the Twelve Chapters received authoritative status.[5]

TEXT

ACO I, 1, 5, pp. 15.16–25.28

[15] An explanation of the twelve chapters given in Ephesus by Cyril, archbishop of Alexandria, when the holy council asked him to provide them with an elucidation of their meaning.

1. 'All things,' as Scripture says, 'are evident to those who understand and right to those who find knowledge' (Prov. 8:9 LXX). For there are some who approach the sacred words of

the inspired Scriptures with the eye of their understanding sharp and clear, and derive from them benefit for their souls like some divine and heavenly treasure. But there are others whose minds are inclined towards falsehood. Enthralled by the garrulity of certain people and enamoured of profane knowledge, they will share the lot of those about whom blessed Paul writes: 'In their case the god of this world has blinded the minds of the unbelievers, to keep them from seeing the light of the glory of Christ' (2 Cor. 4:4). For they are blind and are guides of the blind, and for that very reason they will fall into the pits of destruction. As the Saviour himself says somewhere, 'If a blind man leads a blind man, both will fall into a pit' (Mt. 15:14). For certain people have conducted a campaign of gossip against the doctrines of truth and indeed, having filled their minds with a diabolical perversity, are intent on debasing the mystery of the orthodox faith and make no small criticism of the incarnate dispensation of the only-begotten Son, 'without understanding either what they are saying or the things about which they make assertions,' as Scripture says (1 Tim. 1:7).

2. In earlier times there were many different inventors of such impiety, but now Nestorius and his adherents have not fallen short of their wickedness, opposing Christ like those ancient Pharisees and crying out without restraint: 'Why do you, being a man, make yourself God?' (Jn. 10:33). It was therefore necessary that we ourselves should take issue with their words and condemn their polluted and profane doctrines, mindful of what God has said by the mouth of the prophet: 'Hear O priests and testify to the house of Jacob, says the Lord the Almighty' (Amos 3:13 LXX); and in another place: 'Go through my gates and clear the stones off the road' (Is. 62:10 LXX). For it is incumbent on us who strive on behalf of the doctrines of truth to clear away the stumbling-blocks, so that people should not run any risk of falling over them but travel on a smooth path towards the sacred and divine courts, all but saying with regard to each of them, 'This is the gate of the Lord; the righteous shall enter through it' (Ps. 118:20).

3. Since Nestorius has put into his own books a host of novel and profane blasphemies, we have in our concern for the

salvation of those who read them been compelled to draw up a list of anathemas. We are not dealing with a purely theoretical matter which we could have put into a letter of admonition to him, but as I have just said we are demonstrating that these inventions of his deranged mind are foreign and alien to the doctrines of orthodox faith. Some people are perhaps indignant at my words, either because they have not really understood the significance of what has been written, or because they have become supporters of Nestorius' foul heresy and share in his impiety and think the way he does. The truth, at any rate, cannot fail to be seen by anyone who is accustomed to thinking correctly. But since it is likely that those who have been misled by their specious arguments do not understand how and by what means these things have come about, I have thought it necessary to interpret each of the anathemas briefly and explain its significance in the best way I can. In my opinion this will not be without benefit for the reader.

Anathema 1

4. If anyone does not acknowledge Emmanuel to be truly God and therefore the holy Virgin to be *Theotokos* (for she gave birth according to the flesh to the Word of God made flesh), let him be anathema.

17
Explanation

5. The blessed fathers who gathered some time ago in the city of Nicaea and set forth the definition of our orthodox and unexceptionable faith said that they believed in one God, the Father almighty, maker of all that is, both visible and invisible, and in one Lord Jesus Christ his Son, and in the Holy Spirit. They declared that the Word begotten by God the Father was the same through whom all things were made, light from light, true God from true God, who became incarnate and was made man, suffered and rose again. For since he was God by nature, the only-begotten Word of God took to himself the seed of Abraham, as blessed Paul says (cf. Heb. 2:16), and partook of blood and flesh like us. For he was born according to the flesh from the holy Virgin and became a man like us, not slipping away from being God (God

forbid), but remaining what he was and abiding in the nature and glory of the Godhead. We therefore say that he became man, not undergoing change or alteration into what he was not previously (for he is always the same and he is not susceptible to any 'shadow of change' (Jas 1:17)), and we declare that there was no confusion or mingling or blending of his essence with the flesh. But we say that the Word was united with flesh endowed with a rational soul in a manner that is transcendent and ineffable and known only to himself. Therefore he remained God even in the assumption of flesh and is the one Son of God the Father, our Lord Jesus Christ, the same before all ages and time in that he is regarded as Word and reflection of his being (cf. Heb. 1:3), and in these last days has become man by divine dispensation for our sake.[6]

6. Some people deny his birth according to the flesh that took place from the holy Virgin for the salvation of all, a birth that did not call him into a beginning of being, but he became like us in order to deliver us from death and corruption. It was for that reason that my first anathema inveighed against their erroneous belief and confesses what is correctly held, saying that Emmanuel is truly God and consequently that the holy Virgin is *Theotokos*.[7]

Anathema 2

7. If anyone does not acknowledge the Word of God the Father to be united hypostatically with the flesh and to be one Christ together with his own flesh, that is, the same subject as at once both God and man, let him be anathema.

Explanation

8. The holy Paul, the priest of the divine mysteries, writes: 'Great indeed, we confess, is the mystery of our religion: He was manifested in the flesh, vindicated in the Spirit, seen by angels, preached among the nations, believed on in the world, taken up in glory' (1 Tim. 3:16). What then does 'manifested in the flesh' mean? It means that the Word of God the Father became flesh, not by a change or alteration of his own nature, as we have already said, but because having made the flesh taken from the holy Virgin his own, one and

18

179

the same subject is called Son, before the Incarnation as the Word still incorporeal and after the Incarnation as the same Word now embodied. That is why we say that the same subject is simultaneously both God and man, not dividing him conceptually into a human being with a separate individual identity and God the Word also with a separate identity, that we may exclude any idea of two Sons, but acknowledging that one and the same subject is Christ and Son and Lord.

9. Those who do not hold such a view, or do not wish to believe it, but divide the one Son into two and separate from each other those elements which in reality are united, saying that man has been brought into a conjunction with God only in terms of rank or supreme authority, those we say are alien to our orthodox and irreproachable faith. Consequently, even if he is called an apostle (cf. Heb. 3:1), even if he is said to have been anointed and to have been designated Son of God (cf. Rom. 1:4), that does not cause us any embarrassment with regard to the dispensation of the Incarnation. We say of the Word of God the Father that it was when he became a man like us that he was also called an apostle and was anointed with us on the human level. For having become like us, even though he remained what he was, he will not repudiate what belongs to us, but instead accepts what is human along with the limitations that belong to the human condition, for the sake of the dispensation of the Incarnation, without thereby compromising in any way his glory or his nature. For even in this state he is God and Lord of all.[8]

Anathema 3

10. If anyone with regard to the one Christ divides the hypostases after the union, connecting them only by a conjunction in terms of rank or supreme authority, and not rather by a combination in terms of natural union, let him be anathema.[9]

Explanation

11. Having investigated carefully the mystery of the Only-begotten's dispensation of the Incarnation, we say that the Word of God the Father has been united in a miraculous and

ineffable manner with a holy body endowed with a rational soul and that is how we conceive of the one Son, just as indeed in our own case it is possible to see that soul and body are of different natures and yet together they make up a single living being. There are some, however, who do not consider this to be so. They set the human nature apart for us as a separate individual and say that he was joined to the Word begotten by God the Father only in terms of rank or authority, and not in terms of a natural union, that is a real union, as we ourselves believe. This is also the teaching of the divine Scriptures, which say somewhere: 'we were by nature children of wrath, like the rest of mankind' (Eph. 2:3), taking 'by nature' as equivalent to 'in reality'. Those, then, who divide the hypostases after the union and set each apart separately, that is, man and God, and invent the idea of a 'conjunction' between them only in terms of rank, inevitably set up two sons. And yet the divinely inspired Scriptures say that there is one Son and Lord. Accordingly, if after the ineffable union you call Emmanuel 'God', we understand him to be the Word of God the Father who has become incarnate and been made man, and if you call him 'man', we acknowledge him to be no less God who has by divine dispensation accommodated himself to the limitations of the human state. We say that the intangible has become tangible, the invisible visible. For the body that was united to him, which we say was capable of being touched and seen, was not something alien to him. Those who do not believe this but, as I have said, separate the hypostases after the union, and consider them united by a mere conjunction simply in terms of rank or supreme authority, are excluded by this anathema from those who hold orthodox opinions.[10]

Anathema 4

12. If anyone takes the terms used in the Gospels and apostolic writings, whether referred to Christ by the saints, or applied to himself by himself, and allocates them to two *prosōpa* or hypostases, attributing some to a man conceived of as separate from the Word of God and some, as more appropriate to God, only to the Word of God the Father, let him be anathema.

Explanation

13. Although the Word of God is in the form of God the Father and equal to him, he 'did not count equality with God a thing to be grasped', as Scripture says (Phil. 2:6). On the contrary, he lowered himself to a voluntary self-emptying and willingly condescended to enter into our condition, not abandoning what he is but remaining God even in this state while not disdaining the limitations of the human condition. Therefore everything relating to his divinity and everything relating to his humanity all belong to him. Why did he empty himself if he was ashamed of the limitations of human nature? And if he disdained what was human, who compelled him by necessity and force to become like us?

14. All the sayings in the Gospels, both those with a human colouring and indeed those appropriate to God, we therefore assign to a single *prosōpon*, because we believe that Christ Jesus, that is, the Word of God incarnate and made man, is a single Son. Consequently, if he should say something consonant with the human condition we take these human utterances to have been accommodated to the limitations of his humanity (for after all the human utterance is his also). And if he should speak as God, we likewise allocate the sayings that transcend human nature to the one Christ and Son, since we believe that he who became man was God. Those who divide him into two *prosōpa* inevitably conceive of him as two sons. A human being like ourselves cannot properly be divided into two *prosōpa*, even though he is regarded as consisting of a soul and a body, but in a single human being with a single identity. The same is also true with regard to Emmanuel. Since the incarnate Word of God made man is a single Son and Lord, his *prosōpon* is also necessarily single, and we allocate to it both the human characteristics on account of the dispensation of the Incarnation and the divine on account of his ineffable generation from God the Father. Those who divide him and set apart a distinct human being, who is a different son from the Word of God, and as a distinct God, who is another Son, saying that there are two sons, rightly incur the consequences of this anathema.[11]

Anathema 5

15. If anyone has the temerity to say that Christ is a divinely inspired man instead of saying that he is truly God since he is by nature a single Son, in that the Word became flesh and shared in flesh and blood like us (cf. Heb. 2:14), let him be anathema.

Explanation

16. John the divine Evangelist said that the Word of God became flesh (Jn 1:14) not by some change or alteration transforming his own nature into flesh, as we have already said (for as God he possesses immutability), but because he partook of blood and flesh like us (cf. Heb. 2:14) and became man. For the inspired Scriptures habitually refer to the human being as flesh. They say, for example, that 'all flesh shall see the salvation of God' (Lk. 3:6). But those who devise profane new doctrines, Nestorius and his followers, or those who think like them, pretend to hold this belief and acknowledge the expression 'became incarnate' but do not go on to say that the Word of God became incarnate in reality, that is, became a man like ourselves while remaining what he was. They maintain that the only-begotten Word of God dwelt in someone who was born of the holy Virgin like one of the saints, with the result that it is no longer acknowledged that Christ is One and Son and Lord and to be worshipped. Instead he is regarded as a man set apart on his own and honoured only by a conjunction in terms of a unity of rank and thus is the recipient of joint worship and joint glorification.

17. For the God of all things dwells in us through the Holy Spirit. Indeed he said long ago through one of the holy prophets: 'I will live in them and move among them, and I will be their God and they shall be my people' (2 Cor. 6:16; cf. Lev. 26:12; Ez. 37:27). And blessed Paul writes: 'Do you not know that you are God's temple and that God's Spirit dwells in you?' (1 Cor. 3:16). Christ himself said about the holy prophets or the righteous who preceded him: 'If he called them gods to whom the Word of God came, do you say of him whom the Father consecrated and sent into the world, "You are blaspheming," because I said, "I am the Son of God"?' (Jn 10:35, 36). But God does not dwell in Christ in the same way as he does in us. For Christ was God by nature, who became like us. He was the one and only Son even when he became flesh. Those who have the temerity to say that he was a God-bearing man instead of saying that he was God made man inevitably incur this anathema.

Anathema 6

18. If anyone says that the Word of God the Father is Christ's God or Master, instead of acknowledging the same Christ as simultaneously God and man, since according to the Scriptures the Word became flesh (Jn 1:14), let him be anathema.

Explanation

19. Our Lord Jesus Christ, being the one and only and true Son of God the Father, became flesh. He is the Word and together with his own begetter has sovereignty over all things. 'To him every knee bows, in heaven and on earth and under the earth, and every tongue confesses that Jesus Christ is Lord, to the glory of God the Father' (Phil. 2:10, 11). He is therefore Lord of all things insofar as he is thought of as God and actually is God, even though he is not without flesh after the Incarnation, and is not God or Master of himself. For it is truly most absurd, or rather the height of impiety, to think or speak in this fashion. This anathema is therefore rightly directed against anyone who holds such a view.

22

Anathema 7

20. If anyone says that Jesus is a man controlled by the Word of God and that the glory of the Only-begotten is to be attributed to another existing apart from him, let him be anathema.

Explanation

21. When blessed Gabriel brought the annunciation of the birth according to the flesh of the only-begotten Son of God to the Holy Virgin, he said: 'You will bear a son and you shall call his name Jesus, for he will save his people from their sins'

(Mt. 1:21; cf. Lk. 1:31). He is also called Christ because he was anointed with us in a human fashion, in accordance with the verse of the Psalms: 'You have loved righteousness and hated wickedness; therefore God, your God, has anointed you with the oil of gladness above your fellows' (Ps. 45:7). Even though he himself bestows the Holy Spirit and it is not by measure that he gives it to those who are worthy (Jn 3:34) (for he is filled with it and 'from his fulness have we all received', as Scripture says (Jn 1:16)), nevertheless in view of the dispensation of the Incarnation he is said to have been anointed as a man in a spiritual sense when the Holy Spirit descended upon him, that the Spirit might also abide in us even though it had withdrawn from us in primeval times because of Adam's transgression. Therefore it is the same only-begotten Word of God who became flesh who was called Christ and, possessing the authority appropriate to God as his own, was able to work miracles. Those who say with regard to the authority of Christ that he was endowed with the glory of the Only-begotten, as if the Only-begotten was different from Christ, conceive of two sons, the one controlling and the other being controlled as a man just like ourselves, and therefore incur the consequences of this anathema.

Anathema 8

22. If anyone has the temerity to say that the assumed man should be worshipped along with God the Word and should be glorified and called God along with him as if they were two different entities [for the addition of the expression 'along with' will always necessarily imply this interpretation][12] instead of honouring Emmanuel with a single act of worship and ascribing to him a single act of praise in view of the Word having become flesh, let him be anathema.

Explanation

23. We have been baptized into one God the Father almighty and into one Son and indeed into one Holy Spirit. Do you not then know, says blessed Paul, 'that all of us who have been baptized into Christ were baptized into his death? We were buried therefore with him by baptism into death, so that as Christ was raised from the dead by the glory of the

Father, we too might walk in newness of life' (Rom. 6:3, 4). We have therefore believed in one Son, as I have said, our Lord Jesus Christ, that is, the Word of God the Father who became incarnate and was made man, and were baptized into him. We have been taught to worship him as someone who is one being and truly God and likewise the heavenly powers along with us. For it is written, 'When he brings the first-born into the world, he says, "Let all God's angels worship him"' (Heb. 1:6). The Only-begotten became the first-born when he appeared as a man like us, for then he was also called a brother of those who love him (cf. Rom. 8:29). If anyone therefore says that he worships a man along with but separately from a different being who is the Word of God, instead of bringing them together by a true union into a single Christ and Son and Lord and honouring him with a single worship, he rightly incurs the consequences of this anathema.

Anathema 9

24. If anyone says that the one Lord Jesus Christ has been glorified by the Spirit, in the sense that Christ used the power that came through the Spirit as something alien to himself and received from him the power to operate against unclean spirits and work miracles in human beings, instead of saying that the Spirit by which he also performed the miracles is his own, let him be anathema.

Explanation

25. When the only-begotten Word of God became man he nevertheless remained God, since he is everything that the Father is with the sole exception of being Father. He worked the miracles because he possesses the Holy Spirit, which is from him and essentially innate within him, as his own property. It follows that when he became man he nevertheless remained God, because he performed the miracles through the Spirit by a power that was his own. Those who say that he was glorified as a man like one of us or like one of the saints and that the power by which he operated through the Spirit was not his own but rather was one that was external and appropriate to God, and that he received his

ascension into heaven from the Spirit as a grace, rightly incurs the consequences of this anathema.[13]

Anathema 10

26. Divine Scripture says that Christ became high priest and apostle of our confession (cf. Heb. 3:1) and gave himself up for us, a fragrant offering to God the Father (cf. Eph. 5:2). Therefore if anyone says that it was not the Word of God himself who became our high priest and apostle when he became incarnate and a man like ourselves, but someone different from him who was a separate man born of a woman, or if someone says that he made the offering for himself too instead of for us alone (for he who knew no sin had no need of an offering), let him be anathema.

Explanation

27. Admittedly the things that pertain to human nature are paltry compared to the Word begotten of God, but he did not disdain them on account of the dispensation of the Incarnation. Although he was Lord of all by nature he brought himself down to our level and took the form of a servant. He was called our high priest and apostle because the limitations of the human condition called him to this too. He gave himself up for us as a fragrant offering to God the Father. 'For by a single offering he has perfected for all time those who are sanctified,' as Scripture says (Heb. 10:14). I do not know how those who think differently can maintain that it is not the incarnate Word of God himself who is called both apostle and high priest of our confession, but another human being apart from him. They say that he who was born of the holy Virgin was called both apostle and high priest and arrived at this by a process of development and gave himself up as a sacrifice to God the Father not only for us but also for himself, which is completely alien to our orthodox and irreproachable faith. For he did not commit any sin (cf. 1 Pet. 2:22), and since he is superior to transgression and has absolutely no share in sin, he had no need of sacrifice on his own behalf. But since those who think differently in all likelihood reject this and conceive instead of two sons, the anathema had necessarily to be drawn up, for it made their impiety obvious.

Anathema 11

28. If anyone does not acknowledge that the Lord's flesh is life-giving and belongs to the Word of God the Father himself, but says it belongs to someone else who is joined to him on the basis of rank or simply possesses a divine indwelling, instead of saying it is life-giving, as we have said, because it became the personal property of the Word who is able to endow all things with life, let him be anathema.

Explanation

29. We celebrate the holy and life-giving and bloodless sacrifice in the churches, not in the belief that the offering is the body of an ordinary man like ourselves, and similarly with the precious blood, but instead accepting that it has become the very own body and blood of the Word who endows all things with life. For ordinary flesh cannot endow with life. The Saviour himself testifies to this when he says: 'The flesh is of no avail; it is the spirit that gives life' (Jn 6:63). Because it became the Word's own flesh it is therefore regarded as life-giving and actually is so. As our Lord himself said, 'As the living Father sent me, and I live because of the Father, so he who eats me will live because of me' (Jn 6:57). Since Nestorius and those who think like him ignorantly weaken the power of the mystery, that is why this anathema has rightly been drawn up.[14]

Anathema 12

30. If anyone does not acknowledge that the Word of God suffered in the flesh, and was crucified in the flesh, and experienced death in the flesh, and became the first-born from the dead, seeing that as God he is both Life and life-giving, let him be anathema.

Explanation

31. The Word of God the Father is impassible and immortal. For the divine and ineffable nature transcends suffering and it is this which endows all things with life and is superior to corruption and anything that normally causes us grief. Yet even though the Word of God the Father is these things in his essential being, he made his own the flesh that is receptive of death, that by means of that which is accustomed to suffering he might take these sufferings to himself on our behalf and for our sake and deliver all of us from both corruption and death, having as God endowed his own body with life and become 'the first fruits of those who have fallen asleep' (1 Cor. 15:20) and the firstborn from the dead. He who endured the precious cross for our sake and experienced death was not an ordinary man to be regarded as separate and distinct from the Word of God the Father. On the contrary, the Lord of glory himself suffered in the flesh, according to the Scriptures (cf. 1 Pet. 4:1). Since those who wish to introduce vain and impious doctrines into the orthodox and irreproachable faith say that an ordinary man endured the cross for our sake, this anathema became necessary in order to make plain the degree of impiety existing amongst them.[15]

AGAINST JULIAN

INTRODUCTION

The Emperor Julian's anti-Christian work, *Against the Galilaeans*, had already been in existence for over seventy years when Cyril began to circulate his refutation. We first hear of *Against Julian* in a letter of Theodoret of Cyrrhus, who mentions that Cyril sent a copy to John of Antioch.[1] As John died in 441/2, this provides us with the *terminus ante quem*. The *terminus post quem* cannot be earlier than 433, the year in which Cyril was reconciled with John after the bitter events of 431 (or, perhaps more precisely, 434, when Theodoret himself accepted the council). Within this period, however, the years 437–8 mark a cooling of relations between Alexandria and Antioch as a result of an attack made by Cyril on the Antiochene theologians Diodore of Tarsus and Theodore of Mopsuestia. Of the remaining options, 434–7 or 439–41, scholars tend to prefer the latter because they find it difficult to believe that Cyril could have found the time to compose the work any earlier.[2]

The purpose of *Against Julian* was to counter the continuing influence of the apostate emperor's treatise amongst pagans and also to rally Christians whose faith might have been shaken by his arguments. The three books of *Against the Galilaeans* are now lost.[3] But from the passages that are preserved in Cyril's refutation we can see that Christians must have found it a formidable work. Written at Antioch in the winter of 362–3, as Julian was preparing for the campaign against the Persians that was to cost him his life, it was a devastating attack on Christianity by one who was thoroughly familiar with its teaching. Julian compares the Greek idea of God and his work in creation with the Hebrew, setting the *Timaeus* against Genesis, and concludes that the Hebrew is inferior but nevertheless worthy of respect. Christians, on the other hand, fall between two stools. They have rejected the Greek pantheon for a Hebraic religion yet fail to keep the laws of Moses. Nor do they have anything to compare with the Greek sage, who through philosophical endeavour gains knowledge of the divine essence and becomes like God.

After Julian's death Christian writers wasted no time in reviling him.[4] None of them, however, with the possible exception of Theodore of Mopsuestia, sat down to write a refutation of Julian before Cyril.[5] From Cyril's pen we have ten books refuting Book 1 of Julian, with fragments surviving of a further ten books.[6] The method which Cyril followed was the same as that which he had used in the *Five Tomes against Nestorius*. He works through Julian's text, setting down passages verbatim and responding to each in turn, producing, in effect, a dialogue or disputation.

Cyril must have felt that the countering of the pernicious influence of the apostate was long overdue. Yet in many ways he was not the ideal man for the job. Although a formidable dialectitian, he had not the broad cultural formation that Origen, for example, was able to bring to his refutation of Celsus. Many of his pagan authors are quoted at second hand.[7] But he did have a deep knowledge of the Bible and a thorough grounding in the ecclesiastical tradition, as is demonstrated by the following passages.

The translation is from P. Burguière and P. Evieux, *Cyrille d'Alexandrie, Contre Julien*, tome 1, livres I et II, *SC* 322, Paris 1985, with the exception of the final passage, from Book 5, which is from Migne, *Patrologia Graeca*, vol. 76.

THE SAGES AND SCRIPTURE

C. Jul. 1.1–5 (*SC* 322, 110–116; PG 76, 509A–513B)

509A 1. Those who are wise and intelligent and well versed in sacred doctrines admire the beauty of truth and hold in the greatest esteem the ability to understand an analogy, or an obscure expression, or sayings of the sages, or enigmatic phrases. Only thus will they apply their mind in a precise and coherent way to the divinely inspired Scriptures and fill their souls with divine light. And when they have gained an enviable reputation for an upright and most observant way of life they should be able to procure benefits of the highest kind for others too. For it is written: 'My son, if you become wise for yourself, you shall also be wise for your neighbour' (Prov. 9:12 LXX).

Those whose hearts are perverted, however, and whose minds are deformed, those who have no share whatsoever in the divine light, rise up against the dogmas of orthodox faith, speak most impudently and disparage the ineffable glory, and with abusive words 'utter injustice to the heights' (Ps. 73:8 LXX), as the Psalms say. They are sick, in my view, with a madness of the most extreme kind and with an endemic ignorance, or rather, to tell the truth, as a result of the plotting of the wicked serpent, the originator of evil, who is, of course, Satan.

512A

2. We find confirmation of this in what the divine Paul has written: 'And even if our gospel is veiled, it is veiled only to those who are perishing. In their case the god of this world has blinded the minds of the unbelievers, to keep them from seeing the light of the gospel of the glory of Christ' (2 Cor. 4:3, 4). Therefore the idea that he who is considered to be the god of this age, and who has stolen what he has from the supreme glory, has blinded their hearts is not a difficult one to appreciate. For it is generally admitted that they have been led astray and have set up a vast number of gods, demons and souls of heroes with a life of their own, as they themselves say and are accustomed to think.[8]

B

A sensible person might have shed a tear for those who have not chosen to remain completely silent about things that should make one ashamed. But in fact their enterprise has reached such a pitch of impiety that they seek to infect others too with the disease of this superstition that is so disgusting. They are like serpents that sit by road junctions and spitefully attack those who pass by, pouring the poison of perdition into those whose attention is distracted. It may very appropriately be said of them: 'You brood of vipers! How can you speak good, when you are evil?' (Mt. 12:34). And the Lord is not straying from the truth when he says: 'The good man out of his good treasure brings forth good, and the evil man out of his evil treasure brings forth evil' (Mt. 12:35), and 'Out of the abundance of the heart the mouth speaks' (Mt. 12:34).

C

3. I say these things after reading the books of Julian, who has made intolerable accusations against our holy religion. He

192

says that we have gone astray and have foolishly abandoned the road that is direct and free from reproach, that we have, as it were, gone down onto the rocks, and render worship to the God who is over all things in a manner which is in every respect ill-considered, for it agrees neither with the laws given by the all-wise Moses, nor with the superstitions of the Greeks, that is, with their customs and habits, but we have, as it were, invented an intermediate way of life that fails to achieve the goals of either. For my part, I would say that we have been delivered from the folly of the Greeks, and that there are sound arguments that wall off Christian beliefs from their claptrap: 'For what fellowship has light with darkness, or

D   what has a believer in common with an unbeliever?' (2 Cor. 3:14, 15). That we do not disagree with the books of Moses, nor pursue a way of life that is incompatible with his precepts, I shall attempt to establish as best I can when the proper occasion arises for us to discuss this matter.

4. Leaving that aside, however, I think it is necessary at this juncture to say the following. It is true, as some people parody it, that 'one sage issues from another'. But it is also manifestly obvious that those who come after know the work of their predecessors and not the other way round. Therefore since the sons of the Greeks think very highly of their teachers and suppose they intimidate us by citing their Anaximanders

513A   and Empedocleses, their Protagorases and Platos, adding to them others who have been inventors of their unholy doctrines and, so to speak, founts of ignorance, come now, let us say that one may observe them constructing, as it were, different theories against each other, and proposing irreconcilable arguments in defence of their views on every kind of being. Then let us demonstrate, moreover, that Moses has the advantage of greater antiquity, that he has introduced a doctrine of the ineffable and supreme Essence that is sound and utterly free from error, that he has set down a superlative account of the origin of the world, and that he was a remarkable bestower of laws that are conducive to piety and righteousness. Let us also demonstrate that those whom the Greeks call wise came later and are more recent, that they stole his words and wove them into their own treatises, and that even if they

B   were not entirely able to appropriate a serious body of doctrine in this manner, they did appear to speak the truth in a partial way.[9]

5. Furthermore, some of these were born just after Moses, others flourished at the same time as the holy prophets who came at a later date. Those amongst them who chose to follow their doctrines were rated more highly than the others, even though in their accounts of the doctrine of God they were not entirely free of falsehood.

THE ANTIQUITY OF MOSES

C. Jul. 1. 17–18 (SC 322, 138–142; PG 76, 524A–525B)

[524A] 17. Thus from the precise record of historical periods and genealogies[10] is it not obvious to everybody that the divine Moses was earlier than all the Greek sages, and that the latter were later and comparatively recent? For they lived many years after the beginning of the system of dating by Olympiads.[11] Therefore, in my opinion, it is easy to see and true to say that the Greek sages were not totally unaware of B the doctrines of Moses, nor were they inattentive to the God-given and unadulterated wisdom to be found in him, but utter an occasional note of truth combined with falsehood as if mixing mud with the most fragrant perfume.

What wise teaching, worthy of acceptance, is not found in the Mosaic texts? Or how can anyone fail to admire them? Those who have made a precise study of the vain learning of the Greeks say that philosophy is divided into theoretical knowledge and practical knowledge and if someone becomes competent in both of these he is held to have arrived at a mastery of philosophy.[12] But see here, consider Moses as such a man. For he speaks theologically as no other has done about the supreme essence, the incomparable glory, the pre-eminence over every creature, and demonstrates that the C Creator and Lord of all things is the one and only God. Indeed in those who revere the good, who make every effort to live a virtuous life, Moses may be seen prescribing the best and most honoured laws, which render those who practise them people to be deeply respected.

18. But one may perhaps say: 'Yes, indeed, the teachings of Moses are older than those of the Greek sages. But it does not

follow that the latter have filched the wisdom to be found in him or at any rate have adapted it completely to their own purposes.' Let my readers therefore judge for themselves whether my account of the matter seems the more plausible.

Their own historians, one may say, have toured the whole world in their endless desire for knowledge that they might appear to be well versed in most things, for they considered it an embellishment of their work not to pass over any event in silence. How then would such men, who were accustomed to gather useful knowledge, have neglected to find out about such important historical facts and acquire an explanation of doctrines and laws venerable for their great antiquity? Indeed, Pythagoras of Samos and Thales of Miletus spent a considerable amount of time in Egypt making a collection of what they found there and having assembled the mass of learned facts which they are credited with acquiring took them back to their own country.[13] Moreover Plato himself, the son of Ariston, says in the *Timaeus* that Solon of Athens arrived in Egypt and there heard one of the false prophets, or priests, saying: 'Solon, Solon, you Greeks are always children and an aged Greek there is none, for you are all young in your souls. You have no ancient opinion among you, nor learning hoary with age. Of this you have no knowledge because many generations have died without leaving a written record.'[14]

19. This, in my opinion, also enables one to perceive the venerable antiquity of Christianity. For there was as yet no knowledge of writing among the Greeks. Cadmus had only just brought the alphabet from Phoenicia, whereas the works of Moses had already been written. Solon, who first provided Athens with laws, and indeed Plato himself, who had not only been in Egypt in order to gain the reputation of knowing more than anyone else, will undoubtedly have also admired the works of Moses.

That the Greek historians were well acquainted with Moses may be seen from the very works that they wrote. For Polemon mentions him in the first book of his *Greek Histories*, as does Ptolemaeus of Mendes and indeed Hellanicus and Philochorus and Castor and others besides.[15] Diodorus too, who made a study of Egyptian matters and says that he heard the sages there speak of Moses, wrote as follows: 'After the ancient way of life in Egypt, which legend assigns to the time of gods and heroes, the first they say who persuaded the mass of people to live by written laws was a man of great spiritual stature and of unprecedented quality of life among those commemorated by the Jews, namely, Moses, who was called a god.'[16] It was because some of the Egyptians saw Moses as having come to be full of every virtue that they called him a god, I rather think, as a mark of honour, or perhaps it was because they had learned that the God of all people had said to him: 'See, I have given you as a god to Pharaoh' (Ex. 7:1).

THE CREATION OF MAN IN THE IMAGE OF GOD

C. Jul. 1. 29–34 (SC 322, 162–174; PG 76, 536B–540D)

536B   **29.** Here is another passage I should like to set before my readers as something which, in my opinion, should be of immense profit to them. For it is written with regard to the creation of man: 'And God said, "Let us make man in our image, after our likeness"' (Gen. 1:26), and shortly afterwards: 'So God created man in his own image, in the image of God he created him' (Gen. 1:27). Now the image of God the Father is the Son (cf. Col. 1:15), to whom we too have been conformed spiritually (cf. Rom. 8:29), and human nature was enriched by this in an exceptional way, for it was illuminated by the beauty radiating from the Creator. What then can be said by those who oppose our ideas and make a pretence of piety by confessing with us that God is one and alone, yet
C   maintaining that the Son was not begotten from him? To whom did God say: 'Let us make man in our image, after our likeness?'

Should one not surmise that the holy and consubstantial Trinity addresses these words on this matter to itself, as if the all-wise Moses wanted to demonstrate that the creation of man was not undertaken by God without deliberation but was honoured by his taking counsel, so to speak, beforehand?[17] The divine and uncompounded mind has no need, of course, for reflection, or hesitation, or investigation of any kind. For the moment it wills something, the object of its will comes into being in a correct and perfect manner.[18]

Nevertheless, as I have said, human nature is honoured by a kind of preliminary consultation.

30. But neither shall we keep silent about the arguments of the atheists. For they might perhaps respond at once: 'It is not as you suppose and want to believe, that it is with his own

D   Word and the Spirit that the Father has spoken, but with the secondary and lesser gods that are with him.' Indeed, is it not obvious to everybody that even those who are accustomed to think philosophically in the Greek manner admit that God is one, the creator of the universe who by nature transcends all things, and that certain other gods, as they themselves put it, both those of the intelligible world and those accessible to the senses, were made by him and brought into being? At any rate, Plato says very clearly: 'First then, in my judgement, we must make a distinction and ask, "What is that which always is and has no beginning, and what is that which is always becoming and never is?" That which is apprehended by intelligence and reason is always in the same state, but that which is conceived by opinion with the help of sensation and without reason is always in the process of becoming and

537A   perishing and never really is.'[19] By 'that which always is and has no beginning' he means that nature which is transcendent and beyond creation, by which I understand the God of all things, the God who really exists. So it is that he himself says to Moses, the teacher of sacred truths: 'I am he who is' (Ex. 3:4).[20] As for 'that which is always becoming and never is', this is that which has been brought into existence from non-being by some ineffable and inconceivable power of the God who fashioned our universe. In conclusion, I have demonstrated very clearly, not only from our own sacred Scriptures but also from what they acknowledge that they think and say, that all things were brought into being by God, and that he himself is endowed with a nature of a different kind from that of creatures. For that which has been

B   made is subordinate to its Maker, and by nature is in every way inferior to it.

31. This having been established by our discussion so far, what do those say who have surmised that the God of all things uttered the words: 'Let us make man in our image, after our likeness' to other gods? For if he had wanted to fashion the 'rational earthly animal'[21] after the image of created beings, why did he refer to his own person, saying 'let us make' and 'in our image'? If he thought it right to form man after his own divine beauty alone, why does he accept at the same time the imitation of others, that is to say, their form, or however one can best describe these things? For Creator and

C   creature, or generate and ingenerate nature, or that which is incorruptible and that which is subject to corruption cannot be assigned to the same category with regard to nature, or pre-eminence, or dignity – if indeed one can say without being mistaken that from every possible point of view that which may be regarded as subject to a beginning must necessarily also be subject to decay.

32. The divine Moses, who under the mystical inspiration of the Holy Spirit saw what was to be, had foreknowledge of what concerns us. How this was so I shall now explain. Since the one, ineffable and incomprehensible nature of God is regarded as subsisting as Father, Son and Holy Spirit, that is, as a consubstantial Trinity, in case anyone, swept along out of great stupidity towards matters that do not concern him, should say that man was created in the image and likeness of God but not in that of the Son – or indeed more likely supposes the opposite and says that man was made in the likeness of the Son and not that of the Father also – having

D   foreseen, as I have said, the plausible arguments which one day some people would produce, Moses declares that the Holy Trinity said to itself: 'Let us make man in our image and after our likeness' that he may be understood to have been formed, spiritually of course, on the model of the entire ineffable nature of the Godhead.[22] Our opponents, even though they pretend to make a great display of wisdom, think these arguments are nonsensical. Since on account of their immense stupidity the light of truth is inaccessible to them, they maintain that God is just as likely to have addressed certain spurious, so-called gods. Yet why should it not be worthy of consideration that he who is Creator by nature has granted to the nature of creatures the exalted

540A dignity of his own glory and majesty? We are not saying anything out of malice – why should that be? – but because the nature of created things can never arrive at the pre-eminence of the divine dignities, nor, I think, can it be enriched on the level of essence with that which naturally belongs only and specifically to the ineffable divine nature.

33. It is also absurd from another angle to think that the King and Lord of all things said 'Let us make man in our image and after our likeness' to other gods. For why should he need to make others his colleagues, as it were, and helpers solely for the creation of man, when he had already produced the rest of creation, that is to say, angels and dominions, principalities, authorities and spiritual powers, heaven and
B earth, sun and moon, stars and light, and in short everything that is in heaven and on earth? Is one to say that he suffered from some impotence or that he did not have sufficient energy to accomplish this task without calling on assistance? Yet how would one avoid being accused of the most extreme stupidity if one chose to think in this way? For the divine is all-powerful and self-sufficient in any matter whatsoever; nothing is impossible for it.

Turning now from this nonsense, let us move on to another point, the need to acknowledge that the fullness of the ineffable Godhead is to be understood as present in the holy and consubstantial Trinity, and that we are conformed to the true and exact image of the Father, that is, to the Son, and that his divine beauty is impressed on our souls through
C participation in the Holy Spirit. For he is within us, as the Son himself is, 'because the Spirit is the truth,' as Scripture says (1 Jn. 5:6).

34. In this way the all-wise Moses initiated us into true spiritual knowledge and the holy prophets, apostles and evangelists who came after him did not deviate from his teaching. The same single theological approach may be seen in all of them and one will not find them at odds with each other in any matter whatsoever. Truly inspired by God, they derive what they say from the one Holy Spirit. Our Lord Jesus Christ does not allow us to entertain any doubt on this point, for he says most clearly in their presence: 'It is not you who speak, but the Spirit of your Father speaking through you' (Mt. 10:20). Since we possess an authentic doctrine concerning God that has come down to us from above through the holy
D Fathers, we exult in it and we are not accustomed to yield to the physical descendants of Israel on the grounds that this

doctrine came rather to them. Far from it. We count ourselves too amongst the children of Abraham.[23] For we are the sons according to the promise, and Paul confirms this when he says: 'For not all who are descended from Israel belong to Israel, and not all are children of Abraham because they are his descendants, but the children of the promise are reckoned as descendants' (Rom. 9:6–8).

PAGAN AND CHRISTIAN IMITATION OF GOD COMPARED

C. Jul. 2. 34–36 (SC 322, 272–278; PG 76, 592A–593A)

592A **34.** Our high-minded opponent,[24] so audacious in his attacks on us, pours scorn on the origin of man – the version, that is, proclaimed by the incomparable Moses – and thinks it a small thing that human nature was endowed by God with having been made by him in his image and likeness.[25] Yet how would any sensible person not agree that the question is one of what provides the greatest adornment? What is better, tell me, than our saying that we are stamped with the divine likeness? Do we not say that the divine nature is of all things the most exalted and most sublime, dazzling all around it with its ineffable glory, and of its very self every existing form and beauty of virtue? How is it then that what I have said is not obvious to everybody? Why does he ridicule things that are so remarkable? And why does he mock the fact that a creature endowed with mind and reason, a creature so God-

B like – I mean of course man – has been honoured with dominion over all things?

Indeed, the very nature of things concurs with the teaching of Moses. But he fails to discuss this correlation. He rejects it without argument and simply cleaves to the words of Plato. He expresses his admiration, and in an ill-considered way at that, for the harangue Plato has composed, though on what grounds I do not know, and says that the God of all delivered to the created so-called gods.[26]

35. I think that we should also say something with regard to this. For if Plato is writing the part of a character in this

C
passage and in the manner of the poets is assigning to the role of God the words that he thinks appropriate to him, he has gone wide of the mark, and one could criticize him for not knowing how to construct the part of a character in the proper manner.[27] But if he is pretending to speak in an inspired way, away with his nonsense! For it is not right to say that the God who has dominion over all things allowed false gods to share in the glory that belongs properly to him alone. For he said: 'My glory I shall give to no other, nor my praise to graven images' (Is. 42:8).

Come, let us briefly pit the truth against the words of Plato and say the following. Let it be granted, if you like, that the higher spiritual powers created by God may be honoured by the appellation of 'god'. For we say that there are in heaven certain beings entitled 'gods' and 'lords'. Indeed we ourselves are crowned with such an appellation, since God says to us: 'I
D
said, you are gods and all of you sons of the Most High' (Ps. 82:6).[28] But in this instance there is a very obvious explanation of the matter, and the declaration to us is the clearest evidence of God's benevolence. For when the Creator of all things made that part of creation which is intelligent and rational in accordance with his own image and likeness, in his goodness he also honoured it with the title of 'god'. And there is nothing unreasonable in this. For we ourselves are accustomed to calling a man's portrait, for example, by the same appellation as the original, namely 'a man'.

36. Therefore since that part of creation which is intelligent and rational was given a higher status by God than that which is not rational and intelligent, it appears to have been
593A
assigned the greater glory and gilded with the title of 'god'. No other created being whatsoever has been called a 'god'. The fact that the firmament, that is, the cosmos, is frankly not a living being, nor is it ensouled in any sense, even if none of our own people wishes to say this, is sufficiently proved, in the absence of others whom they hold to be 'wise', by Aristotle, the pupil of Plato himself. For he says, as we have already asserted, that the world is in no sense ensouled, nor is it rational or intelligent.[29] That the cosmos as a whole, or whatever constitutes the All (for that is how Plato puts it) is either ensouled or intelligent, the power of truth prevents Julian from saying, as an entirely adequate refutation has

been provided, as I have said, by his own side and indeed by those dearest to him.

THE TRUE PHILOSOPHER

C. Jul. 5 (PG 76, 772D–776A)

[772D] Julian exalts such things [i.e. the astronomy, geometry and mathematics which he says the Greeks took from the Babylonians, the Egyptians and the Phoenicians and together with music subsequently perfected] and holds them up for admiration.[30] In response to this I would say that he is entirely unaware of what should appropriately be admired by those who are anxious to acquire the best teaching and believe themselves to be enjoying a truly pleasant life.

773A   What makes a man admired and looked up to is not only the ease with which he holds forth, and the charm and attractive rhythm of his diction, which enable him to speak eloquently and thoroughly investigate the meaning of vain and meagre ideas and weave together complex sentences with precision, and endeavour moreover to search out that which transcends the mind and falsifies the true knowledge that comes to us through the senses. In reality a sage is, and is described by us as being, a man who has been enriched by clear and unambiguous doctrine relating to the God of all things, and has made as careful an inquiry as possible into the matters that concern Him. I mean as far as is permissible to human beings, and has acquired along with this a perfect knowledge of all necessary things, so as to be in a position to enable those

B   who follow his teaching with righteousness to conceive a desire for adorning themselves with the splendours of virtue.[31]

What need is there for inquisitive study? What is the use of geometry, musical theory and arithmetic and the other sciences, which are the only things they think fit to honour and on account of them hold their noses in the air? Yet this eagerness for study, I would say, contributes nothing conducive to living an ordered life and keeping oneself free from reproach in one's conduct. For no one will be thus superior to censured pleasures or disdain excessive wealth and vainglory or be free from surges of anger, or be far from censoriousness and envy, or diligently make efforts to practise continence, or

C indeed any of the other virtues that render those to whom they belong or who have assimilated them of greater repute than the rest, and those in whom they are lacking or absent, people of no account. For it is certainly possible to see someone who is intelligent, who has acquired the use of an elaborate style of language, who is extremely fluent, a good Atticist, a master of polished prose, and yet is profane in his way of life and caught in the toils of the most shameful desires. But a man who is wise and sensible has not come to be so by mere words alone. Nor will it satisfy him to establish a reputation through an inventive facility for cutting phrases and an invincible cleverness in using perverted ideas. For such a man is a craftsman with regard to words but has not yet become virtuous in any way. Therefore geometry and astronomy and the rest of such sciences make their practitioner famous and D envied. But only an accurate and detailed and irreproachable knowledge of God, together with the zealous pursuit of virtue and the rejection of its opposite, I would say, can attain the moral splendour of pure and unexceptionable philosophy.

Hellenic learning is vain and pointless and requires much effort for no reward. Perhaps you will not be convinced by my own words. I shall therefore appeal for help, Sir, to your Plato, who wrote in the fifth book of the *Republic*: '"Are we then to designate all these, and other mathematicians like them, and the practitioners of the minor arts as true philosophers?" I said, "No, only those who are fond of contemplating the 776A truth."'[32] For philosophy is not found in geometrical postulates and hypotheses, nor in the academic study of music, nor in astronomy, which is steeped in the principles of nature and flux and probability. On the contrary, philosophy concerns the good itself through knowledge and truth, since these are different paths, as it were, of virtue that lead to the good. Therefore the practice of philosophy is not to be found in the minor arts, which are so derisory, but in knowing the truth, which signifies that which truly exists, which is God.

NOTES

1 THE MAKING OF A BISHOP

1 Attributed to Theodoret of Cyrrhus, (*Ep.* 180 [PG 83, 1489C–1491A]), trans. Prestige (1940), 150.

2 For brilliant portraits of this era see Chuvin (1990), 57–90 and Brown (1992).

3 Isidore of Pelusium, for example, who enjoyed *parrhēsia*, or freedom of speech, with Cyril, warned him not to pursue a family vendetta against the memory of John Chrysostom (*Ep.* 1. 370 [PG 78, 392C]).

4 On Cyril's birthplace, the Coptic Didouseya, see Munier (1947), 200–1, who identifies it with the modern village of Mahalla el Kobra, about 75 miles east of Alexandria. On the date, see Abel (1947), 230. Unlike Augustine or Jerome, Cyril is not at all self-revealing in his writings. For his early career we are dependent on the contemporary ecclesiastical historians, Socrates and Sozomen, and the seventh-century Coptic writer (preserved in a late Ethiopic translation), John of Nikiu. It is John of Nikiu who gives us the name of Cyril's birthplace (*Chronicle*, trans. Charles [1916], 79.11, 12).

5 *Chronicle* 79.1.

6 John of Nikiu, *Chronicle* 79. 2–14.

7 Favale (1958), 45–8.

8 Favale (1958), 47. Favale draws on Jerome, *Apology against Rufinus* 3.18 (PL 23, 470C), who says that Rufinus claimed to be 'a hearer and disciple of Theophilus'. Rufinus spent the years 371 to 377 at Alexandria.

9 A *libellus* (a formal complaint) against Dioscorus of Alexandria by a nephew of Cyril's called Athanasius, which was delivered at Chalcedon, mentions that Cyril had several sisters but makes no reference to any brothers (ACO II, 1, p. [216].24; p. [217].7; p. [218].2–3). Athanasius' mother, one of Cyril's sisters, was called Isidora.

10 For a lively account of a Greek education in Cyril's day, see Marrou

(1956), 142–85, 299–13. Cf. Kaster (1988), 72–95, on Christians as recipients of a literary education.

11 Cyril's style has provoked mainly negative reactions. L.R. Wickham, for example, sees in it 'all the studied ugliness of the Albert Memorial or Second Empire furniture' (Wickham [1983], xiv). My own judgement concurs with that of A. Vaccari, who concludes his study of the technical aspects of Cyril's Greek with the observation that 'Cyril is a real "auctor" in the etymological sense of the word . . . in that he endeavours not only to conserve and revitalize the ancestral treasure-house of the Greek language, rich as it was, but enriches it further with new forms, developing its natural potentiality. As a result his prose has a singular quality, well described by that great connoisseur, Photius: "his prose is his own invention, forcefully adapted to his own personal style, a composition which is, so to speak, unrestrained and disdainful of the mean" (*Bibliotheca cod.* 49). There is an artificiality, a certain touch of poetry, in a prose otherwise characterized by austere argument. All this might be a defect on the aesthetic level but it creates real interest and a powerful attractiveness in the writings of St Cyril' (Vaccari [1937], 38–9).

12 Boulnois (1994), 105–77; Meunier (1997), 27. W.J. Malley observes that a clue that Cyril's 'education did not include a profound study of the Hellenic philosophers is his inability to quote them from memory and paraphrase their doctrine as for example Julian was able to do' (Malley [1978], 260).

13 Siddals (1987); Boulnois (1994), 181–227.

14 On the character of Alexandrian philosophy in the early fifth century, see Wallis (1972) 1, 25, 143–5; cf. Dzielska (1995), 46–65.

15 Boulnois (1994), 85, 186–7. Boulnois speculates (187–8) that Cyril may have had contacts with Hypatia through his uncle's friend Synesius of Cyrene, who had been one of her students – an intriguing possibility.

16 *Against Julian* 5 (PG 70, 733D). Cyril was not the first Christian writer to turn his back on a good secular education. Jerome, for example (who, incidentally, had also made a study of Aristotle's logical treatises and Porphyry's *Isagoge*), came to feel that a Christian should not study pagan authors (cf. Kelly 1975, 39, 42–4, 273–5). Theodoret of Cyrrhus, however, Cyril's contemporary, and after 431 his principal theological opponent, had quite the opposite attitude (cf. Kaster [1988], 79).

17 His sources and pointers towards pagan literature are Eusebius of Caesarea's *Chronicon* and *Preparation for the Gospel*, Clement of Alexandria's *Protrepticus* and *Stromata*, Ps.-Justin's *Exhortation to the Greeks* and Didymus the Blind's *On the Trinity* (Grant [1964], 269–79).

18 ACO 1, 1, 3, p.22.7–9. Wickham suggests tentatively that by 'holy and orthodox fathers' Cyril may have been referring to monks who

gave him a monastic education (Wickham [1983], xii–xiii). (There is a late tradition [recorded in Severus' *Lives of the Patriarchs*, PO 1 (1907), 427–8, but rejected by Hardy (1982), 116] that Cyril spent five years in the desert.) That *tethrametha* ('we have been nurtured', line 9) is intended in a metaphorical sense, however, seems to be indicated a few lines later, when Cyril recapitulates: 'but, as I said, nurtured (*entethramenoi*) by the holy and apostolic doctrines of the Church' (lines 14–15). In a letter written in the following year to Acacius of Beroea (*Ep.* 33.9), Cyril repeats this passage with slight variations: 'I have been nurtured (*etraphēn*) at the hands of an orthodox father' (ACO 1, 1, 7, p.149. 22–3). McGuckin, translating *etraphēn* as 'brought up', thinks he is referring to his uncle Theophilus (McGuckin [1994], 339, n.7). This may be so in view of the fact that Cyril considered Theophilus a Church Father (he included a passage from one of Theophilus' festal homilies in the patristic florilegium presented at Ephesus). It seems to me more likely, however, that he is referring to Athanasius, who besides being the greatest influence on his theological development was also his family's benefactor.

19 Cyril mentions in passing in a letter to Acacius of Beroea (*Ep.* 33.7) that he happens to have been there (ACO I, 1, 7, p.148. 34).

20 Isidore of Pelusium, *Ep.* 1.152 (PG 78, 285A).

21 On the *parabalani* (whose official duties were to transport the sick and destitute to the hospitals), see ODCC³, art. 'Parabalani', and the literature cited there. Cf. also Rougé (1987), 347–9. Other powerful bishops also had their private militias. Pope Damasus succeeded to the papal throne in 366 through the strong-arm tactics of the *fossores*, the guild of grave-diggers who were the excavators of the catacombs. The bishop of Antioch had his *leticiarii*, or pall-bearers for the burial of the poor (Brown [1992], 102–3).

22 Socrates, *Eccl. Hist.* 5.7. The fullest discussion of Cyril's accession to the episcopate is that of Rougé (1987). For a wise and balanced summary of Cyril's early career see esp. Hardy (1982). There are also good summaries in Abel (1947), de Durand (1964), 7–20, Wickham (1983), xii–xix, and McGuckin (1994), 1–20.

23 On the bishop in this period as effectively the political leader of the urban lower classes, see Brown (1992), 71–117.

24 On the subject of John Chrysostom, see the letter of Atticus of Constantinople to Cyril requesting him to restore John to the diptychs (Schwartz [1927], 23–4; trans. McEnerney [1987], ii, Letter 75), the letter of Isidore of Pelusium urging Cyril not to maintain his uncle's policy (*Ep.* 1.370 [PG 78, 392C]) and Cyril's reply to Atticus denying his request (Schwartz [1927], 25–8; trans. McEnerney [1987], ii, Letter 76). On Cyril's public stance against Origenism, see his letter to the monks of Scetis (ACO III, pp. 201–2; trans. McEnerney [1987], ii, Letter 81), where he condemns the denial of the resurrection of the body and the view that embodied existence is a

punishment for the soul's previous sins. On his opposition to anthropomorphism, see *Answers to Tiberius* 2 (Wickham [1983], 141) and *Doctrinal Questions and Answers* 1 (Wickham [1983], 185).

25 For a different view, see Wickham (1983), xiii.

26 Isidore of Pelusium, reporting the view of some of the bishops after the Council of Ephesus (*Ep.* 1. 310 [PG 78, 361C]).

27 John of Nikiu, *Chronicle* 84.102.

28 An act of dubious legality (Socrates, *Eccl. Hist.* 7.7). The Novatianists were a rigorist sect, taking their name from Novatian, a third-century Roman priest who had objected to the receiving back of the lapsed on easy terms. Socrates was especially sympathetic towards them, which is why he has noticed what might otherwise have been an unremarkable act. Celestine did the same as Cyril in Rome (Socrates, *Eccl. Hist.* 7.11). Only in Constantinople did the Novatianists enjoy good relations with their bishop until the arrival of Nestorius (ibid., 7.29).

29 Socrates, *Eccl. Hist.* 7.13; cf. John of Nikiu, *Chronicle* 84.89–99.

30 John of Nikiu, *Chronicle* 84.99.

31 Athanasius, *Encyclical Letter* 4.

32 Theodoret, *Eccl. Hist.* 4.18.

33 Socrates (*Eccl. Hist.* 7.7) says that troops were supplied by Abundantius the commander of the troops in Egypt (presumably the *comes rei militaris*). The prefect of Alexandria (the *praefectus augustalis*, whose area of administration was restricted to the Delta) had no troops at his personal disposal.

34 *Cod. Theod.* 16.8.9. (trans. Linder) issued in 393 and addressed to the Count of the Orient. Cited by Millar (1992), 117.

35 Wilken (1971), 49, who quotes *Cod. Theod.* 13.5.18.

36 Socrates, *Eccl. Hist.* 7.13.

37 On Hypatia and the legends surrounding her, see Dzielska (1995).

38 Brown (1992), 116. *Parrhēsia* was freedom of speech, with an implied freedom of access to the sources of political power. 'It could only be exercised by those who felt that they could count on the friendship of the great.' For a discussion of the term, see Brown (1992), 61–9. In Christian usage *parrhēsia* came by analogy to mean the freedom of approach to God enjoyed by the saints.

39 Socrates, *Eccl. Hist.* 7.14.

40 J. Rougé (1987), 341, points out that stones began to be thrown after Orestes declared that he had been baptized by Atticus, the bishop of Constantinople. Atticus was the prime mover in the campaign to rehabilitate the memory of John Chrysostom, a campaign to which Cyril was vehemently opposed. Orestes' declaration could therefore have been seen as a public statement of support for the Johannite faction. Rougé argues plausibly that the controversy over the status of John Chrysostom was one of the essential factors underlying the animosity between the bishop and the prefect.

41 Socrates, *Eccl. Hist.* 7.14; Chuvin (1990), 88.

42 According to John of Nikiu she was killed by being dragged through the streets; *Chronicle* 84.102.

43 John of Nikiu, *Chronicle* 84.103.

44 Brown (1992), 116. M. Dzielska infers from John of Nikiu's account that the common people regarded Hypatia as a sorceress and a witch (Dzielska [1995], 93–4).

45 Socrates, *Eccl. Hist.* 7.15. For the context of the murder, see Chuvin (1990), 85–90 and Brown (1992), 115–17. Theologians are usually anxious to minimize the role of Cyril (e.g. Wickham [1983], xvi–xvii; McGuckin [1994], 13–15), mistakenly in my view. Cyril may not have been directly involved in Hypatia's death but her influence with the prefect was clearly intolerable and he must have regarded her elimination with satisfaction. It should not be overlooked that the murder took place in the cathedral next to Cyril's residence. Moreover, the leader of the mob was a minor cleric who was presumably convinced that he knew his bishop's mind on the matter. Cf. Rougé (1990) and Dzielska (1995), 83–100.

46 *Cod. Theod.* 16.2.42 (of 416). Cf. Philipsborn (1950), 186; McGuckin (1994), 15 (who translates the quotation). It should be noted, however, that the rescript was given in response to a protest which a delegation from the city council made to Monaxius, the praetorian prefect of the East. Holum (1982), 98–9, attributes Theodosius' lack of support for Orestes to the influence of the emperor's formidable elder sister, Pulcheria (proclaimed Augusta in July 414), who is known for her hostility to Jews and pagans.

47 *Cod. Theod.* 16.2.43 (of 418).

48 For a succinct sketch of the growth of the Egyptian Church, see Bagnall (1993), 278–89.

49 Cyril's official title was 'bishop of Alexandria'. He is addressed thus by the Emperor Theodosius in the sacra summoning him to the Council of Ephesus (ACO I, 1, 1, p. 114.29). His normal style, however, was 'the most holy and most reverend archbishop [or bishop] Cyril' (e.g. ACO I, 1, 2, p. 13.9 and item 45 *passim*). The term 'archbishop' was a courtesy title that could be accorded to a bishop of a great see as a sign of respect without implication of jurisdiction. Bishops of Alexandria could also be referred to as *papas* – 'pope' – the earliest instances occurring in pious references to deceased bishops of blessed memory. The first is from the mid-third century, when Dionysius of Alexandria (248–64) uses the title with reference to his predecessor, 'our blessed pope Heraclas' (Eusebius, *Eccl. Hist.* 7.7.4). In a private letter to Eulogius, his agent in Constantinople, Cyril himself refers to 'the blessed pope Athanasius' (*Ep.* 44, ACO I, 1, 4, p. 36.4; cf. Basil, *Ep.* 258.3). The title 'patriarch', first used with reference to the bishop of Alexandria by Eustratius of Constantinople (died after 582) (*V. Eutych.* 29, PG 86, 2308C), is the normal usage by the time of John of Nikiu (late 7th cent.).

50 At the Council of Chalcedon (451), for example, at which Dioscorus of Alexandria was deposed, the Egyptian bishops refused to subscribe to the Tome of Leo until a new bishop had been appointed, because 'it is customary in the Egyptian diocese not to do such things in contravention of the will and ordinance of their archbishop' (Canon 30, trans. R. Butterworth, in Tanner [1990], 102; also in Percival [1899], 291).

51 On the church's property in Cyril's day, see Bagnall (1993), 289–93.

52 Bagnall (1993), 290–1.

53 Bagnall (1993), 36, 291–2.

54 Isidore of Pelusium comments on Theophilus' 'passion for gems and gold' (*Ep.* 1. 152 [PG 78, 284D–285A]). Theophilus' destruction in 391 of the Serapeum, the most famous temple of the empire, reverberated throughout the Roman world. It is mentioned by all the church historians (Rufinus, *Eccl. Hist.* 2.22–27; Theodoret, *Eccl. Hist.* 5.22; Socrates, *Eccl. Hist.* 5.16; Sozomen, *Eccl. Hist.* 7.15: John of Nikiu, *Chronicle* 78.45) and is also commented on bitterly by pagan writers (e.g. Eunapius, *Lives of the Sophists* 472); cf. Chuvin (1990), 65–9. Theophilus' church building is mentioned by Rufinus (*Eccl. Hist.* 2.27).

55 Bowman (1986), 207; Butler (1978), 372–80. The two obelisks which stood at its entrance were only removed in the nineteenth century, one to the Victoria Embankment, London and the other to Central Park, New York.

56 Rufinus mentions that Didymus was appointed 'master of the church school' by Athanasius (*Eccl. Hist.* 11.7), which is the last we hear of an ecclesiastical school at Alexandria. For the school and the literature on it see ODCC[3], art. 'Catechetical School of Alexandria'.

57 *Encomia on Saints Cyrus and John*, PG 87, 3412B–3413C. Fragments of Cyril's homilies in *Various Homilies* 18, PG 77, 1100–05.

58 PG 77, 1101.

59 For a full account, see McGuckin (1992) and (1994), 16–17; cf. Montserrat (1998). The relics were subsequently taken to Rome, where they now reside in the church of S. Passera (another corruption of Abba Cyrus) on the Via Portuensis. Cf. H. Leclercq, *DACL* 3, 3216–20, and R. Van Doren, *DHGE* 13, 1162.

2 THE EARLY WRITINGS

1 Brown (1992), 8.

2 *Cod. Theod.* 16.8.9; Millar (1992), 117.

3 Millar (1992), 118–19: 'The vocabulary of imperial rhetoric reflects a fundamental shift of attitudes.'

4 *Cod. Theod.* 16.8.2; Millar (1992), 118. Holum (1982), 98 sees in these developments evidence of the influence of the Augusta Pulcheria.

5 PG 68, 113–1125.

6 Wilken (1971), 69–85; Meunier (1997), 8.

7 PG 68, 145Bff; Meunier (1997), 8–16.

8 Cattaneo (1983); Meunier (1997), 16–21.

9 Cf. Wilken (1971), 119: 'it is on the basis of Paul that his central theological ideas took shape.'

10 SC (no. 422, 1997) have published a critical edition of letters 1214–1413. For the remainder one must still consult PG 78. The references to Judaism are collected and discussed by Wilken (1971), 50–3.

11 *Ep.* 1.41 (PG 78, 276C–277A); Wilken (1971), 51.

12 *Ep.* 2.94 (PG 78, 797C–800A); Wilken (1971), 51–2.

13 *Ep.* 4.17 (PG 78, 1064D); Wilken (1971), 52.

14 *Ep.* 1.401 (PG 78, 405D–408A); Wilken (1971), 53. Cf. also Cyril, *In Jo.* 4.2 on Jn. 6:53, 362b–363a, translated below.

15 Millar (1992), 120.

16 The preoccupations of ecclesiastics, however, should not lead us to overstate the element of animosity. There is also an interesting glimpse of Christian–Jewish relations on a social level in an Oxyrhynchos papyrus dating from 400 (*P. Oxy.* XLIV 3203). This is a lease in which a Jew called Aurelius Ioses rents a ground floor room and a basement in Oxyrhynchos from two women described as *monachai apotaktikai*. The text is discussed by R.S. Bagnall, who comments: 'the sight of two Christian nuns letting out two rooms of their house to a Jewish man has much to say not only of the flexibility of the monastic life but also of the ordinariness of intersectarian relationships' (Bagnall [1993], 277–8).

17 Theodoret, *Eccl. Hist.* 3.20.

18 *CCL* LXXVIA, 885, trans. Millar (1992), 114.

19 Jerome's frequent consultation of Hebrew scholars is well known (Kelly [1975], 150–1, 156, 164). There were also others, such as the bishop of Oea in Tripolitania, mentioned by Augustine (*Letter* 71.5), who consulted local Jews on their reading of a difficult verse in Jonah (Millar [1992], 114–15).

20 On the relationship of these senses in Cyril, see Kerrigan (1952), 35–240. Cf. Young (1997), 186–212.

21 *Glaphyra*, Prooem. (PG 69, 16A); cf. Young (1997), 262–3.

22 On Cyril's access to Jerome, see the Introduction to the passages from the *Commentary on Isaiah* translated below.

23 *Glaphyra in Ex.* 1 (PG 69, 400C).

24 *Glaphyra* PG 69, 388–96. There is a slightly different interpretation of the same events in the *Adoration*, PG 68, 245–50.

25 In the *Commentary on John* Cyril argues against the Jewish claim that Moses is superior to Christ (*In Jo.* 3.6 on Jn. 6:35, 324a).

26 *Glaphyra*, PG 69, 415BC. Trans. Wilken (1971), 156–7.

27 *In Jo.* 2.1 on Jn. 3:17, 153d.

28 *In Is.* 45:9, PG 961B.
29 *In Jo.* 9.1 on Jn. 14:20, 819e–820c; cf. Meunier (1997), 109–112.
30 *In Jo.* 1.9 on Jn. 1:13, 92c–e.
31 *In Jo.* 4.2 on Jn. 6:53, 361c.
32 *In Jo.* 3.6 on Jn. 6:35, 324d.
33 On Cyril's eucharistic doctrine, see Chadwick (1951); Gebremedhin (1977); Welch (1994), esp. 104–30.
34 *In Jo.* 4.2 on Jn. 6:53, 362b, 362e.
35 *In Jo.* 2.1 on Jn. 3:6, 147e–148a. Cyril follows Athanasius (rather than Irenaeus and Origen) in making no distinction between image and likeness. Cf. Burghardt (1957), 1–11.
36 *In Jo.* 1.9 on Jn. 1:12, 91c.
37 On Cyril's approach to deification the older studies are still useful: Mahé (1909); Janssens (1938); Gross (1938), 277–97; Du Manoir (1944), 48–52, 163–84, 214–15, 423–8; Liébaert (1951), 229–36. The trinitarian dimensions are brought out in an important article by Sagüés (1947). Burghardt (1957), 65–125, has three excellent chapters on sanctification, incorruptibility and sonship. On Cyril's terminology, one may consult Russell (1988), 57–60. On the double participation (corporeal and spiritual) in the divine, see now Meunier (1997), 161–213.
38 Athanasius, *C.Ar.* 3.27 (trans. Newman).
39 Athanasius, *C.Ar.* 2.1 (trans. Newman).
40 Socrates, *Eccl. Hist.* 2.35.
41 Kelly (1977), 249. On Eunomius and his writings, see Vaggione (1987). The only work that survives in more than fragmentary form is his *Liber Apologeticus*, Vaggione (1987), 34–74 (= PG 30, 835–68).
42 Theodoret, *Eccl. Hist.* 5.35; Socrates, *Eccl. Hist.* 5.23–4.
43 Socrates, *Eccl. Hist.* 1.9.
44 *Letter* 5, PG 66, 1341C–1344C.
45 De Durand (1976), 22.
46 *Dial. Trin.* 1, 389a.
47 Socrates, *Eccl. Hist.* 4.7. Cf. R.P. Vaggione's discussion of this passage and a parallel one in Epiphanius, *Haer.* 76.4.2 (Vaggione [1987], 167–70).
48 Wiles (1989), 164.
49 *Liber Apologeticus* 7–11 (Vaggione [1987], 40–6).
50 Cyril (along with his younger contemporary, Theodoret) is the earliest Christian witness to the use of the term *hyperousios: Thes.* 3, 36B; *Dial. Trin.* 2, 434C; *In Jo.* 1.5 on Jn 1:3, 48c (cf. Theodoret, *Cant.* 2 on Song 3:4, PG 81, 116C). *Hyperousios* was a comparatively recent term. Surprisingly, it is not found in Plotinus, but occurs for the first time in a commentary on the *Parmenides* now attributed (by H.D. Saffrey) to his disciple, Porphyry (*In Parmenidem* 2.11). Boulnois thinks that Cyril may have borrowed the term directly from Porphyry. With Dionysius the Areopagite it was to become a key

term of apophatic theology. For further details, see Boulnois (1994), 229–32, 593.

51 *In Jo.* 3.2 on Jn. 5:37–8, 259d–260a.

52 *Dial. Trin.* 5, 558ab.

53 *In Jo.* 11.2 on Jn. 16:25, 938a.

54 Boulnois (1994), 114.

55 For a detailed discussion of these images, see Boulnois (1994), 115–77.

56 Light and radiance (drawing on Wisd. 7:26 and Heb. 1:3) is the oldest and most widely used image (cf. Justin, *Dial.* 128; Clement Alex. *Prot.* 10, *Strom.* 7.2; Origen, *hom. 9.4 in Jer., Com. Jo.* 13.25; Athanasius, *De Decr.* 23). Hippolytus first mentions water from the spring (*C. Noet.* 11.1). Clement (*Strom.* 4.25) and Origen (*Com. Jo.* 1.38) both compare the Father and the Son to intellect and word. Origen also makes use of the root image (frag. 69 *in Jo.*). With the outbreak of the Arian controversy these images begin to be used with greater frequency. Athanasius presents an especially rich collection, drawn from his predecessor, Dionysius of Alexandria (*De sententia Dion.* 15, 18, 23 and 25). Among the more extended discussions of particular images those of Ps.-Athanasius (= Marcellus of Ancyra) on spring and stream (*Exp. Fidei* 2) and of Gregory of Nyssa on light and radiance (*C. Eunom.* 8.1) are especially noteworthy.

57 On this image, see Boulnois (1994), 159–70.

58 *In Is.* 2.4 on Is. 11:1–3, PG 70, 309C–313A (translated below).

59 *Dial. Trin.* 3, 501e.

60 *Dial. Trin.* 6, 593b.

61 *In Jo.* 11.1 on Jn. 16:14, 929c.

62 *In Jo.* 11.2 on Jn. 16:16, 931e.

63 *In Jo.* 11.2 on Jn. 16:16, 932b.

64 *In Jo.* 11.11 on Jn. 17:20–1, 996e. Cf. Boulnois (1994), 257–60.

65 *Dial. Trin.* 1, 383b, 386ab.

66 The following paragraphs are indebted to Boulnois' detailed discussion of Cyril's trinitarian terminology (Boulnois [1994], 287–331).

67 *Dial. Trin.* 1, 391a.

68 *Dial. Trin.* 1, 392c.

69 *Dial. Trin.* 1, 395a.

70 *Dial. Trin.* 1, 408d–409b.

71 On the Cappadocian contribution, see Boulnois (1994), 296–7, 305–6.

72 Boulnois (1994), 309: 'The first term is more metaphysical, the second more phenomenological.' In the language of Cyril's day one might say that *hypostasis* belongs properly to *theologia* ('knowledge of God'), while *prosōpon* is more appropriate to *oikonomia* (the 'economy of salvation'), *theologia* referring to God as he is in himself, *oikonomia* to God's self-disclosure in time, particularly his

accommodation to the human situation through the dispensation of the Incarnation.

73 On the use of this term, see Louth (1989) and Boulnois (1994) 313–31.

74 Boulnois (1994), 322, dissenting from the sharp contrast between Cyrillian and Cappadocian usage drawn by Louth.

75 Boulnois (1994), 314.

76 *Dial. Trin.* 2, 432c.

77 *Dial. Trin.* 3, 471e; 4, 516d, 523e; *In Jo.* 1.2 on Jn. 1:1, 17a; 11.7 on Jn. 17:6–8, 962a; *C. Jul.* 1.26, 532D–533A. On Cyril's exegesis of these texts and his patristic antecedents, see Boulnois (1994), 134 n.27, 270.

78 I.e. the same approach as that of Athanasius in his *Discourses against the Arians*.

79 *Thes.* 7, 84BC; cf. *Dial. Trin.* 2, 454ab; Athanasius, *C. Ar.* 3.60–6.

80 *Thes.* 11, 149C; 32, 553BC; cf. Athanasius, *C. Ar.* 1.33–4; Boulnois (1994), 394–402.

81 *Dial. Trin.* 2, 423ab; cf. *Dial. Trin.* 7, 640e.

82 *Thes.* 596A; 604B; *Dial. Trin.* 6, 593d; *In Jo.* 9.1 on Jn. 14:16–17, 811a.

83 *In Jo.* 10 on Jn. 14:23, 832a.

84 *Thes.* 596A.

85 *Thes.* 34, 608B.

86 On these and other related terms in Cyril's writings, see esp. Theodorou (1974), who conveniently assembles all the relevant passages.

87 I am aware of only one exception to the rule, dating from the beginning of the Nestorian controversy: in a clear reference to the temporal mission of the Spirit, Cyril says that the Son sends him 'who is from him and is his own' (*to ex autou te kai idion autou*) (*Orat. ad Theod.*, ACO I, 1, 1, p. 66.24). Cf. Boulnois (1994), 510.

88 *In Jo.* 9.1 on Jn. 14:11, 784b.

89 *In Jo.* 5.2 on Jn. 7:39, 472ab; cf. the large number of parallel passages listed by Theodorou (1974), 37–40. In characterizing the Spirit as the *idion* of the Son, Cyril follows Athanasius; cf. *Ep. ad Serap.* 1.2 (PG 26, 533B).

90 *De adorat.*, 148A; cf. *Orat. ad Augustas*, ACO I, 1, 5, p. 56.9.

91 Cf. *Thes.* 33, 569C; *Thes.* 34, 576D–577A, 580BC; *Dial. Trin.* 6, 1012C.

92 The nine passages listed by A. Theodorou are: *In Ps.* 93:14 (PG 69, 1236BC); *In Is.* 57:15–16 (PG 70, 1276B); *In Lc.* 3:21 (PG 72, 521BC); *In Lc.* 11:20 (PG 72, 704AB); *Thes.* 34 (PG 75, 589AB, 617B); *C. Thdt.*, anathema 9, (ACO I, 1, 6, pp. 134.29–135.4); *C. Jul.* 1 (PG 76, 533AB); *Ep.* 55 (ACO I, 1, 4, p. 60.21–4) (Theodorou [1974], 14–18). Whether Cyril knew of the conciliar definition of the procession of the Holy Spirit made at Constantinople in 381 is difficult to determine. The creed read out at the Council of Ephesus (431)

was that of Nicaea, which ends simply: 'And in the Holy Spirit'. The Niceno-Constantinopolitan Creed, which expands the clause on the Spirit ('And in the Holy Spirit, the Lord and Giver of Life, who proceeds from the Father, who with the Father and the Son is worshipped and glorified, who spoke by the prophets') was acknowledged as the creed of an ecumenical council for the first time only in 451, when it was read out at Chalcedon. Cyril never refers to it explicitly, although his treatment of the clause on the Spirit in his letter on the creed (*Ep.* 55) bears some resemblance to it: 'For he is consubstantial with them and is poured forth, or rather, proceeds from God the Father as if from a source, and is bestowed on creation through the Son' (ACO I, 1, 4, p. 60.21–4). Boulnois thinks Cyril may have been aware of the conciliar definition (Boulnois [1994], 509), but this seems to me unlikely. His phraseology is of a piece with his other writings; cf. esp. *Dial. Trin.* 6, 1009B, 1012C.

93 *In Is.* 5.3 on Is. 57:15–16 (PG 70, 1276B).
94 *C. Thdt.*, anathema 9, ACO I, 1, 6, p. 134.9–15.
95 *C. Thdt.*, anathema 9, ACO I, 1, 6, p. 135, 1–4; cf. *Dial.* 6, 1009B.
96 Of all the Greek Fathers Cyril is the easiest to accommodate to the Western position on the *Filioque*. The consensus of scholars today, however, is that the passages often cited in the past in support of the *Filioque* all in fact refer to the economic Trinity: cf. Theodorou (1974); de Halleux (1979); Berthold (1989); Larchet (1998), 44–52. The exception is Boulnois (1994), 500–27. Noting the fluid way in which Cyril passes from the 'economy' to 'theology' and back again, she is the most inclined to assume (in the Western manner) that the economic Trinity must reflect the immanent Trinity, although she too concedes that Cyril cannot be interpreted as a 'Filioquist'.

3 THE NESTORIAN CONTROVERSY

1 Socrates, *Eccl. Hist.* 7.29. The older accounts of Nestorius' career in Bethune-Baker (1908), Loofs (1914), Duchesne (1924), 219–70, and Prestige (1940), 120–49 are still of value; see also Holum (1982), 147–74; Young (1983), 229–40; and McGuckin (1994), 20–53, and (1996).
2 Nestorius' birthplace is given by Socrates, *Eccl. Hist.* 7.29. Germanicia later reverted to its ancient name of Maraş, by which it is still known. Today, as Kahraman Maraş it is the capital of a vilayet in south-east Turkey. The monastery of Euprepius is mentioned by Evagrius, *Eccl. Hist.* 1.7.
3 Socrates, *Eccl. Hist.* 7.29.
4 Memorandum of the bishops in Constantinople, ACO I, 1, 2, p. 65. 25–p. 66.5; cf. Nestorius, *Book of Heraclides* 2.1, 375–7, 382–3 (Nau [1910], 241–3, 245–6).

5 On Pulcheria, see Holum (1982), 79ff; Limberis (1994), 47–61.

6 Barhadbeshabba (Nau [1913], 565–6).

7 *Lettre à Cosme* (Nau [1916], 279). Pulcheria's protest is intelligible in the light of a sermon of Bishop Atticus (who had administered the vow of chastity to Pulcheria and her sisters) who said that the consecrated women would receive Christ in the womb of faith. See Holum (1982), 139–40, who supplies full references.

8 Limberis (1994), 55.

9 Letter of Nestorius to John of Antioch (Loofs [1905], 185); cf. *Book of Heraclides* 1.2, 151–2 (Nau [1910], 91–2).

10 *Book of Heraclides* 1.2, 152 (Nau [1910], 92).

11 Socrates, *Eccl. Hist.* 7.32.

12 Ibid.

13 On the festival of virginity (*parthenikē panēgyris*), which Proclus says is the day's feast, see Limberis (1994), 51–2. The year is given by the *Chronicle* of Theophanes (a.m. 5923) as the first of Nestorius' episcopate.

14 ACO I, 1, 1, p. 103. 14–17.

15 ACO I, 1, 1, p. 107. 17–22.

16 Loofs (1905), 337. For Nestorius' reply, see ACO I, 5, pp. 37–9.

17 Passages are preserved in Cyril's *Against Nestorius*, ACO I, 1, 6, pp. 13–106; Loofs (1905), 225–97.

18 ACO I, 1, 6, p. 18. 24–31; Loofs (1905), 277–8.

19 ACO I, 1, 1, pp. 101–2.

20 *Hom. Pasch.* 17.3, 8 (SC 434, 272 = PG 77, 777C). Cyril uses the 'Theotokos' title only twice before the controversy with Nestorius, at *In Zach.* 5.13 (Pusey [1868], ii. 506.19) and *In Is.* 4.4 (PG 70, 1036D), unless, as is likely, both are interpolations.

21 *Ep.* 1, ACO I, 1, 1, pp. 10–23; trans. McEnerney (1987) i, 13–33; McGuckin (1994), 245–61.

22 ACO I, 1, 1, p. 23. 26–7.

23 *Ep.* 2, ACO I, 1, 1, pp. 23–5; trans. McEnerney (1987), i, 34–6.

24 *Ep.* 3, ACO I, 1, 1, p. 25. 6–16; trans. McEnerney (1987), i, 37.

25 As Pelagianism was a much more important issue in the West than in the East, Nestorius was probably unaware that he was touching a very raw nerve not only on the jurisdictional but also on the dogmatic level. Cyril, by contrast, through an exchange of letters with Augustine of Hippo, was much better informed than Nestorius and was able to use the Pelagian issue to consolidate his relationship with Celestine by drawing a parallel between Pelagianism and Nestorianism. For references and further details see Wickham (1989).

26 E. Schwartz has argued in an influential study that the Nestorian controversy arose from purely political motives. In Schwartz's view, Nestorius welcomed the opportunity to investigate the complaints of the Alexandrian dissidents because he was interested in extending the appellate jurisdiction of Constantinople. Cyril reacted with alarm to what he saw as a threat to the pre-eminence of Alexandria in the

Greek East, and cynically transferred the conflict to the theological arena, where he was on much stronger ground. (Schwartz [1928]. For a more recent statement of this view, see Holum [1982], 151–2.) Political considerations were certainly important. Cyril was as opposed as any Roman pope to having his decisions reviewed by the bishop of Constantinople. But as his *Commentary on John* shows, he was already hostile towards the Antiochene christological tradition before Nestorius appeared on the scene. At most, the need to counter Nestorius' canonical moves prompted Cyril to act sooner rather than later. On this, see the important discussion in Chadwick (1951).

27 *Ep.*11, ACO I, 1, 5, p. 11. 6–10; trans. McEnerney (1987), i, 61; McGuckin (1994), 277.

28 ACO II, 1, p. 104: the month of Mechir (= 26 January–24 February), Indiction 13 (=430).

29 *Ep.* 4.7, ACO I, 1, 1, p. 28. 12–22; trans. Wickham (1983), 9–11. For Nestorius' reply, see ACO I, 1, 1, pp. 29–32; trans. S. Hall in Stevenson (1989), 298–9, McEnerney (1987), i, 43–8, and McGuckin (1994), 364–8. Nestorius was later to claim that the phrase *kath' hypostasin* was unintelligible to him (*Book of Heraclides* 1.3, 226 [Nau (1910), 136]). Like *mia physis* ('one nature'), it has an Apollinarian background. See Richard (1945) and Chadwick (1951), 146–7.

30 The *De Recta Fide*. G.M. de Durand has demonstrated the priority of the *Dialogue on the Incarnation*: '*Theotokos*', for example, is absent from the Dialogue but appears four times in the *De Recta Fide* (De Durand [1964], 42–51).

31 *Oratio ad Augustas*, ACO I, 1, 5, pp. 26–61; *Oratio ad Dominas*, ACO I, 1, 5, pp. 62–118.

32 Letter of Theodosius to Cyril, ACO I, 1, 1, p. 73. 22–4.

33 *Ep.* 11, ACO I, 1, 5, pp. 10–12; trans. McGuckin (1994), 276–9.

34 *Ep.* 144, ACO I, 1, 1, pp. 75–7.

35 ACO I, 1, 1, pp. 77–83.

36 ACO I, 1, 5, pp. 7–10.

37 *Ep.* 17, ACO I, 1, 1, pp. 33–42; trans. Wickham (1983), 13–33.

38 ACO I, 1, 1, p. 89.16.

39 For the date, see Wickham (1983), 13, n.1, who refers to ACO I, 2, p. 51.33. McGuckin gives 6 December 430 but without any reference. He then paints a graphic scene in which the delegates 'entered the cathedral at the most dramatic moment they could choose' and delivered the letters to Nestorius enthroned in the apse (McGuckin [1994], 46). If McGuckin is basing his account on the testimony given by Theopemptus of Cabasa, the leader of the delegation, at Ephesus on 22 June 431 (ACO I, 1, 2, p. 37. 8–22), he has misread the word '*episkopeion*', which in the context must mean the residence, not the throne, of the bishop.

40 Letter of John of Antioch to Nestorius, ACO I, 1, 1, pp. 93–6.

41 In reply to Andrew: *Adversus orientales episcopos* (ACO I, 1, 7,

pp. 33–65); in reply to Theodoret: *Contra Theodoretum* (ACO I, 1, 6, pp. 107–46).

42 It should not be forgotten that Apollinarius, although usually described as belonging to the Alexandrian school, was in fact an Antiochene. He was bishop of the port Laodicea, which along with Antioch, Apamea and Seleucia was one of the great cities of the Syrian tetrapolis. The Antiochenes, after their hard struggle against Apollinarius' Logos-flesh christology, were highly sensitive to anything which seemed to suggest it. Cyril, on the other hand, encapsulated within his Alexandrian tradition, was naturally not worried by it. Cf. Grillmeier (1975), 416: 'Apollinarianism and the church's struggle against it seem to be virtually unknown to the author of the *Thesaurus* and the *Dialogues*.'

43 Letter to Cledonius (*Ep.* 101), PG 37, 181C.

44 Brief but illuminating characterizations of the two approaches may be found in Norris (1982) and O'Keefe (1997). For a good recent account of Cyril's christology, see McGuckin (1994), 175–226. McGuckin is less satisfactory on Nestorius, however, for whom see still Bethune-Baker (1908); Loofs (1914); Sellers (1940), 107–201; Scipioni (1974), 94–148. Cf. Grillmeier (1975), 443–83, whose attribution of a *logos-sarx* christological model to the early Cyril, however, has been widely criticized (e.g. by Welch [1994], 40–2).

45 PGL, s.v. *physis* IIIB.

46 PGL, s.v. *hypostasis* III.

47 PGL, s.v. *prosōpon* XD.

48 Apollinarius' phrase occurs in *Ep. Jov.* 1 (Lietzmann, p. 250.7; PG 28, 28A). On Cyril's relationship to Apollinarius, see Galtier (1956), and Young (1983), 258–63. Cf. McGuckin's comments (1994), 85.

49 *C. Nest.* 2 prooem., ACO I, 1, 6, p. 33.7; cf. *C. Nest.* 2.8, ACO I, 1, 6, p. 46.29.

50 *Adv. Apollin.* 4, cited by Grillmeier (1975), 434.

51 *Ep.* 44, ACO I, 1, 4, p. 35.14; trans. Wickham (1983), 63.

52 *Ep.* 46.3, Second Letter to Succensus, ACO I, 1, 6, pp. 159. 11–160.7; trans. Wickham (1983), 87–9.

53 Wickham (1983), 89, n.3.

54 On the history and use of the term see Michel (1922); Jouassard (1962). The expression itself was first used in the sixth century by the defenders of Chalcedonian christology but the substance of the theory is found before Cyril in Origen (*De Princ.* 1.2.6), Athanasius (*Ep. Adelph.* 3), Epiphanius (*Ancor.* 93), Apollinarius (*Ep. Jov.*) and Gregory of Nyssa (*C. Eunom.* 5). Perhaps the clearest statement by Cyril himself is in *Hom. Pasch.* 17.2 (SC 474, 266 –8 = PG 77, 776AB).

55 *Ep.* 17.8, ACO I, 1, 1, p. 38. 3–22; Wickham (1983), 23–5.

56 *Book of Heraclides* 2.1, 324–5; (Nau [1910], 206–7).

57 Loofs (1905), 280–1; *C. Nest.* 2..6, ACO I, 1, 6, p. 42. 1–3.

58 Loofs (1905), 289; *C. Nest.* 2.4, ACO I, 1, 6, p. 39. 10ff.

59 *Chr. Un.* 732E, de Durand (1964), 362; trans. McGuckin (1995), 73.

60 *C. Nest.* 1, prooem. 1, ACO I, 1, 6, p. 17. 24–7.

61 *C. Nest.* 1.1, ACO I, 1, 6, p. 18. 9–11.

62 *C. Nest.* 2.8, ACO I, 1, 6, p. 46. 35–7.

63 *C. Nest.* 4.5, ACO I, 1, 6, p. 84. 33–5.

64 *C. Nest.* 4.5, ACO I, 1, 6, p. 85. 27–31.

65 *C. Nest.* 3.2, ACO I, 1, 6, p. 60. 16–20.

66 Cyril wrote his first letter home from Rhodes, *Ep.* 20, ACO I, 1, 1, p. 116. Shenoute is not mentioned by Cyril or any Greek source. We know of his attendance at Ephesus only from his own writings (Sinuthius, *De modest. cleric.*, CSCO 96, p. 16.29–30) and the Coptic *Life* (128–30) by his disciple Besa. He was the severe but charismatic abbot of the White Monastery at Atripe in Upper Egypt, which during his abbacy housed more than 2,000 monks. It has been suggested that Cyril took Shenoute to Ephesus simply in order to provide himself with a monastic bodyguard (Bell [1983], 16–17). As a significant theologian in his own right, however, and probably the most powerful ecclesiastic in Egypt after Cyril himself, Shenoute would naturally have been included in Cyril's party. On Shenoute as a theologian, see now Grillmeier (1996), 167–228.

67 On the relative strengths of the parties, see John of Antioch's report to the emperor, ACO I, 1, 5, p. 126. 28–30.

68 The documents are listed in ACO I, 1, 1, pp. 3–9; there is a selection, translated by A. Meredith (with facing Greek text) in Tanner (1990), 40–74, and another selection, by a nineteenth century translator, in Percival (1899), 191–242. For discussions of the council, see Scipioni (1974), 149–298; Grillmeier (1975), 484–7; Wickham (1983), xxii–xxv; de Halleux (1993a); and McGuckin (1994), 53–107.

69 Candidian's duties are laid down in the sacra opening the council (ACO I, 1, 2, pp. 120. 25–121.8). Peter simply appears in the minutes from the start as *primkērios notariōn* (ACO I, 1, 2, p. 7. 34).

70 ACO I, 1, 2, p. 38. 7–11.

71 ACO I, 1, 1, p. 119. 5–19. John elaborates on the difficulties caused by heavy rain and shortage of supplies in his report to the emperor (ACO I, 1, 5, p. 125. 14–21).

72 Reported in Cyril's letter after the council to his clerical and monastic supporters in Constantinople, *Ep.* 23, ACO I, 1, 2, p. 67. 8–9.

73 Cyril gives a sanitized version of this episode in his report to the emperor (ACO I, 1, 3, p. 3.16 ff); cf. his report to Pope Celestine (ACO I, 1, 3, p. 6; trans. Percival [1899], 237–9), where he reveals that he suspected bad faith on John's part. On all the intrigue, see Schwartz (1928).

74 *Book of Heraclides* 1.2, 195 (Nau [1910], 117).

75 ACO I, 4, pp. 27–30; cf. Wickham (1983), xxiii, n.35.

76 ACO I, 1, 3, p. 15. 16–17.

77 ACO I, 1, 1, pp. 120–1. Candidian's account of the affair is given in

his relation to John of Antioch's council (ACO I, 1, 5, p. 119. 10–22, pp. 119. 29–120.3).

78 The ruins of the great double basilica are still to be seen in the north-west of the city. In spite of the crowds visiting Ephesus, it is an unfrequented, atmospheric spot.

79 ACO I, 1, 2, p.10. 1–13.

80 ACO I, 1, 2, pp. 7. 34–8.15. The minutes of the first session of the council (summarized in the following paragraphs) are in ACO I, 1, 2, pp. 3–64. For more detailed accounts, see McGuckin (1994), 75–89, and esp. de Halleux (1993a), who draws attention to the juridical character of the proceedings.

81 ACO I, 1, 2, pp. 8. 29–9.5.

82 ACO I, 1, 2, p. 9. 9–10.

83 ACO I, 1, 2, p. 13. 19–25.

84 ACO I, 1, 2, p. 13.19.

85 ACO I, 1, 2, p. 36. 26–8.

86 The *Explanation of the Twelve Chapters*, translated below.

87 It was the custom of the bishop of Constantinople to entertain the chief officers of state to lunch after the Sunday liturgy.

88 ACO I, 1, 2, p. 37. 8–24.

89 For Cyril, the Fathers, as Wickham remarks, 'are dead, orthodox bishops of unblemished life' (Wickham [1983], 3, n.3). Those quoted here are Athanasius, *C. Ar.* 3, 33 and *Ep. Epict.* 2; Julius and Felix of Rome; Theophilus of Alexandria's fifth and sixth festal letters; Cyprian, *De op. et elemos.* 1; Ambrose, *De fide* 1.94 and 2.77; Gregory of Nazianzus' *Ep.* 101 to Cledonius; Basil the Great, *De spir.* 5. 18; and Gregory of Nyssa, *Or. 1 de beatit.* The Latins were presumably put in to please Rome. The most important testimonies are those of Athanasius and Gregory of Nazianzus.

90 The letter of Capreolus brought to the fathers of the Council the first news of the death of Augustine of Hippo in the previous year (ACO I, 1, 2, p. 52.23).

91 Cyril's proposal: ACO I, 1, 2, p. 54. 11–12. The deed, or *psēphos*, of deposition: ACO I, 1, 2, pp. 54–64; trans. A. Meredith (omitting the signatories) in Tanner (1990), 61–2.

92 *Ep.* 24, ACO I, 1, 1, pp. 117–18, item 28. It was very likely on the following Sunday that Cyril delivered his famous Marian homily in the church of Mary the *Theotokos*. The authenticity of this homily was denied by Schwartz (ACO I, 1, 2, p.102; I, 1, 4, p.XXV; I, 1, 8, p.12) but has been ably defended by M. Santer, who suggests Sunday 28 June or Sunday 12 July (after the arrival of the Roman legates) as likely dates, with the balance of probability falling on the former (Santer, 1975, 149–50).

93 ACO I, 1, 2, p. 64, item 63.

94 Formal notification: ACO I, 1, 2, pp. 64–5, item 65. Cyril's personal letter to the archimandrite Dalmatius and others: ACO I, 1, 2, p. 66, item 67.

95 Synod: ACO I, 1, 3, pp. 3–5; Nestorius: ACO I, 1, 5, p. 13, item 146 (= Loofs [1905], 186–90); Candidian: ACO I, 1, 2, p. 68.5.

96 For the acts of John's council, see ACO I, 1, 5, pp. 119–24.

97 ACO I, 1, 5, pp. 122.15–123.3. For John's report to the emperor, see ACO I, 1, 5, pp. 125–7; cf. Memnon's letter to the clergy of Constantinople, ACO I, 1, 3, pp. 46–7.

98 For the text of the *psēphos*, see ACO I, 1, 5, pp. 122. 15–123.3; for the list of signatories ACO I, 1, 5, pp. 123.5–124.10.

99 ACO I, 1, 7, p. 74. 20–22. For the rescript brought by Palladius, see ACO I, 1, 3, pp. 9–10.

100 ACO I, 1, 7, p. 74. 22–3.

101 ACO I, 1, 7, p. 74. 23–6. For the sacra addressed to the council and delivered by Count John (the government had still not caught up with events at Ephesus, for the sacra is addressed to, amongst others, Pope Celestine, who was not there, and Augustine, who had died the year before), see ACO I, 1, 3, pp. 31–2.

102 For the acts of the second session, see ACO I, 1, 3, pp. 53–63, and for Celestine's letter to the council, ACO I, 1, 3, pp. 55–7. The most significant act of these later sessions was the recognition of the Church of Cyprus as an autocephalous church independent of Antioch (ACO I, 1, 7, pp. 118–22; trans. Tanner [1990], 68–9). Although the minutes do not record it, it is also likely that Pelagianism was formally condemned (cf. Wickham [1989], 200–201).

103 ACO I, 1, 3, p. 67.1. For the names of the delegates: ACO I, 1, 7, p. 77.39–40 (Easterners); ACO I, 1, 7, p. 72.4–5 (Cyrillians).

104 ACO I, 1, 7, p. 77.4.

105 ACO I, 1, 7, p. 77. 23–6.

106 ACO I, 1, 7, p. 70. 15–22.

107 ACO I, 1, 7, p. 71. 5–14; pp. 76.41–77.1. If he had not abandoned the struggle, Theodosius would probably have continued to support him.

108 ACO I, 1, 3, p. 67. 1–9; for the date: Socrates, *Eccl. Hist.* 7.37.

109 ACO I, 1, 7, p. 142.19–33.

110 Nestorius claims that Cyril bought his way out by bribes: *Book of Heraclides* 2.1, 388 (Nau [1910], 249).

111 ACO I, 3, p. 179.11.

112 An account of the events from Cyril's point of view is given in his letter to Acacius of Melitene, *Ep.* 40, ACO I, 1, 4, pp. 20–31; trans. Wickham (1983), 35–61. For modern discussions, see Abramowski (1955/56); Grillmeier (1975), 488–519; Holum (1982), 179–81 (for the political aspects); Wickham (1983), xxv–xxviii; and McGuckin (1994), 107–25.

113 Letter of Maximian to Cyril, ACO I, 1, 3, p. 71; Letter of Cyril to Maximian (*Ep.* 31), ACO I, 1, 3, pp. 72–4.

114 ACO I, 1, 3, pp. 75–90.

115 Letter of Theodosius to John, ACO I, 1, 4, pp. 3–5, esp. p. 4.8–14.

Aristolaus was also carrying a similar letter addressed to Cyril (ACO I, 1, 4, p. 4.15–16).

116 ACO I, 4, pp. 222–5.

117 ACO I, 4, pp. 224–5; cf. Batiffol (1919).

118 On 'tribune and notary', 'a senior officer in the Imperial Secretariat,' see Wickham (1983), 37, n.6. The presence of Maximus, an official on the staff of the Master of Offices, is mentioned by Acacius in a letter to Alexander of Hierapolis, ACO I, 1, 7, p. 146.36. His task was no doubt to implement, if necessary, the threat of coercion contained in the last paragraph of the emperor's letter to John (ACO I, 1, 4, p. 5.4–8).

119 Letter to Acacius of Beroea, ACO I, 1, 7, p. 146; letter to Symeon Stylites, ACO I, 1, 4, pp. 5–6. On the role of holy men as mediators, see Brown (1971) and (1995), 57–78.

120 ACO I, 1, 7, p. 146.29–30.

121 Letter to Acacius of Melitene (*Ep.* 40.3), ACO I, 1, 4, p. 21.22–4; trans. Wickham (1983), 37.

122 Letter to Acacius of Beroea (*Ep.* 33), ACO I, 1, 7, pp. 147–50; trans. McEnerney (1987), i, 128–35; McGuckin (1994), 336–42.

123 *Ep.* 33.8, ACO I, 1, 7, p. 149.32–3; trans. McGuckin (1994), 340. Cf. Archdeacon Ephiphanius' report that the Easterners are seeking that Cyril should anathematize his own chapters, 'which would be to put himself outside the catholic Church' (ACO I, 4, p. 222.17).

124 *Ep.* 33.11, ACO I, 1, 7, p. 150.31–6; trans. McGuckin (1994), 341.

125 *Ep.* 33.10, ACO I, 1, 7, p. 150.17–20; trans. McGuckin (1994), 341.

126 ACO I, 1, 7, p. 164.3.

127 ACO I, 1, 7, p. 163.20–21.

128 ACO I, 1, 7, pp. 151–2.

129 *Ep.* 40.4, ACO I, 1, 4, p. 22.10; trans. Wickham (1983), 39.

130 *Ep.* 40.4, ACO I, 1, 4, p. 22.6.

131 *Libellus* of Paul of Emesa, ACO I, 1, 4, pp. 6–7. Cf. Cyril's letter to Acacius of Melitene (*Ep.* 40.4), ACO I, 1, 4, p. 22. 16–17; trans. Wickham (1983), 41.

132 *Ep.* 39, ACO I, 1, 4, pp. 15–20; trans. McEnerney (1987), i, 147–52; Stevenson (1989), 313–17; McGuckin (1994), 343–8.

133 ACO I, 1, 4, pp. 9–11.

134 ACO I, 1, 4, p. 10.11–12.

135 ACO I, 1, 4, p. 10.15–22.

136 *Ep.* 39.5, ACO I, 1, 4, p. 17.9–20; trans. Wickham (1983), 222.

137 These two points had been emphasized in Theodoret's last sermon at the colloquy at Chalcedon, ACO I, 1, 7, pp. 82–3.

138 ACO I, 1, 4, pp. 7–9, esp. p. 9. 9–14.

139 *Ep.* 40, ACO I, 1, 4, pp. 20–30; trans. Wickham (1983), 35–61; McEnerney (1987), i, 153–67.

140 ACO I, 1, 7, p. 156.34–7; cf. Cyril's remarks to Acacius of Melitene, *Ep.* 40.20, ACO I, 1, 4, p. 29.16–19; trans. Wickham (1983), 57.

141 *Ep.* 40.20, ACO I, 1, 4, p. 29.19–20.

142 *Epp.* 45 and 46, ACO I, 1, 6, pp. 151–62; trans. Wickham (1983), 71–93; McEnerney (1987), i, 190–204; McGuckin (1994), 352–63.

143 *Ep.* 45.2, ACO I, 1, 6, p. 151.15–19.

144 *Ep.* 55, ACO I, 1, 4, pp. 49–61; trans. Wickham (1983), 95–131; McEnerney (1987), ii, 15–36.

145 Text and trans. Wickham (1983), 132–79.

146 Text and trans. Wickham (1983), 180–213.

147 *Ep.* 70, PG 77, 341; trans. McEnerney (1987), ii, 68–9.

148 *Against Diodore and Theodore*: Greek and Syriac frags. in Latin trans., PG 76, 1437–52; additional frags., Pusey (1872), 5, 492–537. Trans. Pusey (1881) (Library of the Fathers of the Church, 47). In M. Richard's judgement it is a hasty work showing lack of erudition on Cyril's part (Richard [1946], 114–15). On Cyril's attitude to Diodore and Theodore in this period, see Abramowski (1955/56).

149 Frags. in Pusey (1872), 5, 476–91; trans. Pusey (1881) (Library of the Fathers of the Church, 47); cf. Wickham (1983), 110, n.5.

150 Text ed. de Durand (1964); trans. McGuckin (1995).

151 Cyril gives indications in his letters of how his books circulated. He would send copies as gifts to his correspondents; see the letters to Celestine (*Ep.* 11, ACO I, 1, 5, p. 12.19–22; trans. McGuckin [1994], 279) and Succensus (*Ep.* 45.12, ACO I, 1, 6, p. 157.9–15; trans. Wickham [1983], 83). His agents in Constantinople also kept copies for distribution; see the letter to Eulogius (Ep. 44, ACO I, 1, 4, p. 37.3–14; trans. Wickham (1983), 67–8).

152 Text: Burguière and Evieux (1985) for books 1 and 2; PG 76, 613–1064 for books 3 to 10 and fragments. Wickham (1983), xix, n.21, suggests that Cyril wanted to cap Theodore of Mopsuestia's refutation of Julian.

153 As Evieux suggests, in Burguière and Evieux (1985), 15.

154 *Ep.* 79, PG 77, 364–5; trans. McEnerney (1987), ii, 97–8.

155 Text and trans. Wickham (1983), 214–21; cf. the definition of the Council of Ephesus against the Messalians, ACO I, 1, 7, pp. 117–18 (trans. Tanner [1990], 66–7). The Messalians, or Euchites, were a spiritualizing sect with dualist tendencies given to a life of intense prayer. The Meletians were another rigorist schismatic group who had originated in 306 in the opposition of Meletius, bishop of Lycopolis, to the bishop of Alexandria's lenient ruling on receiving back Christians who had lapsed under pressure of persecution.

156 PG 65, 160A–C, Daniel 3.

157 *Haer.* 55 (CGS 31); cf. *Nag Hammadi Library*, Melchizedek (IX, 1).

158 Nestorius knew and approved of Leo's *Tome to Flavian* but he died before the Council of Chalcedon (451). On his sufferings in exile and his death, see Evagrius, *Eccl. Hist.* 1.7; 2.2.

159 *The Book of Heraclides*, the title by which Nestorius' apologia is generally known, does not survive in the original Greek. The Syriac version, sometimes called *The Bazaar of Heracleides*, owes its curious

name to a mistranslation (by J.F. Bethune-Baker, and subsequently taken up by Driver and Hodgson) of the Syriac translation (*tegurta*) of the original Greek title, which must have been *pragmateia*, 'treatise'. This version was made in the sixth century and a copy was preserved in the library of the patriarch of the Assyrian Church of the East at Kotchanes (Qodshanes), in Eastern Turkey. The original manuscript perished during the First World War, but a copy had been made in 1888 by a member of the American Presbyterian mission at Lake Urmia in Iran, and another in 1898 from the American copy by a member of the Anglican mission in the same region. The text was brought to Western attention first by Bethune-Baker (on the basis of the Anglican copy) in 1908, and then by P. Bedjan and F. Nau (on the basis of the American copy) in the Syriac edition and a French translation both published in 1910. According to L. Abramowski (1963), the text consists of two works, an apologia by Nestorius and a piece by a later author. This view has been challenged by Scipioni (1974) but not refuted decisively (see the discussion in Grillmeier [1975], Appendix, 559–68).

4 THE CYRILLIAN LEGACY

1 For the history and theological discussions of this period the fundamental studies are the essays in the first volume of Grillmeier and Bacht (1951–2), and the surveys in Frend (1972) and the successive volumes of Grillmeier: (1975), 520–57, (1987), (1995) and (1996). For a brief sketch see Meyendorff (1975), 13–46, and for a helpful diagram of the different theological positions, Brock (1996), 27. Cf. also Sellers (1953); Gray (1979), who argues strongly for the Cyrillian character of Chalcedon; and Torrance (1988).

2 On the meaning of *mia physis* in the fifth and early sixth centuries, see Lebon (1951), 478–91. Cf. Grillmeier (1995), 153–60; (1996), 31–5.

3 Letter to Pulcheria (*Ep.* 95) of 20 July 451 (ACO II, 4, p. 51.4).

4 ACO II, 1, 2, pp. 129–30; trans. Grillmeier (1975), 544; Tanner (1990), 83–7.

5 The problems that followed Chalcedon were due in large part to differing perceptions of what had been achieved there. The West saw it as Leo's council. The Eastern bishops (who had acclaimed Leo's Tome on the grounds that it agreed with Cyril's teaching) saw it as a vindication of Cyril. The popular verdict, however, was that it had exonerated Nestorius. Cf. Frend (1972), 145–9; Gray (1979), 7–16.

6 The West tended to see all opponents of Chalcedon as Eutychians. The Eutychians, however, were a small minority, even in Egypt. The majority were unhappy about the council because it seemed to have betrayed Cyril. They were called by the Syrian Orthodox historian, John of Ephesus, 'the hesitants' (*hoi diakrinomenoi*) (*Hist. Eccl.* 2.37 and 47). It is only after the setting up of a separate hierarchy in the

mid-sixth century that the term 'Monophysites' was used. Cf. Frend (1972), 144.

7 On Timothy Aelurus, see Ebied and Wickham (1985); Grillmeier (1996), 7–35. Pope Leo I was convinced that Timothy was a Eutychian. Timothy, however, 'opposed the *Tome of Leo* and the definition of the council of Chalcedon because he found there the error of Nestorianism' (Lebon [1951], 492). After the council Cyril was quoted somewhat selectively by the anti-Chalcedonians, who made the *mia physis* formula the centre-piece of their christology. 'Timothy is regarded (probably with greater justification than Dioscorus) as the initiator of this development, which not only would produce a pointed, selective Cyrillism among his followers but also would force Chalcedonian theologians to interpret the council of 451 more in Cyril's spirit' (Grillmeier [1996], 16).

8 Evagrius, *Eccl. Hist.* 3.4; Schwartz (1927), 49–51; trans. Grillmeier (1987), 238–40.

9 Evagrius, *Eccl. Hist.* 3.14; Schwartz (1927), 52–4; trans. Grillmeier (1987), 252. Cf. Frend (1972), 177–83.

10 Grillmeier (1987), 288.

11 On the 'theopaschite controversy, see esp. Grillmeier (1995), 317–43. Cf. McGuckin (1984). The formula 'one of the Trinity suffered' is first found in Proclus, *Tome to the Armenians* 21 (ACO IV, 2, p. 192.7). A variant, 'one of the Trinity became incarnate', occurs in the *Henotikon* (para. 7). Severus of Antioch saw in the theopaschite formula 'the touchstone of "true faith"' (Grillmeier [1995], 319).

12 On 'neo-Chalcedonianism', see Moeller (1951), 666–96.

13 On the important figure of Severus of Antioch, see the detailed studies in Lebon (1951) and Grillmeier (1995), 21–175. There are shorter summaries in Frend (1972), 201–8 and Torrance (1988). Severus was leader of the anti-Chalcedonian opposition from 512 to 538. For him Cyril was *the* Church Father, 'the king of the explication of dogmas' (Grillmeier [1995], 21, with refs.).

14 Until Justinian forced their school to migrate eastwards, their intellectual centre was at Nisibis. They are often called the 'Nestorian Church' in spite of the fact that Nestorius did not set up his own church and has little to do with the Syriac-speaking Church of the East, whose fundamental teacher was Theodore of Mopsuestia. On the Western caricature of the Church of the East as the 'Nestorian Church', see Brock (1996) and the literature cited there.

15 In the twentieth century Cyril was also the subject of a papal encyclical. On the occasion of the fifteenth centenary of his death, Pope Pius XII, in *Orientalis Ecclesiae* (9 April 1944), held him up to Eastern Christians as a model of Church unity and cooperation with the Holy See.

16 Cf. Bethune-Baker (1908); Loofs (1914); Amann (1931) and (1949–50); Anastos (1962).

17 Brock (1996), 23.

GENERAL INTRODUCTION TO
THE TEXTS

1 Letter to Pope Celestine (*Ep.* 11), ACO I, 1, 5, p. 12.21.

2 Cardinal Bessarion possessed no fewer than three copies of *Against Julian* on account of its quotations from the Neoplatonist philosopher, Porphyry, which he donated in 1468 with most of his library to the senate of the Republic of Venice. They are now in the Biblioteca Marciana.

3 In a letter to the Venetian senator Francesco Barbaro, dated 25 April 1450 (text in E. Legrand [1962], 103). The manuscript used by George as his exemplar was Vat. gr. 593, which at that time belonged to Cardinal Bessarion.

4 An essay on the *Filioque* by Pusey serves as the introduction to his son's translation of the *Commentary on John* (Library of the Fathers of the Church, 43).

COMMENTARY ON ISAIAH

1 For the date of composition, see Jouassard (1945), 167–70; cf. Fernández Lois (1998), 49. It has been suggested that the commentary was originally a series of lectures given by Cyril to the clergy of Alexandria as part of their theological formation (Cassell [1992]; cf. Welch [1994], 11).

2 *In Is.*, 9A.

3 There were others too. In his own preface Jerome mentions the now lost commentaries of Didymus and Apollinarius. John Chrysostom wrote a commentary, or rather a set of sermon notes, on Isaiah, which now survives in Greek only as far as Is. 8:10 and in a fuller but still incomplete Armenian version. Theodore of Mopsuestia also wrote a commentary that has perished apart from two *catenae* fragments. (For further details, see Dumortier [1983], 11; Gryson and Szmatula [1990]; Hollerich [1999], 14). Apollinarius, however, had been condemned more than thirty years previously; Didymus, whose eighteen volumes dealt only with Is. 40–66, had a highly allegorical exegetical style quite different from that of Cyril; and the Antiochenes, even before the christological controversy, are not likely to have appealed to him.

4 On Eusebius' commentary (ed. Ziegler [1975]), see Hollerich (1999).

5 For Jerome see Adriaen (1963) and PL 24, 9–678; for Ps.–Basil, PG 30, 117–668. R. Gryson (1993–8) has prepared a critical edition of Jerome's commentary.

6 These are in the Prologue (9A, 13B) and in the commentary on Is. 6:2 (173C), 6:3 (176A) and 7:14 (204B). For other passages in the

Commentary on Isaiah not translated here, see Abel (1941), 226–8, Kerrigan (1952), 246–50, 435–9, and Fernández Lois (1998), 61. Further evidence of Jerome's influence on Cyril has been provided by J.J. O'Keefe, with regard to Cyril's commentary on Malachi, and by M.C. Pennacchio, with regard to Cyril's interpretation of Hosea 13:8 (cf. O'Keefe [1993]; Pennacchio [1995]).

7 Cf. Abel (1941); Kerrigan (1952), 435–9; Fernández Lois (1998), 58–62. Kerrigan says that although sceptical at first of Abel's arguments, he became convinced as a result of his own researches that Cyril had indeed been influenced by Jerome (Kerrigan [1952], 435). Fernández Lois, the most recent researcher, has informed me that he believes that although it is not an absolute certainty, there is a strong probability that Jerome's biblical commentaries exercised a direct influence on Cyril. He bases his judgement on (1) the exegetical similarity of various passages in Cyril and Jerome, (2) the cultural interchange between Palestine and Alexandria, and (3) the existence of a group of translators in Alexandria. There is also reason to believe, as Wickham points out, that Cyril knew Jerome's *Dialogues against the Pelagians* (Wickham [1989], 203).

8 Abel (1941), 97; (1947), 227–8. Cf. Kelly (1975), 244–6, 259–61. Jerome had also had contacts with Didymus, who dedicated his commentary on Hosea to him (*De vir. illust.* 109).

9 *Ep.* 11a, ACO I, 1, 7, p. 12.21.

10 ACO I, 2, pp. 5.22–6.3 and p. 7.24.

11 ACO I, 2, p. 7.21–5.

12 I am indebted to Abel Fernández Lois for much of the information summarized in these introductory paragraphs.

13 Cf. Jerome, *In Is.*, Prol. 1 (PL 24, 18B): 'the present scriptural book contains the entire mysteries of the Lord'. On the parallels between the prologues of Cyril and Jerome, see Fernández Lois (1998), 101.

14 Or historical sense: *tēs historias to akribes*.

15 I.e. the inner religious and supernatural dimension: *tēs pneumatikes theōrias tēn apodosin*. The same two hermeneutic levels are mentioned by Jerome: 'Hence after the historical truth, all things are to be received in a spiritual sense' (*In Is.*, Prol. 3, PL 24, 20B).

16 Cf. Jerome, *In Is.*, Prol. 1 (PL 24, 18A): 'I shall expound Isaiah in such a way as to show him to be not only a prophet, but also an evangelist and an apostle'.

17 I have omitted the *historia* as it simply expands the material from Kings and Chronicles which Cyril gives in his preface.

18 On Cyril's opposition to anthropomorphism, see the first of his *Replies to Tiberius*, Wickham (1983), 136.

19 Wisdom (*sophia*) is feminine in Greek.

20 *Emprēstai ētoi thermainontes.* Cf. Jerome: 'The word "seraphim", however, is translated as *emprēstai*, which we may render as "fiery" or "burning", in accordance with that which we read elsewhere: "Who

made his angels spirits and his ministers burning fire"' (Ps. 103:5), (In Is. 6:2, PL 24, 93C–94A). Cf. Kerrigan (1952), 313–14, who remarks that 'the etymology resembles that given by Jerome, but the subsequent applications of the two exegetes differ considerably'.

21 Cyril's interpretation follows that of Jerome: 'they say "Holy, Holy, Holy, Lord God of hosts" in order to demonstrate the mystery of the Trinity in a single divinity' (In Is. 6:2, PL 24, 94BC) who in turn has followed Eusebius. Eusebius corrects Origen, who sees in the seraphim images of the Son and the Spirit. Cyril on this point is followed by Theodoret: 'the "Holy, Holy, Holy" manifests the Trinity; the "Lord God of hosts" indicates the one nature' (Com. Is. 3.70–2, SC 276, 260–2). Cf. Fernández Lois (1998), 140–7.

22 Cyril returns to the symbol of the coal in C. Nest., 2 prooem. (ACO I, 1, 6, p. 33), translated below, and in Schol. Inc. 9 (ACO I, 5, p.221): 'the coal fulfils the function of a type and image for us of the incarnate Word'. The coal, incandescent with heat, is an image expressive of the communicatio idiomatum. Cyril here seems closer to Ps.-Basil (cf. In Is. 183, PG 30, 428C–429B; 186, 436BC) than to Eusebius and Jerome, who attribute to the coal a baptismal symbolism. Cf. Fernández Lois (1998), 203–6. Cyril's coal image later became a point of contention between Chalcedonians and anti-Chalcedonians, the Chalcedonian compiler of the Florilegium Cyrillianum claiming it as evidence for a two-natures teaching in Cyril, Severus of Antioch arguing that it was an image expressing the unity of Christ. See further, Grillmeier (1995), 82–7.

23 Aquila's version has neanis for parthenos. This is discussed at length by Jerome (PL 24, 108A–C), who also gives the Jewish interpretation mentioned below by Cyril: 'The Hebrews think that this is a prophecy referring to Hezekiah the son of Ahaz' (PL 24, 109C). Cf. Also Pseudo-Basil, In Is. 201, PG 30, 464AB. On the history of the exegesis of this verse, see Kamesar (1990).

24 Cyril characteristically connects the bestowal of the name 'Emmanuel' with Jn. 1:14. He returns to the theme in C. Nest. 2 prooem. (ACO I, 1, 6, p. 34), translated below. Cf. Fernández Lois (1998), 241–3, 273–5.

25 Cf. In Is. 3.5 on Is. 42:1–4 below (849C); Eusebius lies behind the image of the Church as the true Jerusalem: cf. Fernández Lois (1998), 349–53.

26 Aaron's rod of almond (or walnut) wood receives a christological interpretation from Cyril that is particularly imaginative. Gregory of Nyssa, for example, contents himself with drawing a parallel between the easy availability of almond wood as fuel for everybody and the efficacy of the wood of the cross as the instrument of salvation for everybody (In bapt. Christi, PG 46, 584A). Isidore of Pelusium, like Cyril, alludes to the astringent nature of the almond, but does not develop it as a christological image (Ep. 1.50, PG 78, 213A).

27 Cyril is alluding to 2 Chron. 29:6 (where 'neck' is translated as 'back' in the English versions); cf. Jer. 19:15. A 'tender neck' suggests itself to Cyril as an image for obedience in contrast to the 'stiff neck' which the biblical writers use as an image for disobedience.

28 Cyril seems to follow Jerome in referring the joy of the new creation to life in the Church. Cf. 'We can say this too, that having turned away from idolatry and abandoned their ancient error, they shall see a new heaven and a new earth' (*In Is.* 18.65 on Is. 65:18, PL 24, 645A). The more eschatological interpretation he mentions is characteristic of Eusebius (cf. *In Is.* 65 on Is. 65:18, PG 24, 513A).

COMMENTARY ON JOHN

1 On the dating see Mahé (1907), Jouassard (1945), and Liébaert (1951), 12–16.

2 On the history of the exegesis of the Fourth Gospel before Cyril, see Wiles (1960), 1–128.

3 Ed. Blanc (1966–92); trans. Menzies, ANF 10, 297–408. On the Gnostic use of John, see Pagels (1989).

4 Didymus, an admirer of Origen, was condemned along with Origen and Evagrius Ponticus by the Fifth Ecumenical Council in 553. Consequently, most of his works have perished. Fragments of his commentary on John are preserved in PG 39, 1645–54.

5 The complete text of Theodore's commentary survives only in a Syriac version (Vosté, 1940) (Greek fragments in PG 66, 728–85). John Chrysostom's homilies occupy PG 59; trans. Stupart, NPNF, 1st series, 14, 1–334.

6 The passages attributable to Didymus in the *catenae* on John are too brief to permit any judgement to be made on whether they have influenced Cyril. The commentaries of Theodore and John Chrysostom appear to have been unknown to Cyril, although both of them were written from an anti-Arian polemical standpoint.

7 *Praef.*, 5cd.

8 *In Jo.* 9 on Jn. 13:21, 734b.

9 *In Jo.* 8 on Jn. 12:27, 705b.

10 *In Jo.* 9 on Jn. 14:10, 785d.

11 On this see Liébaert (1951), 101–38.

12 Grillmeier (1975), 417; cf. 474–6.

13 Welch (1994), 42–60.

14 Caution is necessary with regard to Books 7 and 8, as Pusey bases his text on only one family of *catenae* and has included some non-Cyrilline material. See Liébaert (1951) 133–7, and below, the excerpt from Book 8.

15 Christianity's claim to be the true Israel goes back to Justin Martyr (*Dialogue with Trypho* 123–4, cf. Lieu [1996], 136–7) if not to Paul

himself (cf. Rom. 9:6; Gal. 6:16). The inter-communal strife in Alexandria in Cyril's time lent emotional intensity to the claim (cf. Wilken [1971], 39–68).

16 The analogy of the first person of the Trinity as the sun and the second person as its radiance, which seeks to express the eternal generation of the Son from the *ousia* of the Father, has its roots in Heb. 1:3 but was developed first by Origen (cf. *De Princ.* 1.2.7, PG 11, 135).

17 The connection of Ps. 82:6, 'I said, you are gods' with Paul's teaching on adopted sonship derives from Irenaeus (*Adv. Haer.* 3.6.1; 3.19.1 and 4.38.4) and is taken up by Athanasius in the *Contra Arianos* (e.g. *C. Ar.* 1.9; 1.39; 3.19).

18 The view that the Holy Spirit was a creature and not of the same substance as Christ was first condemned as an Arian opinion at the Synod of Alexandria in 362. The letter of a synod held in Constantinople in 382, addressed to Pope Damasus and his synod in Rome, explaining the decisions of the Ecumenical Council of 381 confirmed the consubstantiality of the Spirit and condemned its opponents as semi-Arians or 'Pneumatomachians' (Tanner [1990], 25–30). In Cyril's day they were known as Macedonians, after Macedonius, deposed from the throne of Constantinople in 360 for holding semi-Arian views (Socrates, *Eccl. Hist.* 2.45). They had their own churches and ecclesiastical organization. Nestorius took action against them in Constantinople and the Hellespont region soon after he became bishop in 428 (ibid., 7.31).

19 Cyril characteristically makes soteriological concerns the starting-point for his theological argumentation. The first to quote 2 Pet. 1:4 as a text supporting the idea of the deification of the Christian was Origen (*De Princ.* 4.4.4; cf. *In Lev.* 4.4 and *In Rom.* 4.9). Athanasius also refers to the text, but it is Cyril who first brings it into prominence and combines it with Ps. 82:6 as the principal biblical text on which the doctrine of deification is founded. On the history of the exegesis of 2 Pet. 1:4, see Russell (1988), 52–60.

20 From a testimony drawing on several Old Testament passages (Ex. 25:8; 29:45; Lev. 26:12; Ez. 37:27; Jer. 31:1) quoted by Paul at 2 Cor. 6:16.

21 At 1 Cor. 3:16; 6:19; 2 Cor. 6:16. Cf. Eph. 2:21.

22 Cyril's second work against the Arians, the *Dialogues on the Holy Trinity*. Proofs of the divinity of the Holy Spirit are set out in Dialogue 7, ed. G.M. de Durand, SC 246 (1978).

23 On Cyril's bipartite anthropology, see Burghardt (1957), 19–24.

24 An image developed by Origen, *De Princ.* 2.6.6.

25 *Hōs idian echōn autēn.* On Cyril's use of the term *idios*, see esp. Louth (1989), and Boulnois (1994), 316–19, 327–9.

26 'One from both' (*heis ex amphoin*) is a phrase used more than once by Cyril in his commentary to sum up the union of the natures in the person of Christ (cf. *In Jo.* 3.5, 301b; 4.2, 363b [translated below]; 9,

747e). He seems to use it less, however, after the outbreak of the Nestorian controversy (cf. *C. Nest* 2, prooem. [ACO I, 1, 6, p. 33.13], translated below).

27 The Greek *en hēmin* is normally translated 'amongst us'. Here I have rendered it literally as 'in us' because Cyril wishes to bring out the reciprocal meanings of the Pauline phrases 'in Christ' and 'in us'.

28 On Christ's divine glory (*doxa*), which is veiled by the flesh yet at the same time manifested by it, see Dupré la Tour (1960–1); cf. Welch (1994), 69–72.

29 Cyril is the first to interpret the sixth chapter of John principally in eucharistic terms.

30 I have accepted Migne's correction and taken *echon* as a neuter, not a masculine, participle. Pusey's text reads: 'since he has within himself the entire power of the Word that is united with him, and it is endowed' etc.

31 Passages from this first chapter of Book 4 were read out at the Sixth Ecumenical Council of 680–1 as a patristic testimony against the Monothelete position.

32 *Hen de tē synodō kai tē aperinoētō syndromē*. On Cyril's use of *synodos* and *syndromē*, see de Durand (1964), 220–2, n.1. Almost the same phraseology is found in *Dial. Christ.* 688d, the passage on which de Durand comments. The two terms express not a coming together of two equal elements but a condescension of the Word towards the flesh.

33 Both senses of the word *logos* are intended here: the Word of God and the spoken word. Cyril presents a powerful argument against the Antiochene (and Leonine) custom of attributing the 'divine' actions and sayings of Christ to the divine nature and the 'human' actions and sayings to the human nature. Both kinds of action, the 'human' and the 'divine' are the work of the same theandric being.

34 On Cyril's use of this analogy with a list of parallel passages in other contexts, see Siddals (1987), 362–3.

35 The same point is developed in Cyril's Third Letter to Nestorius, 7 (Wickham [1983], 22); cf. Louth (1989), 201.

36 On Cyril's eucharistic doctrine in the *Commentary on John*, see esp. Welch (1994). See also Chadwick (1951) and Gebremedhin (1977), both of whom concentrate on the later period of the Nestorian controversy.

37 On Cyril's two-nature exegesis, see Wiles (1960), 129–45.

38 Most of the material omitted, although printed by Pusey as Cyril's text, is from the eleventh-century *catena* of Nicetas and almost certainly not by Cyril (see Liébaert [1951], 131–7).

39 Cyril is aware that there are two different readings of Jn. 12:28. The true reading is 'glorify thy name'. A number of manuscripts, including the one used by Cyril, read 'glorify thy Son', probably through the influence of Jn. 17:1. Modern commentators, unlike

those of an earlier generation, tend now to agree with Cyril that the two readings amount to the same thing, for the Father and the Son are one (cf. Bultmann [1971], 429–30).

40 The concluding paragraph of the Greek text printed by Pusey is omitted, as it has been inserted by the compiler of the *catena* from the *Thesaurus*. See Liébaert (1951), 131.

41 The following paragraphs were among the Cyrilline passages studied at the Council of Florence (1438–9) as patristic evidence for the double procession of the Holy Spirit. This and the other passages cited from the *Thesaurus* and the *Dialogues on the Trinity* were taken from the florilegium of the unionist patriarch of Constantinople, John Veccus (1275–82). The *Commentary on John* as a complete text seems to have been studied intensively only after the council. On the Cyrilline passages in the florilegia, see Meunier (1989).

42 *Idiosystatōs*, 'in his own person', or 'as an individual entity' is an adverbial expression frequently used by Cyril. It seems to be his own coinage unless the treatise *On the Trinity* attributed to Didymus the Blind (which contains a single instance of the word) really is by Didymus. Cf. *PGL*, s.v.

43 The Son's receiving the 'name' of the Father was problematic for the separate identity of the first two persons of the Trinity. Cyril interprets the 'name' in terms of glory by using Phil. 2:9 as a key to understanding John. Cf. M.-O. Boulnois' discussion of this passage (Boulnois [1994], 343–4).

AGAINST NESTORIUS

1 On the dating see Loofs (1905), 21; de Durand (1964), 24, n.1.

2 Paschal Letter 17 (SC 434 = PG 77, 768–98).

3 *Ep.* 1 (ACO I, 1, 1, pp. 10–23).

4 ACO I, 1, 1, p. 23.26 – p. 24.6.

5 First Letter to Nestorius (ACO I, 1, 1, pp. 23–5).

6 ACO I, 1, 1, p. 25.

7 ACO I, 1, 1, pp. 25–8; Wickham (1983), 2–10.

8 On Cyril's handling of the technical aspects of Aristotelian logic, see Siddals (1987); Boulnois (1994), 181–209.

9 The only surviving MS is preserved in the Vatican dossier on the Council of Ephesus (ACO I, 1, 6, p. II).

10 ACO I, 1, 4, pp. 35–7, esp. 37.6–7; Wickham (1983), 62–8, esp. 66.17–19.

11 ACO I, 4 (*Collectio Cassinensis* 294), p. 224; see esp. Batiffol (1919); also Wickham (1983), 66, n.8, and Brown (1992), 15–17.

12 ACO I, 1, 6, pp. 151–7; Wickham (1983), 70–82.

13 ACO I, 1, 6, p. 157.9–11; Wickham (1983), 82.15–17.

14 The Virgin in this instance probably means the Church.

15 *'Theotokos'* was not part of the vocabulary of the Antiochene christological tradition. Nestorius is probably right in treating it (at least in its origins) as an Alexandrian theologoumenon. According to Socrates (*Eccl. Hist.* 7.32) it was first used in the third century by Origen in his (no longer extant) *Commentary on Romans*. In the following century it was used by the Alexandrians Alexander (*Ep. Alex.* 12), Athanasius (*C. Ar.* 3.14, 3.29, 3.33; *V. Anton.* 36; *De Inc. et c. Ar.* 22), and Didymus (*De Trin.* 1.31, 2.4). We also find the term used by the Palestinians Eusebius of Caesarea (*V. Const.* 3.43; *Quaest. ad Marin.* 2.5; *C. Marcell.* 2.1), Cyril of Jerusalem (*Catech.* 10.19) and Epiphanius of Salamis (*Anc.* 75), and by the Cappodocians Gregory of Nazianzus (*Ep.* 101) and Gregory of Nyssa (*Ep.* 3), but not by any Antiochenes. On the early history of the term, see Starowieyski (1989).

16 In other words, the Antiochenes do not accept the typically Alexandrian doctrine of the *communicatio idiomatum*, by which the attributes of the human nature may be predicated of the divine, and vice versa, so that the two natures may he kept distinct and yet both may be referred to a single subject. In fact Nestorius did go some way towards accepting the *communicatio idiomatum*. Although the divine attributes could not be predicated of the human nature, or the human attributes of the divine nature, he held that both could be predicated of the *'prosōpon* of the economy', the God-man Jesus Christ (*Book of Heraclides* 229–34; cf. Kelly [1977], 316). The principle of the *communicatio idiomatum*, clearly enunciated in the Tome of Leo (para. 3), received conciliar endorsement at the council of Chalcedon (451).

17 Modern commentators agree with Cyril on Nestorius' prolixity. Cf. Driver and Hodgson (1925), xxxv.

18 Loofs (1905), 353.1–12.

19 Mani (c. 216–76), of southern Mesopotamian origin, was the founder of an ascetic, dualist religion that was particularly active in the Syriac-speaking world, and by the fourth century seemed to rival Christianity. Because in Mani's view, Christ, 'the messenger of light', had not really descended into the evil world of matter, 'Manichaean' became a general term of abuse for any christological opinions that seemed tinged with docetism.

20 The principle, 'that which was not assumed was not healed' (Gregory of Nazianzus, *Ep.* 101). Cyril consistently anchors his christology in soteriological concerns.

21 *Christotokos*, 'she who gave birth to Christ', is the term proposed by Nestorius in 428 when he was asked to adjudicate between *Theotokos* and *Anthrōpotokos* as suitable titles for the Virgin. It seems to be his own coinage. Cyril finds it unacceptable first because it implies a rejection of Christ's divinity, or at least a union of the divine and the human natures subsequent to Christ's birth, and secondly because it can also be applied to others, such as the mother of John the Baptist and

the mother of Cyrus, who also gave birth to 'christs' or 'anointed ones'.

22 Nestorius is responding to his original audience, which had just expressed its enthusiastic approval of his statement that the Virgin is venerable because she is the mother of the Lord of the universe.

23 Loofs (1905), 277.19–278.2.

24 Loofs (1905), 278.5–7.

25 *Dielthen*, 'passed through', the word that Cyril attributes to Nestorius, is not in fact used by him. What Nestorius actually says is *parelthen*. The change of prefix makes very little difference to the sense, but Cyril's version puts Nestorius, no doubt unconsciously, in a somewhat less favourable light. Cyril's verb, *dielthen*, had already been used by 'Adamantius' (*Dial.* 5.9) and Cyril of Jerusalem (*Catech.* 4.9) with reference to the Gnostic idea that Christ 'passed through' the Virgin like water through a tube (cf. Irenaeus, *AH* 1.1.13). In any event, it was unwise of Nestorius to have used terminology so close to that which was already associated with a docetic christology.

26 This time Cyril does use Nestorius' precise term (*parelthen*).

27 Cyril has chosen the closest parallel he could find in the LXX to Nestorius' use of the verb *parelthen*. The phrase 'the wind passes over it' (*pneuma dielthen en autō*) may also be rendered (out of context) 'the Spirit passed through it'.

28 This was to form the substance of the fourth of Cyril's Twelve Chapters. See *Expl. xii cap.* 4, translated below.

29 'Conjunction', *synapheia*, Nestorius' favourite term for the union of the human and the divine, was not suspected of heterodoxy until it was attacked by Cyril. We find it used by Basil (*Ep.* 210.5), John Chrysostom (*Hom.* 11.2 *in Jo.*), and Proclus of Constantinople (*Or. Laud. BMV,* 8 – according to one manuscript tradition). Athanasius uses the closely related term, *synaphē*, in a passage that must have been familiar to Cyril (*C. Ar.* 2.70). Even Cyril himself uses *synapheia* before the Nestorian controversy as equivalent to *syndromē*, though he qualifies it with the phrase *kath' henōsin*, 'in the sense of union' (*Dial. Trin.* 6, 605d). *Synapheia*, however, was used frequently by Theodore of Mopsuestia, Theodoret of Cyrrhus, and other Antiochenes to emphasize the unconfused aspect of the union of the natures. By 430 Cyril is sensitive only to the discreteness of the natures that the word seems to entail, and chooses to interpret the conjunction as accidental or relative (*schetikē*). He returns to the attack below (*C. Nest.* 2.5 and 2.8), and again in his Third Letter to Nestorius (*Ep.* 17.5). Cf. Grillmeier (1975), 459.

30 This is the first instance in Cyril's writings of the *mia physis* ('one nature') formula, which he took from Apollinarius (*Ep. ad Jovinianum* 1), under the impression that it was Athanasian, but intended in an orthodox sense. On Cyril's use of this expression, see Wickham (1983), 63–4, n.3.

31 Cf. *In Is.* 1.4 on Is. 6:6, 7, translated above.

32 The brilliance of the pearl and the fragrance of the lily are christo-logical images that Cyril has made very much his own. See Siddals (1985), 208–9; Boulnois (1994), 159–70.

33 Loofs (1905), 289.6–15. Nestorius seems to hold a theory of language in which homonymy creates a community of being. Against this Cyril opposes an Aristotelian distinction between what is really held in common and what is merely homonymous (cf. Aristotle, *Categories* 1, 1a1–5; *Topics* 1.15, 107a3ff; 6.2, 139b19ff). See also *C. Nest.* 2.8 (ACO I, 1, 6, p.45), translated below.

34 Cyrus was the Lord's anointed (Is. 45:1), which in the Greek of the LXX is his *christos*.

35 Loofs (1905), 354.7–11. Nestorius here encapsulates his teaching on the symmetrical relationship of the two natures. For the sake of clarity, I consistently translate *axia* as 'rank', *axiōma* as 'dignity' and *synapheia* as 'conjunction'. As noun forms the first two are related as an abstract quality to a specific instance of that quality, but in practice the difference is usually indiscernible. Nestorius sees the union in terms of a common dignity or status shared by the two natures. Cyril objects to this as too extrinsic a factor, as he does to the expression *synapheia*, literally a 'fastening together'. Cyril's views on this matter are summed up in *Expl. xii cap.* 3, translated below.

36 Cyril applies to Nestorius the techniques of Aristotelian logic. The middle, first and third terms refer to the premises of a syllogism. Cf. Aristotle, *Prior Analytics* 1.4: 'If A is predicated of every B, and B of every C, A must be predicated of every C' (26a.1–2).

37 Loofs (1905), 280.17–281.9.

38 *Adiaireton synapheian*. Even this qualified expression is not acceptable to Cyril. He insists on 'hypostatic union' (*henōsin kath' hypostasin*), a union on the deepest level of being, which to Nestorius seems to abolish the distinction between the natures (cf. *Book of Heraclides* 2.1, 225).

39 This passage on oneness and difference is discussed by R. Siddals, who notes: 'When it comes to conceptualizing the oneness that obtains between the man and the divine Word here, Nestorius rejects the notion of numerical oneness, and turns instead to the oneness yielded by the category of relation: there is a kind of uniting relation that binds together the man and the Word into a oneness or union' (Siddals [1985], 207). Cyril concedes that there is a radical difference between the natures, but denies that there is a uniting relation which can be characterized as 'conjunction' (*synapheia*) or equality of 'rank' (*axia*).

40 Loofs (1905), 225.14–21.

41 As in the case of 'rank' and 'dignity', Cyril objects to 'authority' (*dynasteia*) as 'one of the elements forming the ground of the union between Logos and humanity' (PGL s.v. *authentia* A.2., which is used

234

elsewhere by Cyril as a synonym of *dynasteia*). Cyril sums up this argument in *Expl. xii cap.* 7, translated below.

42 Loofs (1905), 275.1–14.

43 'One incarnate hypostasis of the Word' (*mian hypostasin tēn tou logou sesarkōmenē*) is used here by Cyril as an equivalent expression to the *mia physis* formula, 'one incarnate nature of God the Word'.

44 Following Athanasius (see esp. *C. Ar.* 2.70), Cyril sees humanity as a whole taken up in principle into the life of God through the Incarnation. The deification (*theopoiēsis*) of the flesh by the Word makes possible the deification of the individual believer through a personal participation in Christ, above all by means of the sacraments. The Antiochene approach to the mystery of the Incarnation had no room for deification. Hence the application of the pejorative term *apotheōsis*, which was only used for deification in a pagan context.

45 Loofs (1905), 354.22–5.

46 Loofs (1905), 259.16–260.7.

47 *To tēs theias synēgoron authentias. Synēgoros*, translated here as 'advocate', means as an adjective 'speaking with the voice of' or 'speaking with equal authority to'.

48 The sayings of Christ are not to be assigned to two different subjects, those expressing fear and human weakness to the human nature, and those expressing divine power to the divine nature. The Word made flesh is the single subject of all the acts and sayings of Christ. Cf., however, the concession that Cyril was to make to the Antiochene position in the Formulary of Reunion (*Ep.* 39.5), translated above, p. 55.

49 Loofs (1905), 234.5–235.1.

50 Loofs (1905), 228.4–16.

51 Loofs (1905), 355.13–18.

52 The traditional image of the sun and its brightness, as expressive of the unity-in-distinction and co-eternity of the Father and the Son, is here developed by Cyril to suggest that the Son is everything that the Father is except for the Father's being the source of Godhead.

53 Loofs (1905), 356.19–357.4.

54 Cyril turns Nestorius' objection to the Alexandrian doctrine of deification back on him. It is Nestorius who is guilty of deification in a pagan sense by raising an ordinary man to divine status.

55 Cyril explicitly denies the extreme monophysite view that Eutyches was to put forward a few years after his death.

56 Loofs (1905), 229.17–230.5.

AN EXPLANATION OF THE TWELVE
CHAPTERS

1 The best discussions are in Wickham (1983), xxxv–xliii, and Young (1983), 220–9. See also Souvay (1926); Galtier (1933); Du Manoir (1944) 491–510; Diepen (1955); and McGuckin (1994), 44–6, 83–4, 94–5.

2 Cyril replied to Andrew with *Adversus orientales episcopos* (ACO I, 1, 7, pp. 33–65), and to Theodoret with *Contra Theodoretum* (ACO I, 1, 6, pp. 107–46). Theodoret's arguments in particular hit home. It is his objections that Cyril is most anxious to answer in the explanation given at Ephesus.

3 For a detailed account of these events, see McGuckin (1994), 94–107. Cf. de Halleux (1993a).

4 He also pitches his arguments, astutely, on a more popular level.

5 On the reception of the Twelve Chapters after Ephesus, see esp. Wickham (1983), xxxviii–xli; also Galtier (1933) and (1951); Haring (1950); Diepen (1955); Grillmeier (1995), 457–8.

6 Theodoret had said in objection to the first anathema: 'Those of us who follow the teaching of the Gospels do not say that God the Word became flesh by nature or that he was changed into flesh, for the divine is immutable and changeless' (ACO I, 1, 6, p. 108.24–109.1). Besides briefly restating his denial that the Word's becoming flesh implies change in the divine, Cyril adds two points for the benefit of an episcopal readership less attuned than Theodoret to the finer points of dialectics: (i) We take our stand on the faith of Nicaea, and (ii) the manner of the Word's becoming flesh transcends human understanding.

7 Theodoret's objection to the term '*Theotokos*' had been the logical one that if at the Incarnation the Word 'took flesh endowed with life and reason' he cannot himself, as an already existing subject, be said to have been conceived by the Virgin (ACO I, 1, 6, p. 109.11–18). Here Cyril implies that his insistence on the term '*Theotokos*' is primarily to exclude an Arian interpretation of Christ.

8 Theodoret had objected to the expression 'hypostatic union' (*hē kath' hypostasin henōsis*) on the grounds (i) that it was unscriptural and unpatristic, and (ii) that it necessarily implied a mixture or confusion of flesh and Godhead (ACO I, 1, 6, p.114.10–15). Cyril repeats here in summary form what he had said in response to Theodoret, namely, that the expression 'hypostatic union' is simply intended to safeguard the unity of Christ, the incarnate Word. Theodoret himself would surely agree, he says, 'that when he refers to God he is not excluding the human nature, nor does he conceive of the human nature without the deity' (ACO I, 1, 6, p. 115.16–18).

9 The expression that Cyril opposes to *synapheia* ('conjunction'), translated here as 'a combination in terms of natural union', is *synodos*

hē kath' henōsin physikēn. 'Natural', as Cyril goes on to explain, is intended in the sense of 'real'.

10 Theodoret found the meaning of this anathema obscure. He could not see what contrast Cyril was drawing between 'conjunction' (*synapheia*) and 'combination' (*synodos*), nor was he happy with a 'natural' union which seemed to exclude the element of the will (ACO I, 1, 6, p. 116.14–117.2). Cyril omits here his technical discussions of 'conjunction', 'rank' (*axia*) and 'authority' (*authentia*) (developed at length in *C. Nest.* 2.5–6, translated above) and contents himself with saying that by objecting to 'conjunction' he was seeking to exclude the idea of an accidental union, and, conversely, by insisting on 'by nature' he was merely saying 'in reality' (*alēthōs*).

11 The Antiochene exegetical tradition assigned the sayings and acts of Christ which suggested fear or ignorance to his human nature, but his miraculous signs and acts of power to his divine nature, Christ operating thus in two different *prosōpa*, or roles. In 431 Cyril still regarded this as implying an unacceptable duality in the Son, but in the Formulary of Reunion of 433 he conceded the legitimacy of the Antiochene usage. His more extreme followers, however, held fast to this anathema and after 451 rejected Chalcedon partly on account of it.

12 Bracketed by Schwartz as an interpolation.

13 Theodoret was outraged by this anathema, which he said anathematized the archangel Gabriel and even the Lord himself. His biblical citations concerning the Spirit conclude with Jn. 15:26 ('who proceeds from the Father') and 1 Cor. 2:12 ('we have received not the spirit of the world, but the Spirit which is from God'), which were to remain the principal proof texts on the source of the Spirit for the Byzantine tradition (ACO I, 1, 6, p. 133.4–134.15). On Theodoret's conflict with Cyril on this issue, see de Halleux (1979) and Boulnois (1994), 482–92.

14 Theodoret regarded this anathema as Apollinarian in its import because Cyril does not explain that the Lord's flesh is consubstantial with us (ACO I, 1, 6, p. 142.17–19). Cyril does not rehearse here his counter-argument that although consubstantial with us, the flesh of Christ was endowed with divine power, but emphasizes the practical point that Nestorius' christology empties the Eucharist of its efficacy.

15 Everyone agreed that the divine was impassible by definition. Cyril's making the impassible Word the subject of the sufferings of Christ seemed blasphemous to the Antiochenes. Theodoret insisted that it was 'the form of the servant' that suffered, not 'the form of God' (ACO I, 1, 6, p. 144.19–20). Cyril states unequivocally that he does not deny the impassibility of the Word, but reiterates his argument that if the Word is not the single subject of the passion and death of Christ (through making his flesh receptive of suffering), the logical consequence is a deified man alongside the divine Word. On this fundamental point he will concede nothing.

AGAINST JULIAN

1 Letter 83, addressed to Dioscorus of Alexandria, in Azéma (1964), 216–17; 204–5, n.3.

2 On the dating see P. Evieux in Burguière and Evieux (1985), 10–15. The dates, of course, supplied by Theodoret's letter refer only to the circulation of *Against Julian*. Cyril could well have begun the work much earlier, set it aside for more pressing concerns, and then returned to it in later life.

3 Almost the whole of Book 1 has been recovered from *Against Julian*. The surviving fragments have been edited by Neumann (1880), to which should be added the fragments noted by Draguet (1929), and have been translated by W.C. Wright in vol. 3 of the Loeb edition of Julian's works. For an assessment of Julian's anti-Christian programme as set out in *Against the Galilaeans*, see now Smith (1995), 179–218.

4 The list of writers against Julian given by Evieux in Burguière and Evieux (1985), 52–8 includes Gregory of Nazianzus (*Orations* 4 and 5), Apollinarius of Laodicaea (as reported by Sozomen, *Eccl. Hist.* 5.18), Ephraim the Syrian (as reported by Ebedjesus in Assemani, *Bibl. orient.* 3. 1. 63a), John Chrysostom (as reported by John Damascene in the *Sacra Parallela*), Macarius Magnes (his *Apocriticus* refuting a philosopher who is possibly Julian), Theodore of Mopsuestia (fragments in a *catena*), Philip of Side (as reported by Socrates, *Eccl. Hist.* 7.27), Alexander of Hierapolis (as reported by Ebedjesus in Assemani, *Bibl. orient.* 3. 1. 197), and Theodoret of Cyrrhus (two mentions of Julian in the *Cure of Pagan Maladies* 9.25; 10.27).

5 On Theodore, see Evieux's discussion in Burguière and Evieux (1985), 55–6. The fragments which may be from a reply to *Against the Galilaeans* are in Mai, *Nova Patrum Bibliotheca* 6.2 (= PG 66, 95).

6 A critical edition of the first two books has been issued in Sources Chrétiennes 322 (Burguière and Evieux, 1985). For the remaining books we are still dependent on J. Aubert's edition of 1638, which was reproduced by E. Spannheim in 1696, and is the text printed by Migne in 1859 (PG 76, 509–1058).

7 Cyril used Christian authors as a guide to the pagan. As R.M. Grant has shown, Eusebius of Caesarea's *Chronicle* and *Preparatio Evangelica* were the fundamental texts which not only gave Cyril a large number of pagan quotations but also led him to Clement of Alexandria's *Protrepticus* and *Stromata* and Ps.-Justin's *Exhortation to the Greeks*. Cyril followed up the leads given to him by Eusebius and appears to have read further even among some of the pagan authors mentioned by him. Thus, for example, we have a number of quotations from the Hermetic Corpus and from Porphyry's *History of Philosophy* which are not found elsewhere (Grant [1964]. See further, Malley [1978], 258–61, and on Porphyry, Sodano [1997]).

8 Cyril is referring to a Euhemeristic view of the origin of religious cult. Euhemerus of Messene wrote a fictional travel work in the third century BC in which he propounded the view that the gods had all once been human beings, powerful rulers and benefactors who had been deified by their grateful subjects. This view became current in Roman times, largely through Diodorus Siculus (*World History* 6) and proved popular with Christians. Clement of Alexandria refers favourably to Euhemerus (*Protrepticus* 2.24.2). Eusebius of Caesarea regarded his travel work as factual and summarised its contents (*Prep. Evang.* 2.2). Cyril is likely to have picked up Euhemerism from Eusebius, his chief guide in matters pagan.

9 This would not have seemed so far-fetched to Cyril's contemporaries. Many Romans were impressed by the antiquity of the oriental sages, of whom Moses was the best-known representative. Philo taught that Moses had influenced Plato through Pythagoras. The second-century Middle Platonist, Numenius of Apamea, was familiar with the Mosaic books. In the following century Iamblichus mentions in his *Life of Pythagoras* that his hero had consorted in Palestine 'with the descendants of Mochos the prophet and philosopher', a figure who sounds as if he is meant to be Moses. (On these, see Dillon [1977], 143, 365.) Clement of Alexandria (*Strom.* 1, xxv), Ps.-Justin (*Exhortation* 20) and Eusebius of Caesarea (*Prep. Evang.* 11.10) all held that Plato had been inspired by Moses.

10 These we have had to skip, in spite of Cyril's begging us not to (*C. Jul.* 1. 5, 513 BC). They have been taken from Eusebius' *Chronicle*.

11 The Olympic games were founded in 776 BC and had only recently been abolished (by Theodosius I in AD 393). Held every four years for most of this time (each four-year period being an Olympiad), they provided a convenient and widely-used system of dating. Eusebius gives a list of the games with the winners from the foundation to AD 217 (*Chronicle* 1.32–3).

12 The division of philosophy into dialectics, theoretical knowledge and practical knowledge (distinctions going back to Aristotle) had become part of School Platonism by the second century. Theoretical knowledge included theology, physics and mathematics; practical knowledge dealt with ethics (cf. Dillon [1977], 272–304).

13 This is a late tradition which Cyril may have found in Clement, *Strom.* 1.15.

14 *Timaeus* 22b, 23c, which Cyril quotes from Ps.-Justin, *Exhortation* 12 (PG 6, 264A). Cf. Eusebius, *Prep. Evang.* 10.4.19 and Clement, *Strom.* 1.29.

15 Ps.-Justin, *Exhortation* 9 (PG 6, 257B). The 'others besides' are listed by Ps.-Justin as Thallus, Alexander Polyhistor, Philo and Josephus.

16 Diodorus Siculus, *World History* 1.94, quoted by Ps.-Justin, *Exhortation* 9 (PG 6, 260 AB). On Moses as a god, cf. *C. Nest.* 2.4, translated above.

17 Justin Martyr was the first to suggest that Gen. 1:26 indicated plurality in the Godhead (*Dial.* 62). Athanasius made frequent use of the verse in his anti-Arian polemic (e.g. *C. Ar.* 2.31).

18 This is derived from the Aristotelian idea of God as pure actuality (cf. Aristotle, *Metaphysics* 12.7), no doubt through the mediation of a commentator such as Alexander of Aphrodisias.

19 *Timaeus* 27d–28a (trans. B. Jowett, lightly adapted). Cited from Ps.-Justin, *Exhortation* 22 (PG 6, 280C–281B).

20 This also follows the *Timaeus* quotation in Ps.-Justin, *Exhortation* 22 (PG 6, 281A).

21 This is a Stoic definition going back to Chrysippus, for whom rationality was the chief human characteristic, which had long since been accepted by commentators on Aristotle (e.g. Porphyry, *Isagoge* 60, 15 [trans. Strange 38]), that Cyril had used it on other occasions (e.g. *Thes.* 31, 444C and 34, 569B – 'a rational, mortal animal'; *In Jo.* 3.4, 299a – 'a rational animal in the image of the Creator'; *In Jo.* 6, 582d–583a – 'a rational mortal animal capable of understanding and knowledge', the last quotation reproducing Porphyry's exact phraseology). Cf. Burghardt (1957), 19–20, 33–4.

22 Cyril deploys an anti-Arian argument for good measure.

23 This is a favourite theme of Cyril's. See *Commentary on John* 1. 9, translated above.

24 I.e. Julian.

25 Cyril has just reproduced a long passage from the *Timaeus* (41bd) quoted by Julian.

26 Plato's myth, in which the created gods are summoned by their father to assist in the creation of the human race by supplying the mortal element (otherwise humanity would have been entirely immortal and divine if created by the supreme god alone) seeks to account for the dual nature of humanity, its transitoriness on the one hand and its capacity for self-transcendence on the other (*Timaeus* 41a–42e). Cyril, however, is struck more by the dominion of humanity over nature, which is the particular aspect of 'the very nature of things' that supports the biblical narrative.

27 'Role' here renders the Greek *prosōpon*, a useful reminder that for Cyril as well as the Antiochenes a 'person' is fundamentally a character in a drama. It is this concept that lies behind Antiochene scriptural exegesis, in which the starting-point is the identification of the *prosōpon*, the one acting or speaking – the *dramatis persona*. This exegetical approach, in turn, lies behind the two *prosōpa* of Antiochene christology. In Christ, the Antiochenes argue, one must distinguish two *prosōpa*, because Christ sometimes acts as God and sometimes as man. I owe this observation to Andrew Louth.

28 Ps. 82:6 in its remote origins was not so far removed from Plato's myth as Cyril thought. In the course of centuries, however, it had undergone considerable development. The lesser gods of the Ugaritic

divine assembly were adapted by Yahwism and made to serve as angels in the heavenly court. In later Judaism they were seen as human judges condemned because of their corruption. From the time of Justin (*Dialogue with Trypho* 124) Ps. 82:6 was understood to be addressed to the righteous believer. Irenaeus connected the 'gods' of the psalm with the Pauline teaching on adoptive sonship (Rom. 8:16 – cf. *AH* 2.6.1, 3.19.1, 4.38.4). This was taken over by Clement of Alexandria and thereafter became one of the chief biblical proof texts for the doctrine of deification.

29 Cyril is probably basing his statement on a later Aristotelian commentator such as Alexander of Aphrodisias. Aristotle himself, while proposing a mechanical cosmological model, does not entirely exclude popular ideas concerning the divinity of the heavenly bodies (cf. *Metaphysics* 1074a38ff).

30 These are the four liberal arts (the Medieval *Quadrivium*) that were studied along with the classics at secondary-school level and completed a young person's general education (*enkyklios paideia*). Cyril shares his hostility to the liberal arts with pagan Sceptics such as Sextus Empiricus as well as Christian anti-Hellenists such as the third-century author of the *Didascalia Apostolorum*. Most Christians, however, were very happy to benefit from a classical education. On the *enkyklios paideia* and Christian attitudes towards it, see Marrou (1956), 160–85, 314–29.

31 The ideal that Cyril holds up is in fact not far removed from that of Platonism. Ever since the time of Eudorus, the first-century BC Alexandrian scholar who revived the study of Platonism in the Roman Empire, 'becoming like God so far as is possible for human beings' had been defined as the end of man. See Dillon (1977), 122–3.

32 *Republic* 5. 475e, quoted from Clement, *Strom.* I, 93, 5.

BIBLIOGRAPHY

TEXTS OF CYRIL

The first collected edition of Cyril's works, containing the *editiones principes* of most of the surviving texts, was edited by Canon Jean Aubert and published in six volumes in Paris in 1636–8. Some additional texts were published by Cardinal Angelo Mai in vols 2 and 3 of the *Novum Patrum Bibliotheca*, Rome 1844–5. Aubert's edition, together with Mai's additional material, was reproduced by the Abbé J.-P. Migne in 10 volumes (PG 68–77), Paris 1859 (reprinted Turnhout: Brepols 1991).

The first modern critical edition was undertaken by Philip Pusey, the invalid son of the great Tractarian, who in the days before photographic reproductions travelled to Moscow and Mount Athos, besides the great libraries of Western Europe, in order to collate the extant manuscripts. His labours resulted in the following seven volumes:

Pusey, P.E. (1868) *Sancti Patris nostri Cyrilli archiepiscopi Alexandrini in XII Prophetas*, vols 1 and 2, Oxford: Clarendon Press (reprinted Brussels 1965).

Pusey, P.E. (1872)) *Sancti Patris nostri Cyrilli archiepiscopi Alexandrini in D. Ioannis Evangelium. Accedunt fragmenta varia necnon tractatus ad Tiberium Diaconum duo*, vols 3, 4 and 5, Oxford: Clarendon Press (reprinted Brussels 1965). The third volume contains fragments of other NT commentaries and the Doctrinal Questions and Answers.

Pusey, P.E. (1875) *Epistolae tres oecumenicae, Libri quinque contra Nestorium, XII capitum explanatio, XII capitum defensio utraque, Scholia de Incarnatione Unigeniti*, vol. 6, Oxford: James Parker (reprinted Brussels 1965).

Pusey, P.E. (1877) *Sancti Patris nostri Cyrilli archiepiscopi Alexandrini: De recta fide ad imperatorem, ad principissas, ad augustas, de incarnatione, quod unus sit Christus, apologeticus ad imperatorem*, vol. 7, Oxford: James Parker (reprinted Brussels 1965).

Most of the texts in Pusey's vols 6 and 7 together with other material relating to the Council of Ephesus were re-edited earlier this century by the great German scholar, Eduard Schwartz, and published in the first volume of his Acts of the Ecumenical Councils: *Acta Conciliorum Oecumenicorum*, edidit Edvardus Schwartz, tomus primus, volumen primus, pars prima–pars septima *Concilium Universale Ephesinum*, Berlin and Leipzig: Walter de Gruyter 1927–9. Schwartz is critical of Pusey's work, whose judgement, he says, was at fault in many of his emendations (I, 1, 1, p.XX) but he reserves his greatest opprobrium for Migne's Patrology – 'cloaca illa maxima Migneana, quae Patrologiae Graecae nomine gloriatur' (I, 1, 1, p. xviiii). Schwartz also published some Cyrilline material in *Codex Vaticanus gr. 1431. Eine antichalkedonische Sammlung aus der Zeit Kaiser Zenos*, Munich 1927 (Abhandlungen der Bayerischen Akademie der Wissenschaften philosophisch-philologisch und historische Klasse, Vol. 32, Abhandlung no. 6).

After Schwartz, the next series of critical publications was that of Sources Chrétiennes. The following volumes, with valuable introductions and French translations, have been published to date:

de Durand, G.M. (1964) *Deux dialogues christologiques* (On the Incarnation and On the Unity of Christ), SC 97, Paris: Les Editions du Cerf. (De Durand's introduction is an important landmark in the study of Cyril.)

de Durand, G.M. (1976, 1977, 1978) *Dialogues sur la Trinité*, 3 vols, SC 231, 237, 246, Paris: Les Editions du Cerf.

Burguière, P. and Evieux, P. (1985) *Contre Julien*, vol. 1, SC 322, Paris: Les Editions du Cerf.

Lettres festales (I–VI) (1991) introd. P. Evieux, texte W.H. Burns, trad. et notes L. Arragon, M.O. Boulnois, P. Evieux, M. Forrat, B. Meunier, SC 372, Paris: Les Editions du Cerf.

Lettres festales (VII–XI) (1993) texte W.H. Burns, trad. et notes L. Arragon et R. Monnier, sous la direction de P. Evieux, SC 392, Paris: Les Editions du Cerf.

Lettres festales (XII–XVII) (1998) texte W.H. Burns, trad. et notes M.-O. Boulnois et B. Meunier, SC 434, Paris: Les Editions du Cerf.

Of the works of Cyril surviving only in Syriac, the more important are his commentary on Luke, published by J. B. Chabot, CSCO 70, Paris 1912, with a Latin translation by R. Tonneau, CSCO 140, Louvain 1953, and two publications by R.Y. Ebied and L.R. Wickham, 'An Unknown Letter of Cyril of Alexandria in Syriac', *JTS* n.s. 22 (1971), 420–43; *A Collection of Unpublished Syriac Letters of Cyril of Alexandria*, CSCO 359–360, Louvain 1975. For a full bibliography of the texts of Cyril's letters, see McEnerney (1987) i, xi–xii.

ENGLISH TRANSLATIONS

The nineteenth-century translations vary greatly in readability. Those of Philip Pusey, undertaken under the direction of his father for the Library of the Fathers of the Church, are so literal as to be sometimes quite impenetrable without reference to the Greek. The first publication was that of R. Payne-Smith, *A Commentary Upon the Gospel According to S. Luke by Cyril, Patriarch of Alexandria*, 2 vols, Oxford: University Press, 1859, which was translated from the Syriac. Then follow the translations made by Pusey from his critical Greek texts: *The Three Epistles of St Cyril* (the dogmatic letters to Nestorius), Oxford 1872; *The Commentary on St. John*, vol. 1, Oxford: James Parker, 1874 (Library of the Fathers of the Church, 43); *That the Christ is One*, Oxford: James Parker, 1881 (Library of the Fathers of the Church, 46); and *S. Cyril, Archbishop of Alexandria, Five Tomes Against Nestorius; Scholia on the Incarnation; Christ is One; Fragments Against Diodore of Tarsus, Theodore of Mopsuestia, the Synousiasts*, Oxford: James Parker, 1881 (Library of the Fathers of the Church, 47). Pusey was so discouraged by the hostile reception given to the first volume of his *Commentary on St. John* (Jowett called it 'quaint') that he abandoned his work on it. The second volume was translated by T. Randell, *Commentary on St John*, vol. 2, Oxford: James Parker, 1885 (Library of the Fathers of the Church, 48).

Translations of Cyril's dogmatic letters have appeared in the main handbooks: C.A. Heurtley, *On the Faith and the Creed. Dogmatic Teaching of the Church of the Fourth and Fifth Centuries*, 3rd edn., London: Parker and Co. 1889; T.H. Bindley, *The Oecumenical Documents of the Faith*, 3rd edn., London: Methuen 1925; B.J. Kidd, *Documents Illustrative of the History of the Church*, vol. 2, London: SPCK 1923; E. R. Hardy and C.C. Richardson, *Christology of the Later Fathers*, London: SCM Press, 1954 (The Library of Christian Classics, 3); J. Stevenson, *Creeds, Councils and Controversies*, London: SPCK 1966 (revised W.H.C. Frend 1989); N. Tanner, *Decrees of the Ecumenical Councils*, vol. 1, London & Washington: Sheed & Ward and Georgetown University Press 1990.

The publication of modern translations of Cyril's writings was inaugurated by *Cyril of Alexandria. Selected Letters*, edited and translated by Lionel R. Wickham, in the Oxford Early Christian Texts series, Oxford: Clarendon Press 1983. This indispensable collection with an excellent introduction comprises good translations of the Second and Third Letters to Nestorius, the Letters to Acacius of Melitene and Eulogius, the First and Second Letters to Successus, Letter 55 on the Creed, the Answers to Tiberius, the Doctrinal Questions and Answers, and the Letter to Calosirius, with facing Greek critical text based on Schwartz in the case of the dogmatic letters and established by Wickham for the remaining texts.

This was followed by *St. Cyril of Alexandria: Letters 1–50* and *Letters 51–110*, translated by J.I. McEnerney, in the Fathers of the Church series, vols. 76–7, Washington: Catholic University of America Press 1987. All the letters are presented in this collection, including some surviving only in Syriac and Coptic.

The next publication was J.A. McGuckin, *St Cyril of Alexandria: The Christological Controversy. Its History, Theology and Texts*, Leiden: E.J. Brill 1994 (Supplements to Vigiliae Christianae, 23), which contains in addition to the Second and Third Letters to Nestorius and the Letters to Eulogius and Succensus, already in Wickham, Cyril's Letters to the Monks of Egypt, to Pope Celestine, to Acacius of Beroea and to John of Antioch (containing the Formulary of Reunion), the Festal Homily delivered at St John's basilica, Ephesus, and the Scholia on the Incarnation. McGuckin has also published a good translation of the Dialogue on the Unity of Christ, based on the critical text of Sources Chrétiennes: *St Cyril of Alexandria On the Unity of Christ*, translated with an introduction by J.A. McGuckin, Crestwood, NY: St Vladimir's Seminary Press 1995.

OTHER TEXTS AND TRANSLATIONS

Abramowski, L. and Goodman A.E. (1972) *A Nestorian Collection of Christological Texts*, vol. 1: text, vol. 2: introduction, translation and notes, Cambridge: Cambridge University Press.

Adriaen, M. (1963) *Commentarium in Esaiam libri I–XVIII*, in S. Hieronymi Presbyteri, *Opera* pt. I: *Opera Exegetica*, 2 and 2A (CCL 73–73A), Turnhout: Brepols.

Amidon, P.R. (1997) *The Church History of Rufinus of Aquileia. Books 10 and 11*, New York and Oxford: Oxford University Press.

Apophthegmata Patrum, alphabetical series, PG 65, 71–440.

Azéma, Y. (1964) Théodoret de Cyr, *Correspondance* II (SC 98), Paris: Les Editions du Cerf.

Basil, *Enarratio in Prophetam Isaiam*, PG 30, 117–668.

Bell, D.N. (1983) *The Life of Shenoute by Besa*, Kalamazoo: Cistercian Publications (Cistercian Studies series, 73).

Bidez, J. and Parmentier, L. (1989) *The Ecclesiastical History of Evagrius*, London: Methuen & Co.

Blanc, C. (1966–92) *Origène, Commentaire sur S. Jean*, Paris: Les Editions du Cerf (SC 120, 157, 222, 290, 385).

Charles, R.H. (1916) *The Chronicle of John, Bishop of Nikiu, translated from Zotenberg's Ethiopic text*, London: Williams & Norgate.

Draguet, R. (1929) 'Pour l'edition du Philalèthe de Sévère d'Antioche', *BZ* 30, 274–9.

Driver, G.R. and Hodgson, L (1925) *Nestorius. The Bazaar of Heracleides. Newly translated from the Syriac and edited with an Introduction, Notes and Appendices*, Oxford: Clarendon Press. (Unreliable.)

Dumortier, J. (1983) *Jean Chrysostome, Commentaire sur Isaïe*, Paris: Les Editions du Cerf (SC 304).

Eusebius, *Commentaria in Isaiam*, PG 24, 77–525.

Gryson, R. (1998) *Commentaires de Jérôme sur le prophète Isaïe*, Livres 12–15, Freiburg: Herder (VLAGLB 35).

Gryson, R. and Deproost, P.A. (1993) *Commentaires de Jérôme sur le prophète Isaïe*, Livres 1–4, Freiburg: Herder (VLAGLB 23).

Gryson, R. and Coulie J. (1994) *Commentaires de Jérôme sur le prophète Isaïe*, Livres 5–7, Freiburg: Herder (VLAGLB 27).

Gryson, R. and Somers, V. (1996) *Commentaires de Jérôme sur le prophète Isaïe*, Livres 8–11, Freiburg: Herder (VLAGLB 30).

Guinot, J.-N. (1980–4) *Théodoret de Cyr, Commentaire sur Isaïe* (SC 276, 295, 315), *Paris*: Les Editions du Cerf.

Hansen, G.C. (1995) *Sokrates, Kirchengeschichte* (GCS) Berlin: Akademie-Verlag.

Jerome, *Commentarium in Esaiam*, PL 24, 9–678.

Loofs, F. (1905) *Nestoriana. Die Fragmente des Nestorius*, Halle: Max Niemeyer.

Mras, K. (1954, 1956) *Die Praeparatio Evangelica, Eusebius' Werke* vol. 8, pts 1–2 (GCS 43, pts 1–2), Berlin: Akademie-Verlag.

Nau, F. (1910) *Le Livre de Héraclide de Damas*, Paris: Letouzey (reprinted Farnborough: Gregg 1969).

—— (1913) *Barhadbeshabba*, PO 9, Paris: Firmin-Didot.

—— (1916) *Lettre à Cosme*, PO 13, Paris: Firmin-Didot.

Neumann, K.J. (1880) *Juliani imperatoris librorum contra christianos quae supersunt*, Leipzig: B.G. Teubner.

Origen, *Homiliae in Isaiam*, PG 13, 219–53.

Percival, H.R. (1899) *The Seven Ecumenical Councils of the Undivided Church*, Edinburgh: T & T Clark (reprinted Grand Rapids: Eerdmans 1991) (NPNF, 2nd series, 14).

Pharr, C. (1952) *The Theodosian Code and the Novels, and the Sirmondian Constitutions*, Princeton: Princeton University Press.

Preuschen, E. (1903) *Der Johanneskommentar*, vol. 4 of *Origenes' Werke* (GCS 10), Leipzig: J.C. Hinrichs.

Socrates, *Historia Ecclesiastica*, PG 67, 29–872.

Sodano, A.R. (1997) *Porfirio. Storia della Filosofia*, Milan: Rusconi.

Strange, S. K. (1992) *Porphyry. On Aristotle Categories*, London: Duckworth.

Tanner, N. (1990) *Decrees of the Ecumenical Councils*, vol. 1, London and Washington: Sheed & Ward and Georgetown University Press.

Theodoret, *Interpretatio in Isaiam*, PG 81, 215–494.

Torrance, I.R. (1988) *Christology After Chalcedon. Severus of Antioch and Sergius the Monophysite*, Norwich: The Canterbury Press.

Vaggione, R (1987) *Eunomius. The Extant Works*, Oxford: Clarendon Press (Oxford Early Christian Texts).

Vosté, J. M. (1940) *Theodori Mopsuesteni commentarios in Evangelium Ioannis Apostoli* (text: CSCO 115; translation: CSCO 116), Louvain: Durbecq.

Ward, B. (1975) *The Sayings of the Desert Fathers*, Kalamazoo: Cistercian Publications.

Ziegler, J. (1975) *Der Jesajakommentar*, vol. 9 of *Eusebius' Werke* (GCS), Berlin: Akademie-Verlag.

SECONDARY LITERATURE

Abel, F.-M. (1941) 'Parallelisme éxégetique entre S. Jérôme et S. Cyrille d'Alexandrie', *Vivre et Penser. Recherches d'exegèse et d'histoire*, 1re série, 94–119, 212–30, Paris: J. Gabalda.

—— (1947) 'Saint Cyrille d'Alexandrie dans ses rapports avec la Palestine', in *Kyrilliana* (1947), 205–30.

Abramowski, L. (1955/56) 'Der Streit um Diodor und Theodor zwischen den beiden ephesinischen Konzilien', *ZKG* 67, 252–87.

—— (1963) *Untersuchungen zum Liber Heraclidis des Nestorius*, CSCO 242 (Subsidia 22).

Amann, E. (1931) 'Nestorius', *DTC* 11.1, 76–157.

—— (1949–50) 'L'affaire Nestorius vue de Rome', *RSR* 23, 5–37, 207–44; 24, 28–52, 235–65.

Anastos, M.V. (1962) 'Nestorius was orthodox', *DOP* 16, 119–40.

Bagnall, R.S. (1993) *Egypt in Late Antiquity*, Princeton: Princeton University Press.

Batiffol, P. (1919) 'Les Présents de Saint Cyrille à la cour de Constantinople', in *Etudes de Liturgie et d'Archéologie Chrétienne*, Paris: J. Gabalda.

Berthold, G.C. (1989) 'Cyril of Alexandria and the *Filoque*', *Stud. Pat.* 19, 143–7.

Bethune-Baker, J.F. (1908) *Nestorius and his Teaching*, Cambridge: at the University Press.

Boulnois, M.-O. (1994) *Le paradoxe trinitaire chez Cyrille d'Alexandrie. Herméneutique, analyses philosophiques et argumentation théologique*, Paris: Institut d'Etudes Augustiniennes (Collections des Etudes Augustiniennes, Série Antiquité 143). (Indispensable.)

—— (1997) 'Platon entre Moïse et Arius selon le *Contre Julien* de Cyrille d'Alexandrie', *Stud. Pat.* 32, 264–71.

Bowman, A.K. (1986) *Egypt After the Pharaohs 332 BC–AD 642,* London: British Museum.

Brock, S.P. (1996) 'The "Nestorian" Church: a Lamentable Misnomer', *BJRL* 78, part 3, 23–35.

Brown, P. (1971) 'The Rise and Function of the Holy Man in Late Antiquity', *JRS,* 80–101 (reprinted in P. Brown, *Society and the Holy in Late Antiquity,* London: Faber and Faber 1982, 103–52).

—— (1992) *Power and Persuasion in Late Antiquity. Towards a Christian Empire,* Madison: University of Wisconsin Press.

—— (1995) *Authority and the Sacred. Aspects of the Christianisation of the Roman World,* Cambridge: Cambridge University Press.

Bultmann, R. (1971) *The Gospel of John. A Commentary,* trans. G.R. Beasley-Murray, Oxford: Basil Blackwell.

Burghardt, W. (1957) *The Image of God in Man according to Cyril of Alexandria,* Washington: Catholic University of America Press. (Important.)

Butler, A.J. (1978) *The Arab Conquest of Egypt and the Last Thirty Years of the Roman Dominion,* 2nd edn., ed. P.M. Fraser, Oxford: Clarendon Press.

Cassell, J.D. (1992) *Cyril of Alexandria and the science of the grammarians: a study in the setting, purpose and emphasis of Cyril's Commentary on Isaiah,* Charlottesville: University of Virginia dissertation in facsimile.

Cattaneo, E. (1983) 'Formule di fede nelle *Lettere Pasquali* di Cirillo d'Alessandria', *Koinonia* 7, 31–5.

Chadwick, H. (1951) 'Eucharist and Christology in the Nestorian Controversy', *JTS* n.s. 2, 145–64. (Important.)

Chesnut, R.C. (1978) 'The Two Prosopa in Nestorius' *Bazaar of Heracleides', JTS* n.s. 29, 392–408.

Chuvin P. (1990) *A Chronicle of the Last Pagans,* trans. B.A. Archer, Cambridge, Mass: Harvard University Press.

Datema, C. (1982) 'Classical quotations in the works of Cyril of Alexandria', *Stud. Pat.* 17/1, 422–5.

Diepen, H.M. (1955) 'Les Douze Anathématismes au Concile d'Ephèse et jusqu'en 519', *Rev. Thom.* 55, 300–38.

Dillon, J. (1977) *The Middle Platonists,* London: Duckworth.

Drioton, E (1947) 'Cyrille d'Alexandrie et l'ancienne religion égyptienne', in *Kyrilliana* (1947), 233–46.

Duchesne, L. (1924) *Early History of the Christian Church from its Foundations to the End of the Fifth Century,* vol. 3, *The Fifth Century,* trans. C. Jenkins, London: John Murray.

Du Manoir, H. (1944) *Dogme et Spiritualité chez S. Cyrille d'Alexandrie,* Paris: J. Vrin.

Dupré la Tour, A. (1960–1) 'La doxa du Christ dans les oeuvres exégétiques de saint Cyrille d'Alexandrie', *RSR* 48, 521–43; 49, 68–94.

Dzielska, M. (1995) *Hypatia of Alexandria*, trans. F. Lyra, Cambridge, Mass: Harvard University Press (Revealing Antiquity, 8).

Ebeid, R. Y. and Wickham, L. R. (1985) 'Timothy Aelurus: Against the Council Chalcedon' in C. Lage *et al.*, eds, *After Chalcedon: Studies in Theology and Church History offered to Professor Albert van Roey for his Seventieth Birthday* (Orientalia Lovaniensia Analecta, 18), 115–66.

Fatica, L. (1988) *I commentari a Giovanni di Teodoro di Mopsuestia e di Cirillo di Alessandria. Confronto fra metodi esegetici et teologici*, Rome: Studia ephemeridis Augustinianum, 29.

Fernández Lois, A.H.A. (1998) *La cristologia en los commentarios a Isaias de Cirilo de Alejandria y Teodoreto de Ciro*, Rome: Pontificia Universitas Lateranensis, Institutum Patristicum Augustinianum. (Valuable study.)

Fowden, G. (1978) 'Bishops and Temples in the Eastern Roman Empire 320–425 AD', *JTS* n.s. 29, 53–78.

Frend, W.H.C. (1972) *The Rise of the Monophysite Movement. Chapters in the History of the Church in the Fifth and Sixth Centuries*, Cambridge: at the University Press. (Indispensable.)

—— (1990) 'Monks and the End of Greco-Roman paganism in Syria and Egypt', *Cr. St.* 11, part 3, 469–84.

Galtier, P. (1933) 'Les anathématismes de S. Cyrille et le Concile de Chalcédoine', *RSR* 23, 45–57.

—— (1951) 'S. Cyrille d'Alexandrie et S. Léon le Grand à Chalcédoine' in Grillmeier and Bacht (1951–2), vol. 1, 345–87.

—— (1956) 'Saint Cyrille et Apollinaire', *Gregorianum* 37, 584–609.

Gebremedhin, E. (1977) *Life-Giving Blessing. An Inquiry into the Eucharistic Doctrine of Cyril of Alexandria*, Uppsala: Acta Universitatis Upsaliensis (Studia Doctrinae Christianae Upsaliensia, 17).

Gould, G. (1988) 'Cyril of Alexandria and the Formula of Reunion' *DR* 106, 235–52.

Grant, R.M. (1964) 'Greek Literature in the Treatise *De Trinitate* and Cyril's *Contra Julianum*', *JTS* n.s.15, 265–99. (Important.)

Gray, P.T.R. (1979) *The Defense of Chalcedon in the East (451–553)*, Leiden: E.J. Brill (Studies in the History of Christian Thought, 20).

Grillmeier, A. (1975) *Christ in Christian Tradition*. Vol. 1. *From the Apostolic Age to Chalcedon (451)*, trans. J. Bowden, London and Oxford: Mowbrays. (Indispensable.)

—— (1987) *Christ in Christian Tradition*. Vol. 2. *From the Council of Chalcedon (451) to Gregory the Great (590–604)*. Part 1. *Reception and Contradiction. The development of the discussion about Chalcedon from 451 to the beginning of the reign of Justinian*, trans. P. Allen and J. Cawte, London and Oxford: Mowbrays.

—— (1995) *Christ in Christian Tradition*. Vol. 2. *From the Council of Chalcedon*

(451) to Gregory the Great (590–604). Part 2. *The Church of Constantinople in the sixth century,* with Theresia Hainthaler, trans. J. Cawte and P. Allen, London and Louisville: Mowbrays and Westminster John Knox Press.

—— (1996) *Christ in Christian Tradition.* Vol. 2. *From the Council of Chalcedon (451) to Gregory the Great (590–604).* Part 4. *The Church of Alexandria with Nubia and Ethiopia after 451,* with Theresia Hainthaler, trans. O.C. Dean, London and Louisville: Mowbrays and Westminster John Knox Press.

Grillmeier, A. and Bacht, H. (1951–2) eds, *Das Konzil von Chalkedon. Geschichte und Gegenwart,* 3 vols., Würzburg: Echter-Verlag. (Indispensable.)

Gross, J. (1938) *La divinisation du chrétien d'après les Pères grecs: contribution historique à la doctrine de grace,* Paris: J. Gabalda.

Gryson, R. and Szmatula, D. (1990) 'Les commentaires patristiques sur Isaïe d'Origène à Jérôme', *REA* 35, 3–41.

de Halleux, A. (1979) 'Cyrille, Théodoret et le "Filioque"', *RHE* 74, 597–625.

—— (1984) '"Hypostase" et "personne" dans la Formation du dogme trinitaire ca. 375–391', *RHE* 79, 314–69.

—— (1992) 'Les douze chapitres cyrilliens au concile d'Ephès (430–433)', *RTL* 23, 425–58.

—— (1993a) 'La première session du Concile d'Ephèse (22 juin 431)', *Eph. Th. Lov.* 59, 48–87.

—— (1993b) 'Nestorius, histoire et doctrine', *Irénikon* 56, 38–51, 163–77.

Haring, N.M. (1950) 'The character and range of influence of St. Cyril of Alexandria on Latin Theology, 430–1260', *Med. Stud.* 12, 1–19.

Hardy, E.R. (1982) 'The Further Education of Cyril of Alexandria (412–444). Questions and Problems', *Stud. Pat.* 17 (part 1), 116–22.

Hollerich, M.J. (1999) *Eusebius of Caesarea's Commentary on Isaiah. Christian Exegesis in the Age of Constantine,* Oxford: Clarendon Press.

Holum, K. (1982) *Theodosian Empresses,* Berkeley: University of California Press.

Janssens, L. (1938) 'Notre filiation divine d'après S. Cyrille d'Alexandrie', *Eph. Th. Lov.* 15, 233–78.

Jouassard, G. (1945) 'L'activité littéraire de S. Cyrille d'Alexandrie jusqu'à 428', in *Mélanges E. Podechard,* 159–74, Lyons: Facultés Catholiques.

—— (1957) 'Impassibilité du Logos et impassibilité de l'âme humaine chez Cyrille d'Alexandrie', *RSR* 45, 209–44.

—— (1962) 'S. Cyrille d'Alexandrie aux prises avec la "communication des idiomes" avant 428 dans ses ouvrages anti-ariens', *Stud. Pat.* 6, 112–21.

Kamesar, A. (1990) 'The Virgin of Isaiah 7, 14. The Philological Argument from the Second to the Fifth Century', *JTS* 41, 51–75.

Kaster, R. (1988) *Guardians of Language,* Berkeley: University of California Press.

Kelly, J.N.D (1975) *Jerome. His Life, Writings, and Controversies*, London: Duckworth.

—— (1977) *Early Christian Doctrines*, 5th edn., London and New York: Adam Black.

—— (1995) *Golden Mouth. The Story of John Chrysostom – ascetic, preacher, bishop*, London: Duckworth.

Kerrigan, A.S. (1952) *Cyril of Alexandria: Interpreter of the Old Testament*, Rome: Institutum Pontificum Biblicum, (Analecta Biblica, 2). (Important.)

Koen, L. (1991) *The Saving Passion. Incarnational and Soteriological Thought in Cyril of Alexandria's Commentary on the Gospel According to St. John*, Uppsala: Acta Universitatis Upsaliensis (Studia Doctrinae Christianae Upsaliensia, 31).

Kyrilliana (1947) *Etudes variées à l'occasion du XVe centenaire de Cyrille d'Alexandrie (444–1944)*, Cairo: Les Editions du Scribe Egyptien. (Indispensable.)

Larchet, J.-C. (1998) *Maxime le Confesseur, médiateur entre l'Orient et l'Occident*, Paris: Les Editions du Cerf.

Lebon, J. (1951) 'La christologie du monophysisme syrien', in Grillmeier and Bacht (1951–2), vol. 1, 425–580.

Legrand, E. (1962) *Bibliographie Hellénique des XVe et XVIe siècles*, vol. 3, Paris: G.-P. Maisonneuve & Larose.

Liébaert, J. (1951) *La doctrine christologique de S. Cyrille d'Alexandrie avant la querelle nestorienne*, Lille: Facultés Catholiques. (Important.)

—— (1955), 'S. Cyrille d'Alexandrie et la culture antique', *MSR* 12, 5–26.

—— (1970), 'L'evolution de la christologie de S. Cyrille d'Alexandrie à partir de la controverse nestorienne. La lettre paschale xvii et la lettre au moines (428–429)', *MSR* 27, 27–48.

Lieu, J. (1996) *Image and Reality. The Jews in the World of the Christians in the Second Century*, Edinburgh: T & T Clark.

Limberis, V. (1994) *Divine Heiress. The Virgin Mary and the Creation of Christian Constantinople*, London and New York: Routledge.

Loofs, F. (1914) *Nestorius and his Place in the History of Christian Doctrine*, Cambridge: at the University Press.

Louth, A. (1989) 'The use of the term 'idios' in Alexandrian theology from Alexander to Cyril', *Stud. Pat.* 19, 198–202.

McGuckin, J. (1984) 'The "Theopaschite Confession" (Text and Historical Context): a Study in the Cyrilline Re-interpretation of Chalcedon', *JEH* 35, 239–55.

—— (1992) 'The Influence of the Isis Cult on St Cyril of Alexandria's Christology', *Stud. Pat.* 24, 191–9.

—— (1994) *St. Cyril of Alexandria. The Christological Controversy. Its History,*

Theology, and Texts, Leiden: E.J. Brill. (Important, if one-sidedly Cyrillian.)

—— (1996) 'Nestorius and the political factions of fifth-century Byzantium: factors in his personal downfall', *BJRL* 78, part 3, 7–21.

Mahé, J. (1906) 'Les anathématismes de S. Cyrille d'Alexandrie et les évêques orientaux du patriarcat d'Antioche', *RHE* 7, 505–43.

—— (1907) 'La date du Commentaire de S. Cyrille d'Alexandrie sur l'Evangile selon S. Jean', *BLE* 8, 41–5.

—— (1909) 'La sanctification d'après S. Cyrille d'Alexandrie', *RHE* 10, 30–40, 469–92.

Malley, W.J. (1978) *Hellenism and Christianity: The Conflict between Hellenic and Christian Wisdom in the* Contra Galilaeos *of Julian the Apostate and the* Contra Julianum *of St. Cyril of Alexandria*, Rome: Università Gregoriana. (Important.)

Marrou, H.I. (1956) *A History of Education in Antiquity*, trans. G. Lamb, London: Sheed and Ward.

Meunier, B. (1989) 'Cyrille d'Alexandrie au Concile de Florence', *Annuarium Historiae Conciliorum* 21, 147–74.

—— (1997) *Le Christ de Cyrille d'Alexandrie. L'humanité, le salut et la question monophysite*, Paris: Beauchesne (Théologie historique 104). (Valuable study.)

Meyendorff, J. (1975) *Christ in Eastern Christian Thought*, Crestwood: St. Vladimir's Seminary Press.

Michel, A. (1922), 'Idiomes (Communication des)', *DTC*, vol. 7, 595–602.

Millar, F. (1992) 'The Jews of the Graeco-Roman Diaspora between Paganism and Christianity AD 312–438', in J. Lieu, J. North and T. Rajak, eds, *The Jews among Pagans and Christians in the Roman Empire*, 97–123, London: Routledge.

Moeller, C. (1951) 'Le chalcédonisme et le néo-chalcédonisme en Orient de 451 à la fin du VIe siècle, in Grillmeier and Bacht (1951–2), vol. 1, 637–720.

Montserrat, D. (1998) 'Pilgrimage to the Shrine of SS Cyrus and John at Menouthis in Late Antiquity', in D. Frankfurter, ed., *Pilgrimage and Holy Space in Late Antique Egypt*, Leiden, Boston, Köln: Brill.

Munier, H (1947) 'Le lieu de naissance de Saint Cyrille d'Alexandrie', in *Kyrilliana* (1947), 199–201.

Norris, R.A. (1975) 'Christological Models in Cyril of Alexandria', *Stud. Pat.* 13, 255–68.

—— (1982) 'The Problem of Human Identity in Patristic Christological Speculation', *Stud. Pat.* 17/1, 147–59.

O'Keefe, J.J. (1993) *Interpreting the Angel. Cyril of Alexandria and Theodoret of Cyrus: Commentators on the Book of Malachi*, Washington DC: Catholic University of America dissertation in facsimile.

—— (1997) 'Kenosis or Impassibility: Cyril of Alexandria and Theodoret of Cyrus on the Problem of Divine Pathos', *Stud. Pat.* 32, 358–65.

Pagels, E. (1989) *The Johannine Gospel in Gnostic Exegesis. Heracleon's Commentary on John*, Nashville and New York: Abingdon Press.

Papadopoulos, Chr. (1933) *Ho Hagios Kyrillos Alexandreias*, Alexandria: Patriarchal Press.

Pennacchio, M. (1995) '"Quasi ursa raptis catulis". Os. 13,8 nell' esegesi di Gerolamo e Cirillo di Alessandria', *Vet. Chr.* 32, 143–61.

Philipsborn, A. (1950) 'La compagnie d'ambulanciers "Parabalani" d'Alexandrie', *Byzantion* 20, 185–90.

Prestige, G.L. (1940) *Fathers and Heretics. Six Studies in Dogmatic Faith with Prologue and Epilogue*, London: SPCK.

Richard, M. (1945) 'L'introduction du mot "Hypostase" dans la théologie de l'Incarnation', *MSR* 2, 5–32, 243–70.

—— (1946) 'Les Traités de Cyrille d'Alexandrie contre Diodore et Théodore et les fragments dogmatiques de Diodore de Tarse', *Mélanges dédiés à la mémoire de Félix Grat*, 1, 99–116, Paris: En depôt chez Mme Pecqueur-Grat.

Rougé, J. (1987) 'Les débuts de l'episcopat de Cyrille d'Alexandrie et le Code Théodosien' in *ALEXANDRINA. Hellenisme, judaisme et christianisme à Alexandrie. Mélanges offerts au P. Claude Mondesert*, 339–49, Paris: Les Editions du Cerf. (Valuable study.)

—— (1990) 'La politique de Cyrille d'Alexandrie et le meurtre d'Hypatie', *Cr. St.* 11/3, 485–504.

Russell, N. (1988) '"Partakers of the divine nature" (2 Peter 1:4) in the Byzantine Tradition' in *KATHEGETRIA. Essays Presented to Joan Hussey for her 80th Birthday*, 51–67, Camberley: Porphyrogenitus.

Sagüés, J. (1947) 'El Espiritu Santo en la sanctification de hombre segun la doctrina de S. Cirilo de Alejandria', *Estudios Eclesiasticos* 21, 35–83.

Santer, H. (1975) 'The Authorship and Occasion of Cyril of Alexandria's Sermon on the Virgin (Hom. Div. iv)', *Stud. Pat.* 12, 144–50.

Schwartz, E. (1928) *Cyrill und der Mönch Viktor*, Vienna: Akademie der Wissenschaften (Sitzungsberichte der Akademie der Wissenschaften in Wien, Philosophisch-historische Klasse 208, 4). (Important.)

Scipioni, L.I. (1974) *Nestorio e il concilio di Efeso. Storia, dogma, critica*, Milan: Pubblicazioni della Università Cattolica del Sacro Cuore. (Important.)

Sellers, R.V. (1940) *Two Ancient Christologies. A Study in the Christological Thought of the Schools of Alexandria and Antioch in the Early History of Christian Doctrine*, London: SPCK.

—— (1953) *The Council of Chalcedon. A Historical and Doctrinal Survey*, London: SPCK.

Siddals, R.M. (1985) 'Oneness and Difference in the Christology of Cyril of Alexandria', *Stud. Pat.* 18, 207–11.

—— (1987) 'Logic and Christology in Cyril of Alexandria', *JTS* 38, 341–67. (Important study.)

Smith, R. (1995) *Julian's Gods. Religion and Philosophy in the Thought and Action of Julian the Apostate*, London and New York: Routledge.

Souvay, G.L. (1926) 'The Twelve Anathematizations of St. Cyril', *CHR* 5, 627–35.

Starowieyski, M. (1989) 'Le titre *theotokos* avant le concile d'Ephese', *Stud. Pat.* 19, 236–42, Leuven: Peeters Press.

Theodorou, A. (1955) *Hē christologikē horologia kai didaskalia Kyrillou tou Alexandreias kai Theodorētou Kyrou*, Athens: Theologike Schole Panepistemiou Athenon.

—— (1974) *Hē peri ekporeuseos tou hagiou pneumatos didaskalia Kyrillou tou Alexandreias kai Epiphaniou Kyprou*, Athens: Offprint from *Theologia*. (Valuable assembly of texts.)

Turner, H. E.W. (1975) 'Nestorius Reconsidered' *Stud. Pat.* 13, 306–21.

Vaccari, A. (1937) 'La grecità di S. Cirillo d'Alessandria' in A. Gemelli, ed., *Studi dedicati alla memoria di Paolo Ubaldi*, 27–39, Milan: Società editrice "Vita e Pensiero".

Wallis, R.T. (1972) *Neo-Platonism*, London: Duckworth.

Welch, L.J. (1994) *Christology and Eucharist in the Early Thought of Cyril of Alexandria*, San Francisco: International Scholars Publications. (A fresh approach with a useful critique of earlier research.)

Wickham, L. (1989) 'Pelagianism in the East', in Williams (1989), 200–213.

Wiles, M. (1960) *The Spiritual Gospel. The Interpretation of the Fourth Gospel in the Early Church*, Cambridge: Cambridge University Press.

—— (1965) 'The Nature of the Early Debate about Christ's Human Soul', *JEH* 16, 139–51.

—— (1989) 'Eunomius: hair-splitting dialectitian or defender of the accessibility of salvation?' in Williams (1989), 157–72.

Wilken, R. (1971) *Judaism and the Early Christian Mind: A Study of Cyril of Alexandria's Exegesis and Theology*, New Haven and London: Yale University Press. (Indispensable.)

Williams, R. (1989) ed. *The Making of Orthodoxy. Essays in honour of Henry Chadwick*, Cambridge: Cambridge University Press.

Young, F.M. (1971) 'A Reconsideration of Alexandrian Christology', *JEH* 22, 103–14.

—— (1983) *From Nicaea to Chalcedon*, London: SCM Press.

—— (1997) *Biblical Exegesis and the Formation of Christian Culture*, Cambridge: Cambridge University Press.

INDEX OF SCRIPTURAL CITATIONS

2:16–17 107
2:17 160, 164
2:18 160, 164, 167
3:1 180, 187
3:5 146
3:6 108
3:14 100
6:4 100, 124
6:19 154
7:16 166
7:19 165
7:23–5 166
8:1–2 166
9:6 143
9:10 19, 102
10:1 19, 102
10:14 167, 187
10:28 165
13:8 160

James

1:17 179
3:6 140

1 Peter

2:22 187
4:1 165, 189
5:8 117

2 Peter

1:4 45, 103, 111, 124, 163, 229
2:9 100
3:10, 13 95

1 John

2:1–2 123
4:13 104, 139
5:6 199

INDEX OF NAMES AND SUBJECTS